PROBLEM SOLVING WITH FORTRAN

PROBLEM SOLVING WITH FORTRAN

RICHARD W. DILLMAN

Western Maryland College
Westminster, Maryland

Holt, Rinehart and Winston
New York   Chicago   San Francisco   Philadelphia
Montreal   Toronto   London   Sydney   Tokyo
Mexico City   Rio de Janeiro   Madrid

Cover photo of sodium thiosulfate crystal. Courtesy Reginald Wickham, Teaneck, New Jersey.

Library of Congress Cataloging in Publication Data

Dillman, Richard.
  Problem solving with FORTRAN.

  Includes index.
  1. FORTRAN (Computer program language) 2. Problem solving—Data processing. I. Title.
QA76.73.F25D53   1984   001.64'24   84–4458

ISBN 0-03-063734-1

Printed in the United States of America

Printed simultaneously in Canada

5 6 7 090 9 8 7 6 5 4 3 2 1

CBS COLLEGE PUBLISHING
Holt, Rinehart and Winston
The Dryden Press
Saunders College Publishing

CONTENTS

Part III   DATA STRUCTURES

PREFACE

This book will not make you into a computer programmer. Only practice will do that. However, this book will show you how to use the techniques of problem analysis and computer program design that are generally accepted by the commercial programming industry as being the most effective in the writing of "good programs."

LEARNING TO PROGRAM

There is no single "method" to computer programming. Although progress has been made over the last decade in standardizing the way programs are produced, programming is still much less a science than it is an art. Both in analyzing problems and in writing computer programs to solve these problems, the programmer is expected to work on his or her own, to think creatively, and to use good judgment in seeking to develop optimum solutions. Because of this it is difficult, if not impossible to learn to program by reading a book or by listening to someone talk. Programming today is still a craft and like any craft, it can only be learned slowly, with much practice, and with your hands on a keyboard.

If you are a beginner at computer programming, it is essential that you spend quite a bit of time actually *using* the computer. This book wholeheartedly adopts the "hands on" approach (examples are designed to be entered and executed, and each chapter contains exercises to be done at the terminal), but that probably will not be enough. If you are serious about learning to program, you should invent and execute small programs of your own to try out *every* new topic as it appears. The truth is that the only way to learn the material is to write the programs. The more programs you write, the better you will become at writing programs.

LOGIC AND SYNTAX

The chapters of *Problem Solving with FORTRAN* are presented under three basic headings. "Logic" chapters deal with the problem solving, data analysis, and logic construction and representation skills that a programmer needs in order to be able to design algorithms. "Syntax" chapters describe the rules of the FORTRAN language. "Using the Computer" chapters present completed programs that illustrate the material discussed in the preceding sections.

Algorithms are central to the idea of computing, yet the design of algorithms is the skill that is hardest to teach. The syntax of a programming language is fixed. It is embodied in strict rules that are enforced by the computer and, therefore, it must be followed if a program is to run at all. Logic, however, is slippery. In all but the simplest programs there are large numbers of different algorithmic approaches that will produce acceptable output. It is often difficult for beginning students to recognize this fact, and it is particularly difficult for them to do so in classroom situations where the main emphasis is on "getting the program handed in."

In an optimum situation, each student's completed programs would be carefully reviewed for structure and style, each deviation from "good" programming technique would be noted and explained, and the student would be required to correct all errors before credit was given. Although this can sometimes be accomplished in advanced classes, instructors in introductory courses seldom have the luxury of spending that much time with each incoming program, and in any case, the breadth of material to be covered precludes the students having the opportunity to try one program two or three times.

Problem Solving with FORTRAN tries to help with the problem by making a clear distinction between algorithm design and FORTRAN coding. The "logic" chapters develop the techniques of algorithm design without referring to FORTRAN language constructs. This is intended to emphasize the distinction between design and coding as well as to force the students to think about problems in pseudocode rather than in FORTRAN. Each "logic" chapter discusses a particular design-related subject, and each is followed by a "syntax" chapter that presents the FORTRAN instructions needed to implement the design. Then the two are tied together by a "Using the Computer" chapter that demonstrates the creation of an algorithm and its FORTRAN implementation. If the text is used in this way, students should come to see that a well-designed algorithm is a prerequisite to a well-coded program, and the temptation to sit down at the terminal and "bang it out" will be easier to resist.

PROGRAM STRUCTURE AND STYLE

Modern programming is centered on the complementary ideas of structure and style. "Structure" refers to an approach to problem solving, algorithm design, and program coding in which all programs are constructed from a small set of essential logical building blocks called "structures." The three major structures establish logical devices for performing linear sequences, repeating blocks of code, and making decisions within an algorithm or program. Although it is not strictly *necessary* to good programming to use the structured approach, its use does serve to make programs fit a more or less "standard" form. As is discussed in the text, this is a major goal of the programming industry. Programming "style" refers to the visual appearance of the finished program. A well-styled program is logically simple, carefully documented, and very easy to read.

The current emphasis on program structure and style derives from the fact that commercial programs must not only perform the tasks assigned to them, but they must also be easy to change. It is important for student programmers to recognize that commercial programs are very large, have long lifetimes, and are subject to constant modification. ("Classroom" programs often have none of these characteristics.) Because personnel costs make up a major part of the cost of software, and because maintenance of existing software is a continuing need, many organizations now strongly support structured, well-styled programming as the approach most likely to produce effective software at minimum cost. Students who are planning to seek jobs in the programming industry should be aware that "getting it to work" is only one of many factors upon which their programming will be evaluated.

THE FORTRAN SYNTAX USED IN THIS BOOK

Problem Solving With FORTRAN uses ANSI FORTRAN 77. On the assumption that FORTRAN 77 is now the *de facto* FORTRAN standard, no attempt has been made to reconcile the text with FORTRAN IV or any earlier version. Students using FORTRAN IV, WAT V or other FORTRANs will find that some of the examples given in the text do not compile properly on their systems. However, all program examples are preceded by well-documented algorithms clearly written in pseudocode. Students should have little difficulty in locating the offending statements, comparing them with the algorithms, looking up the proper syntax in the FORTRAN *User's Manual*, and making the corrections. In fact, this would be excellent practice for the kind of work that professional programmers actually do.

USING THE MANUALS

Quite often the first contact between a professional programmer and a new computer that he or she is to use is through the system's manuals. It is not unusual for a new programmers' supervisor to hand the programmer a stack of manuals and say "Spend a couple days reading these, and then we'll get you on the system." Employers cite "reading the manuals" as the one major skills in which apprentice programmers are most often deficient.

Granted, most computer language manuals are poorly conceived and badly written, and true, good programmers know their language syntax thoroughly. Nevertheless, each system has its quirks, and when the compiler is generating error messages, there is no substitute for the ability to put one's finger on the section of the manual that gives the exact rules for the statement in question. It is imperative that students learn how to use manuals, and this can only be achieved through practice.

To that end this text makes frequent reference to the *Computer User's Guide,* the manual that discusses the operating system and its commands; and the FORTRAN *Reference Guide*, the manual that discusses the FORTRAN syntax rules. We suggest that students be given early formal assignments in using the manuals, and that differences between the text and the user's system be treated as a minor problem which the student is expected to resolve on his or her own.

FORTRAN SYNTAX OMITTED FROM THIS BOOK

FORTRAN was the first of the "high level" computer languages to be implemented for general use. It has been in existence for some thirty years, and in that time it has gone through several evolutionary changes. Since FORTRAN is a "standardized" language, the changes have been under the control of the American National Standards Institute (ANSI), and ANSI has tried to keep each newer version compatible with the versions that preceded it. One of the results of these attempts is that FORTRAN is a language composed of both rules and exceptions to rules.

An expert programmer, knowing how to make use of the exceptions, can do strange and wonderful things with FORTRAN. More than most computer languages, FORTRAN lends itself to the use of "tricks" and "gadgets." Modern practice frowns on this approach, however, stressing instead the use of simple, easily followed, structured codes. Since this book is designed for beginners, it sticks to the structured approach, and in order to keep the ideas simple, it omits a number of FORTRAN instructions. Here is a brief list of the omissions.

COMPLEX, DOUBLE PRECISION, and other advanced TYPE statements. The combination of default, implicit and explicit typing—with or without accompanying dimension statements—provides extensive flexibility for the expert, but can be very confusing to beginners. This book uses only the INTEGER, REAL, and CHARACTER type statements, and always dimension arrays in DIMENSION statements. Once students have mastered these, variations are easy to introduce, so we doubt that instructors will find this approach limiting.

COMMON and BLOCK DATA. When beginners are introduced to COMMON, their eyes light up. Here is a statement that solves all of their problems having to do with thinking through the interfaces between subprograms. We doubt that beginning students will be working on programs with the large numbers of interface variables needed to make COMMON necessary, and we feel that without COMMON, they will have to put more effort into the study of interfacing—a skill that we think is valuable. Once subprograms have been studied, instructors who wish to introduce COMMON can do so with little effort. (It makes an excellent exercise in FORTRAN manual reading.)

Unusual ENTRY to and EXIT from subprograms. To preserve the idea of modular programming, we omit reference to ENTRY and to multiple exits from subprograms. Beginners don't need these statements, and they lead to unnecessary complexity.

Unusual or advanced FORMAT codes; some forms of READ, WRITE and PRINT. The large number of FORMAT codes, along with the various forms of READ, WRITE, and PRINT, give the FORTRAN programmer exceptional control over the program's input and output. In order to keep things simple we have chosen to use:

READ ∗ —as the standard unit input instruction, formatted input (e.g. READ [unit, format]) is used only with data files;

PRINT ∗ —as the standard unit unformatted output instruction;

WRITE (unit, format) —as the formatted output instruction for the standard output unit and for data files.

In addition we restrict our use of FORMAT codes to those that are strictly necessary to produce the outputs of the example programs. We feel that beginners should spend the majority of their time on algorithm design and structured coding, and to this end we try to keep the I/O syntax as simple as possible.

ACKNOWLEDGMENTS

I would like to thank John and Vikki Cleckner, Brete Harrison and his staff, and Cobb/Dunlop, Inc. for their help in the creation and production of this book. Thanks also to the many reviewers for the insights gained from their analysis of the text.

I
INTRODUCTION: WHAT IS PROGRAMMING?

1
USING THE COMPUTER: SYNTAX AND LOGIC

DEFINITIONS

Computer
: A set of electronic devices that manipulate information by following instructions given to them by people called programmers.

Instruction
: A statement, written in a language the computer can understand, that will cause the computer to perform a specific activity.

Program
: A collection of instructions which, when executed by the computer, will produce the solution to a problem.

Execute
: The process of carrying out an instruction or set of instructions.

FORTRAN
: A computer "language"; a particular set of instructions that can be used to create computer programs.

FORTRAN Syntax
: The rules that must be followed when writing instructions with the FORTRAN language.

Program Logic
: The order in which the instructions in a program are executed; if the instructions are not executed in the proper order, the computer will not produce correct solutions.

Syntax Error Message
: A message printed by the computer when it finds an instruction in which the *syntax* rules have been violated.

FORTRAN Language Reference Manual	A book, put out by the company that made your computer, that contains all the syntax rules for the FORTRAN language on your computer system.
Computer User's Manual	A book, put out by the company that made your computer, that explains how to type in, correct, and execute programs on your computer system.

WRITING PROGRAMS

You are about to learn how to use a computer to do things such as print out messages, add up sets of numbers, and sort words into alphabetical order.

The computer can do none of these things by itself. It can *only* act if it has been given detailed instructions that tell it *exactly* how to carry out each task it is expected to perform. These sets of instructions are called *programs*. They are written in a special language the computer can understand and then given to the computer to be executed.

It is not always easy to choose the set of instructions that will solve a particular problem. Problems are usually written in English. Before a problem can be *programmed* and *executed* by the computer, it must be translated into a language the computer can understand. This work is done by a person called a programmer.

But programmers are not just translators; they are also *problem solvers*. Computers cannot think. They cannot solve problems. They can *only* follow instructions. It is the programmer who actually solves the problem and then instructs the computer so that the computer can solve it too.

You can see, therefore, that there are two parts to the writing of any computer program:

1. The problem must be solved. The programmer must come up with a sequence of steps that the computer will be able to follow to get the solution to the problem. This is known as developing the *program logic* or *designing* the program.
2. The programmer must translate the sequence of steps into a language the computer can understand. In doing this the programmer must follow the *syntax* rules of the language. This part of writing a program is called *coding* and *testing* the program.

The *syntax* rules are the rules the computer follows when it is evaluating instructions to be executed. Each computer language has different rules. In this book we will deal with the FORTRAN computer language and so we will talk about *FORTRAN syntax*.

EXECUTING PROGRAMS

There are many different brands of computers, and the procedures you must follow to have the computer execute a program differ from brand to brand. When you have written your first program, your instructor will show you how to enter the program into your particular brand of computer and how to tell the computer to begin executing the program.

Your instructor will also have access to a book called the *Computer User's Manual*. This book includes all of the operating instructions for your computer. If the computer does something that you don't understand, or if there is something you want to do but don't know how to, you will usually be able to find the answer in the *Computer User's Manual*.

FORTRAN SYNTAX ERRORS

When you tell the computer to begin executing your program, it will first look over your program to see if you have correctly followed rules of FORTRAN syntax. If there are statements in your program in which you have violated the rules, the computer will print *syntax error messages* to notify you that something is wrong.

Your first programs will produce a large number of error messages. Don't let this frustrate you. The computer only accepts statements that are *perfectly correct*. Even experienced programmers spend a good deal of their time correcting errors.

Most of the syntax errors you will see will be the result of typing mistakes. For example, if you mean to type the word READ but accidentally type REMD instead, the computer will identify that as an error. You can correct the error simply by retyping the line. If the computer says there is an error in a certain line, but the line looks correct to you, look up the instruction in the *FORTRAN Language Reference Manual* and make sure that you have remembered the rule correctly. If you still aren't sure what's wrong, then ask someone to help you. Often another person will be able to spot an error that you can't see.

The computer will not *execute* your program correctly until all the syntax errors have been removed. Just because a program executes, however, does not mean that it is correct. You should always check the output to make sure that the program is doing what you expect it to.

If your program's output is incorrect, then you will have to go back and check the program's logic. The best way to do this is to take a pencil and sheet of paper and go through the program line by line, keeping track of what happens at each line, just as if you were the computer. This is a slow and sometimes tedious job, but if you do it well, you will always find your mistakes.

PRACTICE

Your instructor should be able to tell you where to find a copy of the *FORTRAN Language Reference Manual* for your computer system. Look in the index at the back of this manual and find the section called "errors" or "error messages." Glance through this section. The words may not mean much to you now, but as you begin to write programs, you will need to look there whenever your programs have errors in them.

A SAMPLE PROGRAM

In the next two chapters we'll be talking about problems and problem solving, and we'll be seeing how programmers go about developing program logic. But just to give you an idea of what the finished product looks like, here is an example of a completed FORTRAN program:

```
*       THIS PROGRAM COMPUTES THE SUM OF
*       THE FIRST TEN INTEGERS
        INTEGER N,SUM
        N=1
        SUM=0
100     CONTINUE
        IF (N .GT. 10) GOTO 200
        SUM=SUM+N
        N=N+1
        GOTO 100
200     CONTINUE
        PRINT*,'THE SUM IS',SUM
        END
```

In FORTRAN:

- Lines starting with * or with a number begin in column 1.
- Others begin in column 7.

This program adds up the numbers $1 + 2 + 3 + \ldots + 9 + 10$ and prints out the sum. If you type the program into your computer and have the computer execute it, the words

```
THE SUM IS 55
```

should print out on the screen.

This program probably makes little sense to you now, but that's all right. The next chapter will show you how such programs are created.

PRACTICE

Type the sample program into your computer and execute it. The *Computer User's Guide* for your computer system should have a section that explains how to do this. If you run into any problems, your instructor will be able to help you out.

2
LOGIC: PROBLEM ANALYSIS

DEFINITIONS

Problem Statement | A request, written in English, for a computer programmer to write a program.

Problem Analysis | The process of studying a problem statement to be sure that enough information has been given to allow a program to be written; the first step in the program development process.

PROBLEMS

The word "problem" has a special meaning to computer programmers. "Problem" is used to describe any situation in which a programmer is expected to create a new program.

Such situations are called problems because there is no guarantee that a given request for a program can be satisfied. For example, the request:

> Write a program to compute the sum of the first 50 odd numbers.

can be very easily programmed (you'll see what the program looks like in a later chapter). The request:

> Write a program to predict what tomorrow's weather will be.

cannot be programmed, however. The reason it can't be programmed is that we don't understand weather prediction well enough to be able to give the computer the right instructions. To write a computer program to do something, we must first be able to understand how to do it ourselves.

Thus while there are many problems a programmer can be asked to program, there are only certain ones that can actually be solved. When a programmer is given a problem to program, the first job is to analyze the problem to see if it can be solved.

PROBLEM ANALYSIS

Since the objective is to write a program, and since the problem statement is usually written in English, the programmer's first job is to *organize the information* given in the problem statement in a way that will let the programmer decide whether a solution is possible. Organizing the information given in a problem statement is called *problem analysis*.

The first step in problem analysis involves a very simple rule:

EVERY PROGRAM HAS A PURPOSE

The problem statement should include information that describes what the program is to do. For example, for the two problem statements given on page 6, the purpose of the first program would be:

PURPOSE   Sum the first 50 odd numbers.

The purpose of the second would be:

PURPOSE   Predict tomorrow's weather.

Being able to write down the purpose of a program does not mean that the program can be written. However, if you *can't* write down the purpose of a program, then you don't know what the program is supposed to *do*. That's the second basic rule of programming:

> IF YOU DON'T KNOW WHAT A PROGRAM IS
> SUPPOSED TO DO, YOU DON'T KNOW ENOUGH TO
> WRITE THE PROGRAM.

As an example, here is a typical problem statement:

PROBLEM   ABC Company produces plastic seat covers and sells them to depart-
               ment stores. The company does about $2,000,000 worth of business
               each year. The company has 25 employees, and all employee records
               are done by hand by a secretary and two bookkeepers. Write a pro-
               gram to help the company save money in the way it processes em-
               ployee records.

PURPOSE   ?????

This problem statement does give information about the ABC Company. It does not, however, give any *specific* information that a programmer can use to identify the problem. "Save the company money" may be the company's purpose for hiring a programmer, but "save the company money" does not say anything about what the program is supposed to *do*. The problem statement is *incomplete*.

Here is an example of a more complete problem statement:

PROBLEM   To save money on the processing of employee records, ABC Company has decided to computerize its payroll procedures. The company employs 25 people, including a secretary and two bookkeepers who currently handle the payroll. All employees are paid by the hour. Each employee has a Social Security number, a regular hourly rate, an overtime hourly rate, and a deduction rate. Anything over 40 hours a week is considered overtime. Paychecks are issued every two weeks. The formula for computing pay is:

$$\text{GROSS PAY} = \text{REGULAR HOURS} \times \text{REG. RATE} + \text{OVERTIME HOURS} \times \text{O.T. RATE}$$
$$\text{TAKE-HOME PAY} = \text{GROSS PAY} - (\text{DEDUCTION RATE} \times \text{GROSS PAY})$$

PURPOSE   COMPUTE TAKE-HOME PAY FOR EACH EMPLOYEE.

Once the purpose of the program has been identified, the programmer then continues to *organize* the information given in the problem statement to see if the problem can in fact be programmed. Since computer programs in general are designed to accept data in one form, process the data according to some set of rules, and print out the results, it is usually a good idea to organize the information given in the problem statement into these three categories.

OUTPUT

When a program is executed by the computer, the results that are printed out are known as the *output*. The output may include lists of numbers and names and will always include headings and titles that describe the output.

If you don't know what the output of a program is supposed to look like, you cannot write the program.

Because the output is so important in determining how the program will be designed, it is usually the first of the three categories to be organized. The *best* way to organize the output information is to write out a sample page that shows what the output *should* look like. The sample output is also very useful later on to check and make sure that the final program is correct.

A good problem statement *includes* a description of the output. For example:

PROBLEM   The local weather bureau measures the amount of rain that falls each day. Write a program to summarize the rainfall data. Print the total rainfall for each month from January to date. Print the average monthly rainfall for the year so far.

SAMPLE
OUTPUT

```
DATE:   JULY 5, 1985
MONTHLY RAINFALL TO DATE
JAN  1.34
FEB  1.05
MAR  1.13
APR  2.20
MAY  2.04
JUNE 6.61
MONTHLY AVERAGE: 1.56
```

Except for the numbers (which will change depending on the month and the amount of rain), the sample output shows *exactly* what the final program output will look like. In this case the programmer knows that the date must appear at the top of the page and be followed by the heading MONTHLY RAINFALL TO DATE. The programmer also knows that the program should print out the monthly rainfall figures correct to two decimal places and that the average rainfall figure should come last on the page. In this way, the sample output will serve as a guide for decisions to be made later as the program is developed.

If no sample output is given in the problem statement, the programmer will have to create one. Here is another example:

PROBLEM   A company keeps an alphabetical list of all of its current customers. The company is planning to open a new store and wants to mail an announcement to each customer living in the area where the new store will be. Write a program to print the customer list, sorted by the customer's Zip Code number.

In this case no sample output is provided. To create a sample output, the programmer needs to establish two things:

1. What information needs to appear in the printout.
2. How that information should be arranged on the page.

In this example the information to be printed includes the name, address, and Zip Code of each customer. We know this because the problem says that the output is to be used for mailing an announcement to the customers. The information will be arranged in groups according to Zip Code. The output will have a title (let's choose: CUSTOMER LIST, BY ZIP CODE), and each type of information to be printed should be labeled. The exact form of this output would vary from programmer to programmer. One way to set it up would be like this:

SAMPLE
OUTPUT

```
                    CUSTOMER LIST, BY ZIP CODE

    ZIP CODE     NAME         STREET         CITY      STATE
    33602     J. SMITH    2121 MAIN ST.    TAMPA       FLA
              T. JONES    6 MAIN ST.       TAMPA       FLA
              K. FIRST    12 BACK ST.      TAMPA       FLA
    33515     B. THOMAS   18 FLOWER AVE.  CLEARWATER   FLA
    46802     S. JONES    36 MAVERN AVE.   FT WAYNE    IND
              K. FROST    19 TENTH ST.     FT WAYNE    IND
              F. TIMMONS  2 MAIN ST.       FT WAYNE    IND
                               .
                               .
                               .
                         And so on
```

If possible, the programmer's sample output should be given to the person who wrote the problem statement for verification. This is done to make sure that the programmer has included everything that needs to be included in the final printout.

Once the sample output has been specified, the programmer's job is very clear.

> THE PROGRAMMER IS EXPECTED TO WRITE A PROGRAM WHICH WHEN EXECUTED BY THE COMPUTER WILL PRODUCE OUTPUT THAT MATCHES THE SAMPLE OUTPUT.

That is, the output sample shows what the final product is supposed to be. To determine how to generate the final product, the programmer must now look at the problem statement to see what data is available for the computer to process and what processing rules are specified.

PROCESSING RULES AND DATA

Data is information that the computer will have to work with while it is executing the program. *Processing rules* explain how the data is to be manipulated by the computer in order to produce the output. Data is often referred to an *input,* and the idea of data processing is often illustrated in a diagram like this:

Once the programmer knows what the output should look like, the problem statement can be reexamined in order to organize the data and the processing rules.

As an example, let's look at a very simple problem:

PROBLEM   Write a program to compute the sum of the integer numbers starting at 12 and ending at 23.

SAMPLE   `THE SUM IS 210`
OUTPUT

PURPOSE   Sum the whole numbers from 12 to 23.

DATA

Initial value of the sum	0
First number to be summed	12
Last number to be summed	23

RULES   The second number to be summed is found by adding 1 to the first number, that is, the second number is $12 + 1 = 13$.

The *next* number to be added into the sum can always be found by adding 1 to the number that was added into the sum *this* time.

If the next number to be added into the sum is bigger than 23, then there is no more summing to do.

When there is no more summing to do, the words "THE SUM IS" and the final sum should be printed out.

Here are some questions that people often ask when they see this problem for the first time.

QUESTION 1

This is a dumb problem. Why can't I just have the computer print out `THE SUM IS 210` and leave it at that?

Answer

This particular problem is so simple that in real life you would never bother to take the time to program it. It is used here to help show you the *idea* of thinking about a problem to discover what data and rules are available. Suppose, however, just for the sake of argument, that the problem said to find the sum of the odd numbers from 2113 to 6223149. This is still a very simple problem, but now it's easier to write a program and execute it than it is to do the addition by hand.

QUESTION 2

What is the difference between data and rules?

Answer

A piece of data is an object; a number or a name; a *thing*. A rule is a statement that either describes a piece of data or tells you how to process the data.

QUESTION 3

How do you find the data and the rules?

Answer

One of the most important skills a programmer needs to have is the ability to read and understand English. The person who writes the problem statement is trying to convey information about the problem. The programmer must be able to identify the information that is present in the problem statement and decide if there is enough of it to allow the solution of the problem.

In this example the first piece of information is that a sum is to be computed. Since the programmer knows that a sum is a set of numbers added together, he or she knows that there must be a first number in the set and a final number in the set, and that the beginning value of the sum will be zero.

The word "integer" tells the programmer that only whole numbers will be included in the sum. "Integer" also means that the next number in the set to be summed will always be 1 bigger than whatever the current number is. This tells the programmer that the second number will be $12 + 1$, the third number $12 + 1 + 1$, the fourth $12 + 1 + 1 + 1$, and so on. Since the problem says to print the sum, the programmer knows to stop the addition after the last number, 23, has been added to the sum, and to print the output at that point.

It is important to read the problem carefully. Suppose, for example, the problem statement had said to find "the *product* of the integers *between* 12 and 23." Although this is a similar problem, there are two very significant changes. First, since a product is required instead of a sum, the set of numbers must now be multiplied together instead of added, and the initial value of the product must be 1. Second, the use of the word "between" to describe the set of numbers to be multiplied is ambiguous. It isn't clear whether the set should include 12 through 23 inclusive, or 13 through 22. The programmer would need to talk to the person who wrote the problem statement to find out which set of numbers to use.

QUESTION 4

How do you know if you've correctly organized all of the data and rules?

Answer

You don't always know whether you have or not. It isn't always clear at the beginning of the program development process that there is enough information available in the problem statement to write a program that will solve the problem. Neither is it always possible to be sure that the information given in the problem statement is fully correct. A program is written in stages:

1. *Problem analysis*. Find the program's purpose; define the sample output; establish as clearly as possible the data and rules.
2. *Algorithm design*. Write out as clearly as possible the detailed series of steps the computer must go through in order to produce the desired output.
3. *Program coding*. Translate the algorithm (the series of detailed steps) into a computer language.
4. *Program debugging*. Execute the coded program to find and eliminate language errors.
5. *Program testing*. Execute the coded program with different sets of data to make sure the program will work correctly under all conditions.
6. *Program documentation*. Write an explanation of how the program works so that other people will be able to use it.

So far we have only looked at step 1, problem analysis. As the program moves through the other steps, the programmer will constantly review the program's progress. At the beginning there will be many uncertainties, but the programmer will question these, and think about them and eventually remove them. At the end of the process will be a program that does exactly what it is supposed to do.

> THERE IS NO "MAGICAL," EASY WAY TO WRITE
> PROGRAMS. EVERY SINGLE PROBLEM IS
> DIFFERENT, AND EVERY PROBLEM WILL REQUIRE
> READING, THINKING, AND UNDERSTANDING.

Luckily, however, even though each problem is different, many problems have similar aspects. The first computer language is the most difficult to learn. As programmers work, they gain experience. And with experience they find programming easier and easier to do.

ALGORITHMS

The preceeding section described the problem analysis part of the program development process. Now we will take the information that we have extracted from the problem statement and develop a logical plan, or algorithm. The next step beyond that will be to translate the algorithm into a FORTRAN program.

As a preview of what comes next, here is the algorithm for the last problem we looked at:

PURPOSE   Sum the integer numbers from 12 to 23

ALGORITHM   (1)   Set sum to zero
            (2)   Set number to 12
            (3)   Add number into sum
            (4)   Add one to number
            (5)   If number is less than or equal to 23, then go to step (3) else go to step (6)
            (6)   Print out "THE SUM IS" followed by the sum
            (7)   Stop

And here is the FORTRAN program as translated from the algorithm:

```
*       SUM THE INTEGERS FROM 12 TO 23
*           INTEGER N,SUM
            SUM=0
            N=12
30          CONTINUE
            SUM=SUM+N
            N=N+1
            IF (N .LE. 23) GOTO 30
            PRINT*, 'THE SUM IS',SUM
            END
```

Both of these will be explained in detail in Chapter 3.

PRACTICE

1. Type the last program into the computer and execute it. The output should be:

    ```
    THE SUM IS 210
    ```

2. Change the fifth line to read:

    ```
    N=1
    ```

    and then execute the program again. What does the printout tell you?
3. Delete the line that begins with PRINT, and execute the program again. What happens now? Why?

3
LOGIC: ALGORITHM DEVELOPMENT

DEFINITIONS

Algorithm

A step-by-step, detailed plan that gives the specific procedure a computer must go through to produce the desired output.

Algorithm Development

The process of translating a problem statement into an algorithm. Since not all problems can be programmed, it is always a good idea to do a problem analysis before beginning the algorithm development.

PROGRAMS

A *program* is a set of instructions, *written in a language that the computer understands,* that explains to the computer how to solve a particular problem.

If computers could understand English, then writing computer programs would be easy. We could just say, "Computer, print out the sum of the numbers from one to twenty-nine," and out would come the answer.

But English is a very complex language; in fact, it is too complex for today's computers to understand. Because of that we must give our instructions to the computer in one of the *computer languages* that have been created for just that purpose.

In this book you will be learning the FORTRAN language. Beginning in Chapter 5, the rules for using FORTRAN (also called the FORTRAN syntax) will be presented. It is not enough, however, just to know the rules for writing FORTRAN instructions. You also have to know how to put the instructions together in order to build programs that will work.

As Chapter 1 explained, two different skills are required of a programmer:

1. *Syntax*. Knowing the rules of the particular computer language.
2. *Logic*. Deciding what sequence of steps to follow to get the solution to a problem.

Of these skills, the syntax is easier to learn. Syntax rules never change. They can be memorized once and kept forever.

Every problem is different, however, and each new problem requires a new logical design. There are no exact rules that can be memorized and applied every time. There are, though, some basic tools that programmers use to help them organize their logic. One of these tools, "problem analysis," was shown in Chapter 2. Another tool is called algorithm design.

ALGORITHMS

Problem analysis is used to organize the information given in a problem statement in order to make it easier to understand and solve the problem. *Algorithm design* is used to specify the *exact* set of steps the computer will have to go through to produce the correct output.

An *algorithm* is a *detailed plan*, written to be understood by humans, that *describes in a step-by-step way* the instructions that will be given to the computer in order to solve a particular problem. The algorithm is *not* a program. It is written *prior* to writing the program. It is then checked out for accuracy and completeness, and finally translated into a computer language and executed.

Many techniques are used in designing algorithms. Flowcharts, pseudocode, top-down design, and modular design are among those that will be discussed later in this book. For now, we will concentrate on the *process* of constructing the logical plan from the information given in the problem statement.

As an example, let's look at the problem that was given near the end of Chapter 2.

PROBLEM   Write a program to print out the sum of the integers starting at 12 and ending at 23.

SAMPLE   `THE SUM IS 210`
OUTPUT

PURPOSE   Sum the whole numbers from 12 to 23.

DATA

Initial value of the sum	0
First number to be summed	12
Last number to be summed	23

RULES   The second number to be summed is one bigger than the first number; the third is one bigger than the second, and so on.

After the last number to be summed is added in, the answer should be printed.

In developing the algorithm, or plan, for the solution of this problem, you must remember that the computer will only recognize two kinds of entities:

Data   Objects; things; usually numbers or characters

Instructions   Actions; usually commands to do something to pieces of data.

So in developing an algorithm, your job is to decide what actions the computer should take to produce the sample output. The actions must be taken *using* the data given in the problem analysis. The actions must *follow* the rules given in the problem analysis.

In this case our objective is to print out the sum of the numbers from 12 to 23. Therefore, we are going to have to give the computer a step-by-step plan that will show it how to compute that sum.

In looking over the problem analysis we see that we have a piece of data called SUM and that it needs to start out with an initial value of zero. Thus the *first* action we'll tell the computer to take is:

(1)   Set SUM to be 0

The (1) indicates that this is the first step in the algorithm. To help keep track of the steps, we will number each one.

How do we know that this should be step (1)? Well, we know that eventually the SUM has to be printed out, and we know that the SUM has to start out at zero before anything else happens to it. So it seems logical to do that first. It may be, of course, that this analysis is wrong, but we have to start *somewhere*. If later we decide that some other step should come first, we'll make a correction. It is *unusual* for a programmer to get an algorithm perfectly correct the first time through. More often an algorithm will require a lot of trial-and-error thinking and rewriting before it is ready to be used.

(1)   Set SUM to be 0

What will step (2) be?

To get the final answer, we must add a set of numbers into the sum. First 12 must be added in and then 13, and then 14, and so on up to 23.

One way to look at this is to think of an instruction:

SET SUM TO BE 12 + 13 + 14 + 15 + · · · + 22 + 23

But the problem won't let us do it this way. The problem *only* gives us the data pieces 12 (the first number to be added in) and 23 (the last number to be added in); we don't have 13, 14, 15, . . ., 22 to work with. We *do,* however, have a rule for computing the second, third, fourth, and so on, numbers to be added in. In the algorithm we need to add 12 into the SUM and then apply the rule to get the next number. One way to do this would be:

(1) Set SUM to be 0
(2) Add 12 to SUM
(3) Add 1 to 12
(4) Add 1 + 12 to SUM
(5) Add 1 to 1 + 12
(6) Add 1 + 1 + 12 to SUM
    .
    .
    .
And so on

You can see that step (2) adds the first number into the SUM, and step (3) applies the rule to get the next number to be summed. Step (4) adds that number in, and step (5) applies the rule to get the next number.

This algorithm will work, but it's very hard to read. Since algorithms must be read by people (to be tested and corrected), they should be easy to understand.

In looking at what we have so far, we see that steps (2), (4), and (6) each adds a number into the SUM. To make things a little simple, we'll define a new piece of data called NUMBER. NUMBER will always contain the next value to be added to the sum.

(1) Set SUM to be 0
(2) Set NUMBER to be 12
(3) Add NUMBER to SUM
(4) Add 1 to NUMBER
(5) Add NUMBER to SUM
(6) Add 1 to NUMBER
(7) Add NUMBER to SUM
    .
    .
    .
And so on

Now we can check the algorithm by *tracing* through it to see if it works.

STEP	VALUE OF SUM	VALUE OF NUMBER
1	0	—
2	0	12
3	12	12
4	12	13
5	25	13
6	25	14
7	39	14
.		
.		
.		
	And so on	

If we were to follow this all the way out, we would see that when NUMBER is set to 23 and added in, SUM would become 210.

That would tell us that the algorithm works, but it is still hard to read, and it is very long. Let's see if we can simplify it further by making it shorter.

In reading over what we have so far, we see that steps (3) and (4), (5) and (6), (7) and (8), and so on, are identical. Why don't we just have the algorithm *repeat* those additions by doing the same set of steps over again and again?

(1) Set SUM to be 0
(2) Set NUMBER to be 12
(3) Add NUMBER to SUM
(4) Add 1 to NUMBER
(5) Go back to step (3)

Now step (5) sends the algorithm back to do step (3) over again. Notice that in doing this we have developed rules for how algorithms work. In an algorithm:

1. Step (1) is always performed first.
2. Steps are always done in order unless specific instructions are given to do otherwise.
3. The "go to step" instruction may be used to change the order in which the instructions are performed.

Thus this algorithm will be performed in this order: (1), (2), (3), (4), (5), (3), (4), (5), (3), and so on.

As before, we can trace the algorithm to see if it is correct:

STEP	SUM	NUMBER
(1)	0	—
(2)	0	12
(3)	12	12
(4)	12	13
(5)	12	13
(3)	25	13
(4)	25	14
(5)	25	14
(3)	39	14
(4)	39	15
	•	
	•	
	•	
	And so on	

If you follow this out, you will see that it computes the same sum as the earlier versions Its advantage is that it is much shorter, and much easier to read.

Now we have a plan that shows how to compute the sum the problem statement asked to see. The question is: Are we finished?

The answer is: No. The problem statement says to *print out* the SUM. Our algorithm doesn't specify that yet, but it seems easy to fix:

(1)   Set SUM to be 0
(2)   Set NUMBER to be 12
(3)   Add NUMBER to SUM
(4)   Add 1 to NUMBER
(5)   Go to step (3)
(6)   Print out "THE SUM IS" and the value of SUM

But there's a problem here. Do you see what it is?

Each time step (5) is performed, the algorithm jumps back to step (3). Because of this, step (6) will never be reached. Not only this, but the algorithm will run on forever. There is nothing that tells it to stop.

To fix this problem, we need to introduce a new type of instruction, the IF test. The IF test is used whenever we need to have the algorithm make a *decision:*

(1)   Set SUM to be 0
(2)   Set NUMBER to be 12
(3)   Add NUMBER to SUM
(4)   Add 1 to NUMBER
(5)   IF NUMBER is less than or equal to 23
      THEN go to step (3)
(6)   Print "THE SUM IS" and the value of SUM
(7)   Stop

Now the algorithm is complete. Each time step (5) is executed, a question is asked. The question is, "Is NUMBER less than or equal to 23?" If the answer to the question is "yes," then the algorithm performs the "go to" part of step (5) and goes back to step (3). If the answer to the question is "no," then the algorithm proceeds to steps (6) and (7). Notice that step (7) indicates where the algorithm is to stop.

As before, we trace the algorithm to see if it is correct:

STEP	SUM	NUMBER	ANSWER AT STEP (5)	PRINTOUT
(1)	0	—	—	—
(2)	0	12	—	—
(3)	12	12	—	—
(4)	12	13	—	—
(5)	12	13	YES	—
(3)	25	13	—	—
(4)	25	14	—	—
(5)	25	14	YES	—
(3)	39	14	—	—
		•		
		•		
		•		
(3)	187	22	—	—
(4)	187	23	—	—
(5)	187	23	YES	—
(3)	210	23	—	—
(4)	210	24	—	—
(5)	210	24	NO	—
(6)	210	24	—	THE SUM IS 210
(7)	210	24	—	—

Since the correct output will be printed, the algorithm is alright and can be coded into FORTRAN and executed.

It is important to see that there was more than one possible algorithm that could have been written to solve this problem. Different programmers will develop their logic in different ways. It is *not* important that you learn to develop algorithms that are exactly the same as the ones in this book. But it *is* important that you learn how to analyze problems, organize information, and develop logical plans. Without these skills, you will not be able to write good programs.

Before we see how to translate algorithms into FORTRAN, it is worthwhile to restate the general rules for building algorithms:

1. Step (1) is always performed first.
2. Steps are always performed in order unless specific instructions are given to do otherwise.
3. The "go to" instruction may be used to change the order in which instructions are performed.

4. The IF/THEN instruction may be used to ask a "yes/no" question. If the answer is "yes," the THEN part of the instruction is performed. If the answer is "no," the THEN part of the instruction is not performed.
5. Every algorithm must be able to stop.

TRANSLATING ALGORITHMS INTO FORTRAN PROGRAMS

Once the algorithm has been written and tested, it is ready to be translated into FORTRAN. The translating process makes use of the programmer's knowledge of the language's syntax to produce a working program. We will begin discussing FORTRAN syntax in Chapters 5 and 6. Right now we are concerned mostly with the translating process rather than with the specific rules.

Here is the algorithm we just developed:

(1) Set SUM to be 0
(2) Set NUMBER to be 12
(3) Add NUMBER to SUM
(4) Add 1 to NUMBER
(5) IF NUMBER is less than or equal to 23 THEN go to step (3)
(6) Print "THE SUM IS" and the value of SUM
(7) Stop

To translate this into a program, each step must be turned into a FORTRAN statement or set of statements. The statements must follow the rules of FORTRAN syntax.

One of the FORTRAN rules is that each statement must have a number. Another rule specifies how arithmetic is to be done. Another specifies how data items are to be stored in the computer's memory. All of the rules will be covered in detail in Chapters 5 and 6. For now, however, the descriptions will be very brief.

Data items in the algorithm are represented in FORTRAN by things called *variable names*. In this algorithm there are two data items that need variable names—SUM and NUMBER.

DATA ITEM	FORTRAN VARIABLE NAME
SUM	S
NUMBER	N

The rules for choosing variable names are given in Chapter 5. For now just remember that anytime you see an S, it means SUM, and anytime you see an N, it means NUMBER.

The program looks like this:

REFERENCE NUMBER	STEP	FORTRAN PROGRAM STATEMENT
1		`* PROGRAM TO SUM NUMBERS: 12 -- 24`
2		`INTEGER S,N`
3	(1)	`S=0`
4	(2)	`N=12`
5		`10    CONTINUE`
6	(3)	`S=S+N`
7	(4)	`N=N+1`
8	(5)	`IF (N ,LE, 23) GOTO 10`
9	(6)	`PRINT *, 'THE SUM IS ', S`
10	(7)	`END`

The reference numbers are used to identify the lines of the program to make it easier to refer to them. They are not part of the program itself. Although it is possible to number lines *within* a FORTRAN program, it is not required. We will usually refer to the reference numbers as *line numbers*. If we do number lines in the program, we will refer to those as *statement numbers*. The *step* column is used to show which lines in the program are translations of which steps in the algorithm. The *step* numbers are not part of the program either.

The rules for forming a FORTRAN program will be discussed at length in Chapter 5, but we will mention one or two of them here. First, there are three *column positions* that are important when you are typing FORTRAN programs into the computer. These column positions are the first, the seventh, and positions 1 through 5. Here are the rules:

1. Any line that has an asterisk (*) in column 1 will be treated as documentation, or comment, line. Documentation lines are used to write messages to other programmers who can be expected to look at your program after it is finished. These messages are usually called comments. All programs should have comments, and we will discuss them later.
2. If a line is to be numbered, the number must appear in columns *1 through 5*. Only certain kinds of lines should be numbered. We will explain those as we go.
3. All other FORTRAN instructions should begin in column 7.

In this program line 1 is an example of a comment line—notice that it begins with an * in column 1. Line 5 is an example of statement number. Notice that the number is in columns 1 and 2—and the FORTRAN statement begins in column 7.

Now let's look at how the program works. The programmer enters the lines in the order they are to be performed. The computer executes programs by performing the first instruction, then going on to the next one; then to the next one, and so on. It is the programmer's job to put the instructions in the proper order. Notice that the last instruction is END. The last instruction in every FORTRAN program *must* be an END. This is to tell the computer where the end of the program is. (Computers are not too bright; they can't figure this out for themselves.)

In this program, line 2 tells the computer that S and N are to contain integer numbers. Notice that this statement doesn't have a corresponding step in the algorithm. This is so because in the algorithm we *knew* that the numbers were integers, so we didn't worry about writing it down. We have to *tell* the computer this, however, and that's what the INTEGER instruction is for. It is unusual for a programmer to create an algorithm in which every step turns out to have exactly one line in the program. This is why we refer to program coding as a *translation* process.

Line 3 instructs the computer to set the *value* of a *variable* named S to zero. Line 4 sets the variable N to 12. Line 6 instructs the computer to add the value of the variable N *into* the value currently stored in the variable S. (We will skip line 5 for a moment.) Here is a trace of what happens as the computer executes these lines.

AT REFERENCE LINE NUMBER	THE VALUE IN N IS	THE VALUE IN S IS
3	(undefined)	0
4	12	0
6	12	12
7	13	12

At line 7, one is added to the value of N.

Notice that each line in the program causes something to happen. Each line is an instruction to the computer telling it to perform a specific activity. The difference between an algorithm and a program is that an *algorithm* is a plan and is written for people to understand; a *program* is a set of instructions written for a computer to execute.

Going back to the example, line 8 checks to see if the value of N is less than or equal to 23. If it is, then statement number 10 (line 5) will be executed next. If it is not, then the following line (line 9) will be executed next. Line 9 prints out the message THE SUM IS on the screen, and follows that by printing out the current value of variable S. Line 10 stops the program.

You can type this program into the computer and tell the computer to execute it. The output should be:

```
THE SUM IS          210
```

Don't worry if you don't understand exactly how the FORTRAN syntax works. Chapters 5 and 6 will describe those rules. Chapter 4 will give you another example of a problem analysis, algorithm design, and FORTRAN program. Remember that from now on *all* programming problems, no matter how easy they seem to be, should be analyzed and written out as algorithms before they are coded into FORTRAN.

PRACTICE

Write an algorithm that will explain how to compute the sum of the *even* numbers beginning with 24 and ending with 72. This algorithm is a variation of the one we just developed, so you can use page 22 as a guide.

Chapter 4 gives an answer to the problem, but you should try to work it out on your own first.

4
USING THE COMPUTER: A SAMPLE PROBLEM

PROBLEM Write a program to print out the sum of the even numbers starting with 24 and ending with 72.

PROBLEM ANALYSIS

SAMPLE
OUTPUT `THE SUM IS  xxxxx`

PURPOSE Sum the even numbers from 24 to 72.

This problem is similar to the problem we programmed in Chapter 3. Its purpose is to compute and print out a sum. What makes this problem different is that the program is supposed to sum only the *even* numbers from 24 to 72.

The sample output is also similar to the output in the problem from Chapter 3. Here, though, instead of specifying the exact number to be printed, we've written down "xxxxx." "xxxxx" is what we call a *format code*. The string of x's is used in the sample output to indicate that a number is to be printed out when we aren't sure what the *exact* value of the number will be. "xxxxx" means that we expect to see a number, and that we don't know exactly what the number will be, but that it shouldn't have more than five digits.

Some other examples of the "xxxxx" formatting convention are:

CODE	MEANING
xxx	A three-digit integer
x	A one-digit integer
xxx.x	A three-digit number, rounded to one decimal place
xxxx.xx	A four-digit number, rounded to two decimal places

SAMPLE   THE SUM IS   ×××××
OUTPUT

In this problem, then, we expect the output number to be an integer of up to five digits. Of course, we can find the actual value of that number by doing the sum by hand or with a calculator. That will be a useful thing to do once we've finished the program because at that point we will want to check the program's output to see if it is correct. For now, however, we don't really *need* to know what the *exact* answer will be.

DATA AND RULES

In reading the problem statement we find three pieces of data and one special rule. As data, we know that the first value to be added into the sum is the value 24. We also know that the last value to be added into the sum is the value 72. And, of course, we know that the sum itself starts with a value of zero.

DATA   Initial value of the sum   0
                First number to be summed   24
                Last number to be summed   72

      The new *rule* we have concerns the fact that the program will sum a set of *even* numbers. The rule for even numbers says that if you start with an even number, you can always get the *next* even number by adding 2 to the number you have. We also have the rule that once the sum has been computed, it should be printed out.

RULES   Once an even number has been added into the sum, the next even number
                can be found by adding 2 to the number that was just added in. After the
                final sum has been computed, it should be printed out.

ALGORITHM

First, a summary of the problem analysis:

PROBLEM   Write a program to print out the sum of the even numbers starting with 24
                and end with 72.

PURPOSE   Sum the even numbers from 24 to 72

SAMPLE   THE SUM IS   ×××××
OUTPUT

DATA   Initial value of sum   0
      First NUMBER to be summed   24
      Last NUMBER to be summed   72

RULES   If NUMBER is an *even* number, then the *next* even number is NUMBER
      + 2.

When the final value of SUM has been computed, it should be printed out.

As you remember, the *algorithm* is a set of steps that shows the computer exactly how to produce the desired output. Step (1) of the algorithm is always performed first, and all other steps are always performed in order, unless specific instructions are given to do otherwise.

The two specific instructions are the "goto" instruction, which always changes the order in which the steps are performed, and the "if/then" instruction, which asks a yes/no question and only changes the order if the answer to the question is yes.

Our first job is to decide what step (1) will be. In looking at the data, we see two things that can be done first:

1. We will be adding up a set of numbers and storing the result in a place called SUM. SUM should start out at zero.
2. The first number to be added into the sum is the number 24. NUMBER should start out at 24.

So our first two steps will be:

    (1) Set SUM to be 0
    (2) Set NUMBER to be 24

Since the final sum is equal to "first even number + next even number + next even number + $\cdots$ + last even number," we can think of the set of steps as being:

• Get the first even number.
• Add it into the sum.
• Get the next even number.
• Add *it* into the sum.
• Get the next even number.
• Add *it* into the sum.
• Repeat this until the last number has been added into the sum.

We have a rule that tells us how to get the *next* even number, and we know that the *last* number is 72, so we can put the algorithm together like this:

    (1)   Set SUM to be 0
    (2)   Set NUMBER to be 24
    (3)   Add NUMBER into SUM
    (4)   Add 2 to NUMBER
    (5)   IF NUMBER is less than or equal to 72 THEN go to step (3)
    (6)   Print THE SUM IS and SUM
    (7)   Stop

Notice that step (3) adds the current "even number" into the sum. Step (4) computes the next even number and step (5) checks to see if the last number has been added in. Step (6) prints the string of letters THE SUM IS followed by the final value of SUM. Step (7) stops the algorithm.

Next we have to check the logic of the algorithm to make sure it will work the way we think it will. We do this by tracing through at least some of the steps by hand:

STEP	SUM	NUMBER	ANSWER AT STEP (5)	PRINTOUT
(1)	0	—	—	—
(2)	0	24	—	—
(3)	24	24	—	—
(4)	24	26	—	—
(5)	24	26	YES	—
(3)	50	26	—	—
(4)	50	28	—	—
(5)	50	28	YES	—
(6)	78	28	—	—
(7)	78	30	—	—
		•		
		•		
		•		
		And so on		

We see that each time step (4) is performed, NUMBER gets bigger. This tells us that eventually NUMBER will grow to be bigger than 72. When this happens, the answer at step (5) will be "NO," and steps (6) and (7) will be performed. So everything looks alright.

CODING THE PROGRAM

The next thing we have to do is to translate each step of the algorithm into one or more lines of FORTRAN code. Remember (from Chapter 3) that *data items* in the algorithm become *variable names* in FORTRAN.

DATA ITEM	FORTRAN VARIABLE NAME
SUM	S
NUMBER	N

Since the problem is very similar to the problem we programmed in Chapter 3, we will use the same variable names. Remember that when you see a SUM in the program it means SUM; and when you see an N it means NUMBER.

The program looks like this:

STEP	FORTRAN PROGRAM
	INTEGER N,SUM
(1)	SUM=0
(2)	N=24
	100 CONTINUE
(3)	SUM=SUM+24
(4)	N=N+2
(5)	IF (N .LE. 72) GOTO 100
(6)	PRINT *,'THE SUM IS',SUM
(7)	END

The next two chapters will explain most of the syntax rules of the FORTRAN language used in this program. One thing you should notice is that some of the lines in a FORTRAN program start in the first column while others start in column 7.

Of the lines that start in column 1, some begin with an integer number, and others begin with an asterisk. The ones that begin with an asterisk are called *comment lines*.

Because it is important that programs include information about what they do and how they work, FORTRAN provides an * as a special instruction that allows programmers to include *comments* within their programs. Comments *do not execute*. The computer ignores them. They are put there for *people* to read.

The general form of a comment is:

* THE REST OF THE LINE IS A COMMENT.

Comments are used to make programs easier to read. In particular, they make it easier for someone other than the original programmer to correct or modify a program. We will discuss program commenting techniques in more detail in later chapters, but at the very least your programs should always have comments to:

• State the purpose of the program.
• Give your name and the date.

Your instructor may ask you to include additional comments, but for now our programs will look like this:

```
Column    Column
1         7

*    SUM OF EVEN NUMBERS, 24 TO 72
*
*    R.W. DILLMAN
*    OCT. 1984
*
          INTEGER N,SUM
          SUM=0
          N=24
100       CONTINUE
          SUM=SUM+N
          N=N+2
          IF (N .LE. 72) GOTO 100
          PRINT *,'THE SUM IS',SUM
          END
```

You can see that these comments *identify* the program. You can also see that blank comment lines are used for spacing.

Remember that the object is to make the program easy to read. Each programmer has his or her own *style* of doing this. Style is very important in programming, and we will discuss it again in Chapter 16.

Other than comment lines, all lines of a FORTRAN program that begin in column 1 begin with an integer number. These numbers are called *statement numbers*.

Statement numbers are used to identify those lines which, for one reason or another, will be referred to by instructions elsewhere in the program. In the example program, the CONTINUE statement must be numbered because it is the *destination* of an IF / THEN / GOTO instruction later on in the program. CONTINUE statements are often used as destination markers and are always numbered. There are other FORTRAN instructions that require numbers; these will be described in later chapters. For now it is enough to know that GOTO must direct the computer to a *numbered* CONTINUE line elsewhere in the program.

Statement numbers must be integers. The biggest possible statement number is 99999. Statement numbers need not come in any particular order, but most programmers tend to choose their statement numbers in ascending order.

You should notice that all lines other than numbered lines and comment lines begin in column 7. You should also notice that all three of the programs you've seen so far have END as their last statement. *Every* FORTRAN program should have END as its last statement. This is a rule of the FORTRAN language.

PRACTICE

1. Type this program into the computer and execute it:

```
          INTEGER N,SUM
          S=0
          N=24
100       SUM=SUM+N
          N=N+2
          IF (N .LE. 72) GOTO 100
          PRINT *, 'THE SUM IS',SUM
          END
```

What does it print out? Verify that the answer it prints out is correct.

2. Look at the program at the end of Chapter 3. Which lines in that program are different from the lines in this chapter's program? Explain why each of the different lines is different.

3. Suppose the problem in this chapter said: "Write a program to print out the sum of the even numbers from 24 to *71*." How would that change the problem analysis? How would it change the algorithm? How would it change the program? Prove that your answers are correct.

4. Suppose the problem said: "Write a program to print out the sum of the even numbers from *23* to 71." How would that change things?

5. Write an algorithm to compute the sum of the *odd* numbers from 1 to 105. Code and execute the corresponding program.

6. Write a program to perform this algorithm:

    (1) Set SUM to be 0
    (2) Set NUMBER to be 10
    (3) PRINT "NUMBER", "SUM"
    (4) Add NUMBER to SUM
    (5) PRINT NUMBER, SUM
    (6) IF NUMBER is less than 100 THEN goto step (4)
    (7) Stop

Sample output:

```
NUMBER          SUM
    10           10
    20           30
    40           70
     .            .
     .            .
     .            .
```

7. Write an algorithm and then a program to print a *list* of the odd numbers from 1 to 9.

Sample output:

```
ODD NUMBERS
1
3
5
7
9
```

SUMMARY
FOR PART I

A computer program is a set of statements each of which instructs the computer to perform a specific task. The set of statements, when executed by the computer, produces the answer to a question or the solution to a problem.

To create competent programs, a programmer must be able to handle two different mental activities. First, the programmer must acquire a clear understanding of the problem to be solved and, based on that understanding, develop an algorithm that demonstrates a logical solution to the problem. Second, the programmer must translate the algorithm into a computer language, enter the translation into the computer, and test it to show that it works.

The first of these two skills is called *algorithm* or *logic design*. The second is called *coding*. Because they are very different activities, it is better to do the logic design first, and then the coding and testing. Programmers who attempt both at the same time will usually be able to create small programs very quickly, but more complicated programs will take them much longer to write, and the most complicated programs will be more than they can handle.

Algorithm design involves quite a bit of *thinking*. Since people think differently, there are no real rules for how to find the best algorithms in the shortest amount of time. One of the better approaches may be to organize the available information into three categories: outputs, inputs, and processing rules; and then just start trying to think up a solution. The only way to learn how to make good algorithms is to practice making them.

To code efficiently, a programmer needs to know the rules, or syntax, of the computer language. The syntax rules are very strict—in fact if they are violated, the computer will stop. There are a fairly small number of rules, however, and with practice they are easy to learn.

The message here is that programming is a skill. To learn how to do it, you have no choice but to practice it. It probably will be frustrating at first, but as you learn the syntax rules, and as you begin to see the kind of logic that computers need, things will make more and more sense. And, of course, the more you practice, the easier it will become.

PROGRAMMING PROBLEMS

You don't really know enough FORTRAN syntax to begin creating your own programs just yet. We'll begin with syntax in the next chapter.

Before we go on, however, there *are* some things that you should know how to make the computer do. All of these have to do with typing in, saving, and printing copies of programs. Use one of the example programs, and make sure that you can instruct the computer to do each of the following.

1. Sitting at the terminal, type the program into the computer.
2. Have the computer save the program from the terminal onto disk (or tape).
3. Sign off the computer. Then sign back on and have the computer load the saved program back from the disk (or tape) to the terminal.
4. Have the computer print a listing of the program on the screen. (If your terminal doesn't have a screen, skip this one.)
5. Have the computer print a listing of the program on paper.
6. Run the program.
7. Delete some lines from the program.
8. Add some lines to the program.
9. Make a change to an existing line in the program.
10. Erase the program from the disk (or tape).

II
ELEMENTARY
SKILLS

5
SYNTAX: OUTPUT, VARIABLES, AND ASSIGNMENTS

DEFINITIONS

Terminal
: The electronic device the programmer uses to communicate with the computer.

Output
: What a program instructs the computer to print out at a terminal.

PRINT*
: The FORTRAN instruction that tells the computer to do output.

String
: A set of characters enclosed in single quote marks.

Variable
: A name that identifies a location in the memory of the computer. Data that has been stored in a variable can be printed out by using a PRINT* statement. The contents of a variable may change during the execution of a program.

Assignment
: The act of storing data in a variable. In FORTRAN the equal sign is used to do assignment.

Separator
: The comma (,) is used to separate items to be output by a PRINT* statement.

SYNTAX

Syntax rules are the rules which the computer insists that you follow whenever you use the FORTRAN language. The syntax rules must be followed exactly. If you break one of the rules, the computer will print out a message that tells you that you made a *syntax error*. It will also tell you where in the program the error was found. The computer will not execute your program until all of the syntax errors have been corrected.

The syntax rules that follow are the rules for what is known as *FORTRAN 77*. FORTRAN is one of the oldest computer languages, and FORTRAN 77 is the latest standard version, replacing the older standard FORTRAN IV (also known as FOR-TRAN 66). "Standard" means that the American National Standards Institute (ANSI) has published an official set of rules which any computer that claims to have FORTRAN 77 must be able to follow.

There are many different kinds of computers, however, and you may find an occasional difference between the rules shown in this book and the rules your computer uses. If the computer insists that you have an error in a line that you think is correct, you can check the rule by looking in the *FORTRAN Language Reference Manual,* which is supplied by the manufacturer of your computer. Your instructor will be able to tell you where to find a copy of the manual.

INSTRUCTIONS

Remember that each line of a computer is an *instruction* that tells the computer to *do* something. In Chapters 3 and 4 are examples of computer programs that use a series of instructions to have the computer find the answer to a problem. This instruction, for example,

        N = 24

uses the equal sign, or "assignment operator," to store the *value* 24 into the *numeric variable* N. And this instruction:

        PRINT *,'THE SUM IS',S

tells the computer to display the *character string* 'THE SUM IS' and the *value* stored in the variable S at the terminal.

In this chapter we will look at the syntax rules for the PRINT* instruction. We will also look at the rules for assigning values to variables. It is impossible to write FORTRAN programs without knowing the language's syntax rules, but you should also remember that the order in which the FORTRAN instructions are executed, the logic of the program, is equally important to the solution of the problem.

LAYOUT OF FORTRAN PROGRAMS

The instructions that make up a FORTRAN program must be arranged in a particular way. Each line of a FORTRAN program may contain only one instruction. There are up to 72 columns of characters per line. Instructions must begin at (or after) the seventh column of a line.

```
COLUMNS 1        2        3        4        5        6        7
123456789012345678901234567890123456789012345678901234567890123456789012
     PRINT *, 'MY NAME IS CAROL'
```

If an instruction starts in columns 1 through 6, the computer will not accept the program. Instead it will print out an error message to indicate that something is wrong.

Computer terminal screens usually display up to 80 columns of characters, but FORTRAN will only use 72 of these. Any characters typed in columns 73 through 80 will be ignored. (There is no good reason for this. FORTRAN is a very old language, and some of its rules are holdovers from the days when computers weren't as powerful as they are now.) If an instruction needs to go beyond column 72 of a line, it can be continued on the next line. This is done by putting any character in column 6 of the next line and then continuing to type the instruction.

```
COLUMNS 1        2        3        4        5        6        7
123456789012345678901234567890123456789012345678901234567890123456789012
     PRINT *, 'THIS IS A PRETTY LONG INSTRUCTION. WHEN IT REACHES THE
    #END OF THE FIRST LINE, IT WILL HAVE TO CONTINUE ON TO THE NEXT LIN
    #E AND THEN ON TO THE ONE AFTER THAT.'
```

If a FORTRAN line has anything other than a blank in column 6, that line will be treated as a continuation of the line before it. We will use the number sign (#) as our continuation marker, but any character will work. Notice that the first character of a continuation line also starts in column 7, and that column 7 of the continuation line is treated just as if it were column 73 of the line before it.

Occasionally it is necessary for the programmer to identify a FORTRAN line for some particular use. A line can be marked for identification by giving it a label. Labels must consist entirely of digits and must be placed in columns 1 through 5.

```
COLUMNS 1        2        3        4        5        6        7
123456789012345678901234567890123456789012345678901234567890123456789012
 136 PRINT *, 'THIS LINE IS LABELED AS LINE 136'
  84 PRINT *, 'THIS LINE IS LABELED AS LINE 84 AND CONTINUES ON TO THE N
    #EXT LINE (WHICH IS NOT LABELED).'
```

A label can be any integer number from 1 to 99999. Labels can come in any order the programmer wants. To help keep programs simple and easy to read, lines should not be assigned labels unless this is absolutely necessary.

The particular brand of computer that you are using may have slightly different rules for entering FORTRAN instructions. We will assume that instructions begin in column 7, that column 6 is used to mark continuation lines, and that labels use columns 1 through 5. You should read the *Computer User's Manual* for your system to be sure that these rules apply to your computer.

THE PRINT INSTRUCTION AND DATA

The PRINT* instruction has the general form:

PRINT *, data to be printed

If the first word in a FORTRAN line is the word PRINT*, then the computer will attempt to display the "data to be printed" at the terminal.

One FORTRAN syntax rule is that instruction words must be spelled correctly. Only PRINT* will be accepted. PRNT*, PRIN*, PRENT*, or *any other* misspelling will not be accepted. If the instruction is misspelled, the computer will print an error message and you will have to correct the instruction.

In FORTRAN the "data to be printed" can be a number of different *types*. *Numeric* data is made up of numbers, and is also divided into two major types, *integer* and *real*. An integer number is a number that contains no decimal point. A real number is one that does contain a decimal point. Character, or string, data is made up of characters. To make it easier for the computer to identify it, character data is always enclosed in single quotation marks.

Here are some examples of legal numeric data.

Value	Type
27.6	Real
–203	Integer
54917	Integer
–6	Integer
0	Integer
0.0	Real
–9.0	Real

Some numeric data which humans accept is not acceptable to the computer. Here are some examples of illegal numeric data.

3,702	Computer does not accept the comma.
$2000	Computer does not accept the dollar sign.
37.50–	Minus sign must come in front.
4 1/2	Computer accepts decimals, but not fractions.

Any characters that can be typed will be accepted as string data as long as the string is enclosed in single quotation marks.

Here are some examples of legal string data:

'SUSAN SMITH'	A name
'JUNE 3, 1994'	A date
'200356'	*Not* a number, but a string of digits
'ABCDEFGHI'	A string of letters
' '	A string of blanks
' '	The "null" string; contains no data

The PRINT* instruction is used to display data items at the terminal:

        PRINT *, 36.2

Printed at the terminal: 36.2

        PRINT *, 59216

Printed at the terminal: 59216

        PRINT *, $3,107.24

Printed at the terminal: ERROR MESSAGE

        PRINT *, 3107.24 (previous line corrected)

Printed at the terminal: 3107.24

        PRINT *, 'ABCDE'

Printed at the terminal: ABCDE

Notice that although strings must have single quotation marks around them in the PRINT statement, they are printed without them.

        PRINT *, 'JULY 4, 1999'

Printed at the terminal: JULY 4, 1999

        PRNT 'HELLO'

Printed at the terminal: ERROR MESSAGE

        PRINT* 'HELLO' (previous line corrected)

Printed at the terminal: ERROR MESSAGE

        PRINT *, 'HELLO' (previous line corrected)

Printed at the terminal: HELLO

The PRINT* statement can also be used to print out the contents of special computer memory locations called variables. We will look at variables next; then we will see how PRINT* is used to display more than one data item at a time.

VARIABLES AND ASSIGNMENT

The equal sign is used to assign data to a variable name. The form is always:

> Variable name = data to be stored

Some examples:

```
I=2931
B3=341.29
F5=-27.0
K=0
C=-.92
M3=-1
```

All of these instructions assign data to *numeric variables*. This means that the number on the right side of the equal sign (=) is *stored* in the computer's memory in a location identified by the variable name on the left side. A *variable name* may be a letter (A-Z) or a letter followed by any combination of up to five letters and digits (A-Z, 0-9). Another way of saying this is that a FORTRAN variable name may be any combination of from one to six letters and digits, but that it must begin with a letter.

Legal names

> X, BOXTOP, R213B, M5, MYNUM

Illegal names

> 3ZIP   Doesn't begin with a letter.
> FX?   ? is not a letter or digit.
> TESTDATA   Too many characters.

In FORTRAN numeric variable names must specify whether the numbers they contain are *integer* or *real*. This specification is controlled by the letter that *begins* the variable name. The standard *type* specifications are:

LETTER THAT BEGINS THE VARIABLE NAME	NUMERIC TYPE
A through H	Real
I through N	Integer
O through Z	Real

Thus FROG and ZIP18 are real variable names, while INDEX and M345 are integer. On most computers numeric variables contain the number 0 or 0.0 until some other value is assigned. You should check your *FORTRAN Language Reference Manual* to see if this is true for your particular computer system.

The programmer can change the types of variable names by using one of the FORTRAN *type* statements. Two of the *type* statements are INTEGER and REAL, and they are used like this:

```
INTEGER FROG, P27, INSET
REAL M88, JSTOP, XYZ
```

Now FROG, P27, and INSET will be treated as *integer* variable names, while M88, JSTOP, and XYZ will be treated as *real*. The INTEGER and REAL statements can be used to override the standard typing (as with FROG, P27, M88, and JSTOP), or to confirm the standard (as with INSET and XYZ). Although FORTRAN does not require it, many programmers use the type statements to define *all* of their variables. Doing this makes their programs easier to read, and easier to correct if there are errors.

We remind you again that the rules might not be *exactly* correct for your computer. Check your *FORTRAN Reference Manual* to be sure.

Notice that there is a difference between the variables P0, which is the letter P followed by the digit zero, and PO, which is the letter P followed by the letter O. Many programmers omit the letter O entirely from their programs in order to avoid this kind of confusion.

Character, or string, data is stored in variables of type *character*. Character variables *must* be explicitly defined by using the CHARACTER type instruction.

```
CHARACTER*30 FROG, INSET, BX72
```

This defines FROG, INSET, and BX72 as character variables each of which is able to hold a string of up to 30 characters. (None of them may now be assigned numeric data.) Data which is to be assigned to a character variable must be enclosed in single quote marks.

```
FROG='THIS IS THE FIRST STRING'
INSET='MY PHONE NUMBER: 212-4476'
```

String variables may be assigned to one another.

```
BX72=FROG
```

In this case, BX72 now contains the string 'THIS IS THE FIRST STRING'. Strings may also consist of digits and/or blanks.

> INSET=' '   This stores a string of five blanks.
>
> FROG='234078'   This stores a string of six *digits*. Notice that '234078' is not a *number*. Neither it nor the variable FROG can be used to do arithmetic.
>
> BX72=''   This stores the *null string* into BX72. The null string contains no characters. On many computers when a character variable is first defined, it is initially set to contain the null string.

The computer processes string data somewhat differently than it does numeric data. In this book we will be mostly concerned with numeric processing, but string operations are fully discussed in Chapter 30.

IMPLICIT TYPING

The FORTRAN instruction IMPLICIT can be used along with the other type instructions to define the type of a set of FORTRAN variable names. For example:

        IMPLICIT REAL(K)

will override the standard typing and make all variables that *begin* with the letter K be real variables. Here are some examples of the use of IMPLICIT.

        IMPLICIT INTEGER(A-H), REAL(I-Z)

Now variables beginning with any of the letters A through H will be integer, and variables beginning with any of I through Z will be real.

        IMPLICIT INTEGER(I-N), REAL(A-H, O-Z)

This is the standard typing.

        IMPLICIT CHARACTER*50(A-H)

Here variables beginning with the letters A through H will be string variables of size 50, those beginning with I through N will be integer (the standard has not changed for them), and variables beginning with the letters O through Z will be real.

In this book the standard typing will be used for numeric variables. Character variables, of course, *must* be defined before they can be used, but in our example programs, we will follow the convention of typing all variable names. This is a good programming practice, and we recommend it. When variables are used in examples of FORTRAN that are not parts of entire programs, we will assume that the variables have been correctly defined prior to their use.

PRINTING VARIABLES AND
LISTS OF DATA

```
R = 6.34
PRINT *, R
```

The first line causes the value 6.34 to be stored in the variable R. The second line causes the computer to print out the value stored in R. In this case 6.34 will be printed at the terminal.

```
JWORD='ABCDEFG'
PRINT *, JWORD
```

The first line causes the string ABCDEFG to be stored in the string variable JWORD. The second line causes the computer to print out the contents of JWORD. In this case ABCDEFG will be printed at the terminal.

The comma is a separator that is used to allow the output of more than one variable or string in the same PRINT* statement.

Strings should be used to label the values being printed out.

```
PRINT *, 'R =' ,R
```

will print out:

```
R= 6.34
R3 = 2000
PRINT *, 'THE SUM IS',R,'AND THE PRODUCT IS',R3
```

will print out:

```
THE SUM IS 6.34 AND THE PRODUCT IS 2000
```

It is difficult to read unlabeled computer output. Good programmers always include labels in their PRINT* statements.

FORMATTED OUTPUT

When you use the PRINT * instruction to print out the values of variables, you will notice the output does not usually come out in a nice, orderly way. This is so because the * part of the PRINT * instruction is a general command that lets the computer decide the final form of the output. FORTRAN programmers can override the * output by replacing the * with special codes that give an exact description of the form the output is to take. These codes are called *format* codes.

If, for example, you execute the following program,

```
REAL RES
RES=10.0/3.0        This is ten divided by three.
PRINT *, RES
END                 This marks the last line in the program. Every
                    FORTRAN program must end with END.
```

the printout will be

        3.333333

The long string of 3s is there because since the computer doesn't know how many digits of precision are to be displayed, it displays as many as it can. To specify the form of the output, you need to use the F format command. In this case that would look like this:

```
REAL RES
RES=10.0/3.0
PRINT '(F4.2)', RES      The format code replaces the *.
END
```

The format code F4.2 specifies that the output value is to be a real (F stands for "floating point") number, and that the number is to be printed as four digits with two digits to the right of the decimal point. So now the output will be:

        3.33

The general form of the F code is:

        Fa.b

where a is an integer number that indicates the *maximum* number of digits to be printed (including the decimal point), and b specifies the number of digits to the right of the decimal point.

For example, if we assign a value to RES:

            RES=123.456789

then

            PRINT '(F10.6)',RES

will print out: 123.456789

            PRINT '(F9.5)',RES

will print out: 123.45679   The number will be rounded up.

        PRINT '(F5.1)',RES

will print out: 123.5

        PRINT '(F4.0)',RES

will print out: 123.   Here there are *no* digits to the right of the decimal point.

        PRINT '(F7.0)',RES

will print out: 123.   Since the maximum number of digits is seven while only four are used, the remaining three are filled out with blanks.

        PRINT '(F2.5)',RES

will print out: **   If the maximum size specification is not big enough to hold all of the significant digits, a field of *s will be printed.

Integer values are specified by using the I format code. The I code is similar to the F code. It has this general form,

        Ia

where a is the maximum number of digits to be printed. Integer values have no decimal points.

String data are specified by using the A (for "alphanumeric") format code. The A code has this general form,

        A

There is no maximum size specified. The exact number of characters contained in the variable will be printed.

EXAMPLE   RES=123.45678   A real number
           NUM=12345   An integer number
           PRINT '(A,F6.2,A,I5)','THE RESULTS ARE ',RES,' AND ',NUM

will print out:

        THE RESULTS ARE 123.46 AND 12345

In the PRINT statement notice that there are blanks after the letter E in ARE and around the word AND. If these blanks are left out, like this:

```
PRINT '(A,F6.2,A,I5)','THE RESULTS ARE',RES,'AND',NUM
```

the output will run together like this:

```
THE RESULTS ARE123.46AND12345
```

Three additional format codes can be used to control spacing. The T command tells the computer to *tab* over to a particular column before printing. For example:

```
PRINT '(A,T17,F6.2,T25,A,T30,I5)','THE RESULTS ARE',RES,'AND',NUM
```

will print out:

```
THE RESULTS ARE 123.46 AND 12345
```

In this case, 123.46 begins in column 17, AND begins in column 25, and 12345 begins in column 30. The general form of the tab code is:

```
Ta
```

where a is the number of the print column at which the first character of the next output value is to be printed.

The X code tells the computer to print blanks. The general form of the X code is:

```
aX
```

where a is the number of blanks to be printed. For example:

```
PRINT '(A,1X,F6.2,2X,A,2X,I5)','THE RESULTS ARE',RES,'AND',NUM
```

will print out:

```
THE RESULTS ARE 123.46  AND   12345
```

Notice that unlike the other codes, the specification number for the X code comes before the code rather than after it. Also notice that the X code prints a specified number of blanks, while the T code tabs out to a specified column.

The final format code that we will look at here is the slash (/). When a slash is encountered in a format specification, the computer prints a line feed and a carriage return. This means that the next value after the slash will be printed beginning at the front of the next line. For example:

```
PRINT '(A,1X,F6.2,//,A,1X,I5)','THE RESULTS ARE',RES,'AND',NUM
```

will print out:

```
        THE RESULTS ARE 123.46
        AND 12345
```

Multiple slashes will produce multiple line feeds. For example:

```
PRINT '(A,1X,F6.2,///,A,1X,I5)','THE RESULTS ARE',RES,'AND',NUM
```

will print out:

```
        THE RESULTS ARE 123.46

        AND 12345
```

One final note. FORTRAN 77 contains a number of holdovers from earlier versions of the language. One of these holdovers has to do with something called *carriage control*. Basically, *carriage control* means that the computer expects that the *first* character in each line of output will be a code that tells it where to begin printing the line. This means that some computers will actually *use* the first character in each output line. In our last examples, the output might actually look like this:

```
        HE RESULTS ARE 123.46
        ND 12345
```

The code for *normal* printing is a blank, and all of the output we will be doing can be handled by using the X command to supply a blank at the beginning of each output line. We would rewrite the last example like this:

```
PRINT '(1X,A,1X,F6.2,//,1X,A,1X,I5)','THE RESULTS ARE',RES,'AND',NUM
```

to make the output come out properly. Notice that the first code blank for the first line, and the first code after the / / is also an 1 X. The second one is needed because the values printed after the / / will be on a new line.

IMPORTANT   Format codes are very powerful tools that allow programmers to specify very complex output forms. Creating the correct set of formats is often a very time-consuming task, however. You should *create* your programs using the PRINT * instruction. Then, once you are sure that the *values* of the outputs are correct, you can go back through the program and substitute format codes for the *s. (Formatted output is discussed in more detail in Chapter 33. Character processing is discussed in Chapters 30 and 31.

PRACTICE

1.  ```
    PRINT *, 'ABCXYZ$'
    END
    ```

    Type in this program and run it. What prints out? What happens if you leave out the END line?

2.  ```
    I43=200
    K=2B
    R3 EQUALS 1.29
    PRINT R3,K;I43
    ENX
    ```

    Run this program. Fix the syntax errors and see what prints out.

3.  ```
    A9=400
    B9=6.3
    PRINT *, 'A9 IS ',A9,' AND B9 IS ',B9
    END
    ```

    Run this program. The output should be:

    ```
    A9 IS 400 AND B9 IS 6.3
    ```

    Now change the program to make the output say:

    ```
    THE SMALLEST IS 6.3 AND THE BIGGEST IS 400
    ```

4. Run this program and see what prints out.

    ```
    CHARACTER*10 TEST, DRIP, FROG
    TEST='ABCDE'
    DRIP='..........'
    FROG='1234567890987654321'
    PRINT *,TEST,DRIP,FROG
    END
    ```

    Change the PRINT* statement to be:

    ```
    PRINT '(X,A,2X,A,6X,A)',TEST,DRIP,FROG
    ```

    and run the program again. What is different about the second output?
    ```

5. Using formatted output, write programs that will print out the following:

    a. `123.4      69.2      105.0`
    b. `123.4`
        `  69.2`
        `105.0`
    c. `123.4      69.2`
        `  105.0`
    d. `123.4`
        `  69.2`
        `105.0`

6. Write programs that will print out the following:

    a. `THE TIME IS 2:30 AM`
    b. `NUMBERS FROM 1 TO 10:`
        `   1`
        `   2`
        `   3`
        `   .`
        `   .`
        `   .`
        `  10`
    c. `NUMBERS FROM 1 TO 10:`
        `   1 2 3 4 5 5 6 8 9 10`

6
SYNTAX:
ARITHMETIC

DEFINITIONS

Integer
: A number with no decimal part, also called a *fixed point* number. On output integers are printed without decimal points.

Real
: A number that has a decimal part, also called a *floating point* number. On output real numbers are printed with decimal points.

Constant
: An integer or real number used in a program statement. The value of a constant does not change during the execution of the program.

PARAMETER
: The FORTRAN instruction that is used to define constants.

Numeric Variable
: A name that identifies a memory location into which integer and real numbers can be stored. The value stored in a variable can be changed at any time during the execution of the program.

Type
: One of the FORTRAN statements INTEGER and REAL that are used to define numeric variables.

Assignment
: The operation of storing a number into a memory location.

Operator
: One of a set of symbols (+, -, /, *, **, =) which are used to do arithmetic and assignment in FORTRAN.

ARITHMETIC

In FORTRAN there are five arithmetic operators:

Addition	Plus sign (+)
Subtraction	Minus sign (-)
Multiplication	Asterisk (*)
Division	Slash (/)
Exponentiation	Two asterisks (**)
	A**B means A to the B power

The *results* of an arithmetic operation *must be assigned* to a *numeric variable name*.

EXAMPLES   These are legal:

J = 4*2	The result is 8.
K = 3**2	The result is 9 (3 squared).
R4 = 3.6-2.7	The result is 0.9.

These are not legal:

4 + 9 = C	Backward, should be C = 4 + 9.
A3 + D9*5	Result not assigned to a variable.
4B = 9.3+6	4B is not a legal variable name.
B3 - C = X4*Y+3	B3-C is not a legal variable name.

If more than one arithmetic operation is to be performed in a line of FORTRAN code, the operations are *always* executed in this order:

- First, all exponents are done.
- Next, all multiplications and divisions are done.
- Last, all additions and subtractions are done.

EXAMPLES   J=9+2-10/5+3*2
becomes J=9+2-2+6 which becomes J=15.
R=4-6/3+2**3
becomes R=4-6/3+8 which becomes R=4-2+8 and finally R=10.

Parentheses can be used to change the order in which the operations are done. Operations within parentheses are done first.

EXAMPLES   A=2+3*4.1   The result is 14.3.
B=(2+3)*4.1   The result is 20.5.
C=2+(3*4.1)   The result is 14.3.

The arithmetic operations follow the same rules that you use when you do arithmetic. The computer, however, does impose some restrictions that you are not used to.

- There are no fractions.

  X = 3 1/2   This is not "three and a half." It is "thirty-one divided by two."
  X = 3.5   This is "three and a half."

- All operators must be specified.

  Y = 2(X + 1)   This is an error. There must be an operator between the 2 and
                 the (.
  Y = 2*(X + 1) This is "two times X plus one."

- Division by zero is illegal.

  M = 5/(2*3 - 6)   This works out to 5/0. Any time division by zero is
                    attempted, the computer will print an error message.

- Positive decimal exponents are alright, but negative decimal exponents are illegal.

  X = 9**(.5)   This is "9 to the one-half power" or "square root of nine."
                  The result is 3.
  Q = 6**(-.5)   This produces an error message. Negative fractional roots
                  are undefined.

Once a value has been assigned to a variable name, the variable can be used in other arithmetic expressions.

EXAMPLES   S = 3.1   2*S = 2*3.1 since 3.1 was
             Q9 = 2*S   stored in S. The result is
             PRINT *,Q9   6.2, which is stored into Q9.

                Prints out: 6.2

             K = 4   Here one is added to the value
             K = K + 1   of K and the result is stored
             PRINT *,K   back into K.

                Prints out: 5

             A = 8   A - 2*B becomes 8 - 2*4 which,
             B = 4   works out to be zero. Division
             Q = 9/(A - 2*B) by zero is illegal.
             PRINT *,Q

                Prints out: ERROR

```
X = 16
B = -2
R = 16**(1/B)
PRINT *,R
```
(1/B) works out to be 0.5. 16 to the 0.5 power is the same as the square root of 16.

Prints out: 4

```
X = 16
B = -2
R = 16**(1/B)
PRINT *,R
```
The value of B is now negative. (1/B) works out to -0.5, and the negative fractional roots are illegal.

Prints out: ERROR

PRACTICE

1. Have the computer print the value stored in each of the variable names. Why does it print what it does?

```
K  = 103          M3 = 103.33402179
TO = 26.192       F4 = 2693177204
```

2. Find and correct the errors in this program:

```
A3-B9=27
B3+6-7.1*2
C3=X+2*(9.4
Z3=B4*-3.2+7
PRINT *,A3,B3,C3,Z3
END
```

3.  ```
    K = 4
    S9 = 8
    ```

    Add lines to this program to do the following:

    Compute A = the product of K and S9
    Compute B = S9 minus K
    Compute C = K minus S9
    Compute D = K plus S9 divided by 2
    Print out A, B, C, and D
    ```

4. Have the computer print the value stored in each of these variables. Why does it print what it does?

```
A  = 6 +  (2 - 3)*(4**2)
I  = 9.3+  10.7 - 2
F8 = 8/3  + 5.4
```

7
USING THE COMPUTER: A SAMPLE PROBLEM

PROBLEM ANALYSIS

PROBLEM Write a program to print out the sum of the first 13 even integers.

PURPOSE Sum the first 13 even integers.

SAMPLE   `SUM OF THE FIRST THIRTEEN EVEN INTEGERS:   XXX`
OUTPUT

This problem differs from the other problems we have seen in that it does not *specify* what the beginning and ending even numbers are. What it tells us instead is to find the sum of the *first 13* even numbers. We know that the first even number is 2, so that part is easy. We also know (from Chapter 4) the rule for finding the next even number. So it looks as though our only real problem will be to figure out how to tell the computer to stop after it's added in the thirteenth number. To do this we will have to show the computer how to *count*.

  If we summarize the data and rules, we get:

DATA   Initial value of the sum   0
       First number to be added   2

RULES   The *next* even number can always be found by adding 2 to the *current* even number.
        After 13 numbers have been added into the sum, the sum should be printed out.

  It is important to see that the problem does not tell us what the *value* of the last number to be added into the sum is. It does, however, specify a rule that tells us *how many* values to add. As you will see, this will work out just as well.

ALGORITHM

For a first try, we can set up an algorithm similar to the ones we've done before. Since this problem is a little different from the others, we don't really expect this algorithm to be correct, but we have to start somewhere.

     (1)   Set SUM to 0
     (2)   Set NUMBER to 2
     (3)   Add NUMBER into SUM
     (4)   Add 2 to NUMBER
     (5)   IF NUMBER $<=$??? THEN go to step (3)
     (6)   Print "SUM OF THE FIRST THIRTEEN EVEN INTEGERS:" and SUM
     (7)   Stop

Step (1) initializes SUM to zero. Step (2) gets the first even number. Step (3) adds it into the sum, and step (4) gets the next even number. Our problem comes with step (5).

    Since we don't know what the *value* of NUMBER will be when it reaches the thirteenth even number, we can't test the value of NUMBER to see if the sum is finished. We have to test something else.

    What we would like to say is something like this:

     (5)   IF the thirteenth number hasn't been added in yet, THEN go back to step (3)

The trouble is that the computer won't know what the term "the thirteenth number" *means*. Before we can ask it to make this kind of a decision, we have to show it how to *count*.

    When you count, you always count *things*. If, for example, you sit by a window and count the cars that go by, what you are doing is *adding up* the *number* of cars you see. What you actually *do* is something like this:

- When you see the first car, you think to yourself "one."
- When you see the next car, you remember that the count is "one" and add one to it to get a new count of "two."
- Each time another car comes by, you add one to your count.

    Now, if I were to tell you, "Sit by the window and tell me the color of the eighth car that goes by," you'd be able to do that. The first car to go by would be car number "one." Each one after that would add one to the count. Each time you added one to the count, you would check to see if the count was up to "eight." When the count reached eight, you would write down the color of that particular car. This is what we have to show the computer how to do.

    You can see that when we talk about the *count*, we are talking about a thing that the computer will have to remember. This tells us that the count will be a data item in the same way that SUM and NUMBER are data items. You can also see that we have developed a rule for *counting:*

- Decide what "thing" you are going to count.
- Set the initial value of COUNT to 0.
- Each time the "thing" you want to count occurs, add one to COUNT.

EXAMPLE   Write an algorithm for printing out the first ten integers.

(1)   Set COUNT to 0
(2)   Add 1 to COUNT
(3)   Print COUNT
(4)   IF COUNT is less than 10 THEN go to step (2)
(5)   Stop

Step (1) initializes COUNT to zero. Step (2) adds 1 to the value of COUNT and step (3) prints out the new value. Step (4) checks to see if the tenth value has been printed. If not, then steps (2), (3), and (4) are executed again. If the tenth value has been printed, then the algorithm stops. As always, we can check this algorithm to see if it is correct:

STEP	COUNT	PRINTED AT STEP (3)	ANSWER AT STEP (4)
(1)	0	—	—
(2)	1	—	—
(3)	1	1	—
(4)	1	—	YES
(2)	2	—	—
(3)	2	2	—
(4)	2	—	YES
(2)	3	—	—
•	•	•	•
•	•	•	•
•	•	•	•
(4)	9	—	YES
(2)	10	—	—
(3)	10	10	—
(4)	10	—	NO
(5)	(STOP)		

Notice that at step (4) the answer to the IF question will be "YES" as long as the value of COUNT is less than 10. As soon as COUNT becomes 10 [at step (2)], and is printed out [at step (3)], the answer to the IF question will change to "NO" and the algorithm will stop.

To find the sum of the first thirteen integers, then, we need to combine the counting algorithm with the summing algorithm.

(1) Set sum to be 0
(2) Set COUNT to be 0
(3) Set NUMBER to be 2
(4) Add NUMBER into SUM
(5) Add 2 to NUMBER
(6) Add 1 to COUNT
(7) IF COUNT is less than 13 THEN go to step (4)
(8) Print "THE SUM OF THE FIRST THIRTEEN EVEN INTEGERS:" and SUM
(9) Stop

The two new steps are steps (6) and (7). Step (6) adds 1 to COUNT *each time* NUMBER is added into SUM. Step (7) tests to see if the count is less than 13. If it is, then fewer than thirteen numbers have been added into the sum. As soon as COUNT is equal to 13, the algorithm moves on to steps (8) and (9) to print out the result and stop.

To check the algorithm:

STEP	SUM	NUMBER	COUNT	ANSWER AT STEP 7
(1)	0	—	—	—
(2)	0	—	0	—
(3)	0	2	0	—
(4)	2	2	0	—
(5)	2	4	0	—
(6)	2	4	1	—
(7)	2	4	1	YES
(4)	6	4	1	—
(5)	6	6	1	—
(6)	6	6	2	—
(7)	6	6	2	YES
(4)	12	6	2	—
(5)	12	8	2	—
(6)	12	8	3	—
(7)	12	8	3	YES
		•		
		•		
		•		
	And so on		

This much is a reasonable (though not complete) check of the algorithm. The third time we get to step (7), COUNT is equal to 3, and SUM is equal to the sum of the first three even numbers ($2 + 4 + 6 = 12$). It's a pretty good bet that the algorithm will work out for all thirteen even numbers, so rather than take the time to figure out the whole table, we'll go ahead and code the program. Then, of course, we'll execute the program. If it doesn't give us the correct answer, we may have to come back and finish the algorithm checkout. If it does give the right answer, however, we will have saved quite a bit of time.

PROGRAM

We have added one new variable, but other than that there is nothing in this program that we haven't seen before.

DATA ITEM:
COUNT   VARIABLE NAME: COUNT

STEP		FORTRAN PROGRAM
		INTEGER NUMBER, SUM, COUNT
(1)		SUM=0
(2)		COUNT=0
(3)		NUMBER=2
	10	CONTINUE
(4)		SUM=SUM+NUMBER
(5)		NUMBER=NUMBER+2
(6)		COUNT=COUNT+1
(7)		IF (COUNT .LT. 13) GOTO 10
(8)		PRINT *, 'THE SUM OF THE FIRST THIRTEEN EVEN #INTEGERS: ',SUM
(9)		END

DOCUMENTED PROGRAM

As always, we need to add comment statements to identify the programmer and program. In addition, we will also add comments to identify the variable names that are used in the program.

REFER-ENCE		FORTRAN PROGRAM
1	*	SUM OF FIRST THIRTEEN EVEN NUMBERS
2	*	
3	*	R. W. DILLMAN
4	*	FEBRUARY 1984
5	*	
6	*	VARIABLES:
7	*	NUMBER=CURRENT EVEN INTEGER
8	*	SUM=SUM OF NUMBERS, COUNT=COUNT OF NUMBERS
9	*	
10		INTEGER NUMBER, SUM, COUNT
11		SUM=0
12		COUNT=0
13		NUMBER=2
14	10	CONTINUE
15		SUM=SUM+NUMBER
16		NUMBER=NUMBER+2
17		COUNT=COUNT+1
18		IF (COUNT .LT. 13) GOTO 10
19		PRINT *, 'THE SUM OF THE FIRST THIRTEEN EVEN
20		#INTEGERS: ',SUM
21		END

Lines 6 to 8 represent a *variable dictionary*. It is very useful, especially in larger programs, to have this information available when you are debugging your programs. You should try to develop the habit of including a variable dictionary in every program you write.

PRACTICE

1.   Execute the program and verify that its answer is correct.

2.   What is the *value* of the thirteenth even number? Change the program to print that value along with the sum.

3.   Change the problem analysis, algorithm, and program in order to find the sum of the first 229 even numbers. How can you verify that the answer printed by this new program is correct *without* adding up the 229 numbers by hand?

4.   Add a new line to the program after line 12:

```
L = 13
```

and change line 18 to read:

```
IF (COUNT .LT. L) GOTO 10
```

then execute the program. What prints out? Why is this a better way of writing the program than the way we did it in the example?

5.   There is a limit to the number of even numbers whose *exact* sum you can have the computer print out. Why is there a limit? How would you go about finding the limit?

8
LOGIC: THE LOOP STRUCTURE

DEFINITIONS

Structures
The name given to a set of special forms that are often used to simplify program design and coding.

Simple Structure
The programming structure in which a set of instructions is executed, each immediately after the one before it.

Loop Structure
The programming structure in which a set of instructions is repeated some number of times.

STRUCTURES

Most computer professionals agree that there are *only three* basic things you need to be able to do to write good computer programs.

1. You need to be able to have the computer execute a series of instructions in sequential order (i.e., one after another).
2. You need to be able to have the computer repeat a set of instructions as many times as you want.
3. You need to have the computer be able to execute I F tests.

We refer to these three activities as *logical structures*, and each structure has a name.

ACTIVITY	STRUCTURE
Execute a sequence	Simple
Repeat a sequence	Loop
Execute an I F test	IF/THEN/ELSE

We will talk about the IF/THEN/ELSE structure in Chapter 14. Here we will concentrate on simple structures and loops.

SIMPLE STRUCTURES

The simple structure is the easiest to understand. Anytime you ask the computer to perform one or more activities in a row, you are using a simple structure. For example, in the algorithm for summing the numbers from 1 to 10:

(1) Set COUNT to be 1
(2) Set SUM to be 0
(3) Add COUNT into SUM
(4) Add 1 to COUNT
(5) IF COUNT is less than 10 THEN go to step (3)
(6) Print "THE SUM IS" and SUM
(7) Stop

Here steps (1) and (2) are a simple sequence. This is so because they are always performed in the order (1), (2), and are only performed once. Steps (6) and (7) also fit this description.

Steps (3), (4), and (5), however, are performed over and over again. They are an example of a repeating, or *loop*, structure.

LOOP STRUCTURES

We could rewrite the summing algorithm to look like this:

(1) Set SUM to be 0
(2) LOOP with COUNT going from 1 to 10
    (2.1) Add COUNT to SUM
(3) Print "THE SUM IS" and SUM
(4) Stop

Although this is a different way of writing the algorithm, it still performs the same activities. Step (1) initializes the sum to zero. Step (2) is a loop. A loop is always repeated some number of times. In step (2) the repeating is controlled by the data item COUNT, which starts at 1 and stops at 10. By being able to say:

(2) LOOP with COUNT going from 1 to 10
    (2.1) Add COUNT to SUM

we give ourselves a way of *specifying* the loop within the algorithm.

Notice, in this example, that step (2) *defines* the loop. That is, it says to you, "This is a loop." It also tells you that the data item COUNT will control the number of times the loop is to be repeated.

When we say that COUNT will go from 1 to 10, we assume that COUNT will start at 1 and go up in steps of 1 until its value is *bigger* than 10. That is, each time step (2) is performed, 1 is added to COUNT. As soon as COUNT is bigger than 10, the loop is finished and the algorithm goes on to step (3). As always, we can check this algorithm by tracing it:

STEP	COUNT	SUM	OUTPUT
(1)	—	0	—
(2)	1	0	—
(2.1)	1	1	—
(2)	2	1	—
(2.1)	2	3	—
(2)	3	3	—
(2.1)	3	6	—
(2)	4	6	—
(2.1)	4	10	—
(2)	5	10	—
(2.1)	5	15	—
(2)	6	15	—
•	•	•	•
•	•	•	•
•	•	•	•
(2)	10	45	—
(2.1)	10	55	—
(2)	11	55	—
(3)	11	55	THE SUM IS 55
(4)	(STOP)		

It is important to understand *exactly* what happens when step (2), the loop step, is performed.

The *first* time step (2) is performed, COUNT is initialized to 1. Then the instruction that is to be repeated, step (2.1), is performed. After step (2.1) is completed, the algorithm *automatically* goes back to step (2). We don't need an IF test to do this because the act of going back and repeating is built into the idea of using the LOOP.

Each time the algorithm *comes back* to step (2), 1 is added to the value of COUNT. If COUNT is *not* bigger than 10, then step (2.1) is repeated again. As soon as COUNT gets to be *bigger* than 10, the LOOP is finished, and step (3) is performed.

Now let's look at a slightly more complicated problem. The problem we did in Chapter 4 said:

PROBLEM Write a program to print out the sum of the even numbers starting with 24 and ending with 72.

The algorithm we developed looked like this:

  (1) Set the SUM to be 0
  (2) Set NUMBER to be 24
  (3) Add NUMBER into SUM
  (4) Add 2 to NUMBER
  (5) IF NUMBER is less than or equal to 72
       THEN go to step (3)
  (6) Print "THE SUM IS" and SUM
  (7) Stop

As in the algorithm we just did, this algorithm contains a loop. This one is different, though, in that the loop is not repeated a *specified number* of times. That is, it is not repeated as the value of a counter goes from 1 to some final value. Instead, it is repeated as the value of the data item NUMBER goes through the even numbers from 24 to 72.

Since we know the rule for finding even numbers, we can say that the data item NUMBER goes from 24 to 72 in *steps* of 2 (i.e., 24, 26, 28, 30, 32, . . . , 70, 72). If we decide to use this as part of the LOOP structure, we can rewrite the even-number algorithm like this:

  (1) Set SUM to be 0
  (2) LOOP with NUMBER going from 24 to 72 in steps of 2
      (2.1) Add NUMBER into SUM
  (3) Print "THE SUM IS" and SUM
  (4) Stop

Checking the new version of the algorithm, we get:

STEP	NUMBER	SUM
(1)	—	0
(2)	24	0
(2.1)	24	24
(2)	26	24
(2.1)	26	50
(2)	28	50
(2.1)	28	78
(2)	30	78
•	•	•
•	•	•
•	•	•
	And so on	

Steps (2) and (2.1) will be repeated until NUMBER has taken on each of the even values from 24 to 72, and each of those values has been added into the sum.

We can see from this that there are *two* parts to every loop structure:

1. The word LOOP.
2. A *control* statement that describes how the loop will work and when it will be finished.

All loops have these two parts.

As a final example, let's look at the problem we did in Chapter 7. That problem statement said:

PROBLEM   Write a program to print out the sum of the first thirteen even integers.

The algorithm looked like this:

     (1)   Set SUM to be 0
     (2)   Set COUNT to be 0
     (3)   Set NUMBER to be 2
     (4)   Add NUMBER into SUM
     (5)   Add 2 to NUMBER
     (6)   Add 1 to COUNT
     (7)   IF COUNT is less than 13 THEN go to step (4)
     (8)   Print "THE SUM OF THE FIRST THIRTEEN INTEGERS:" and SUM
     (9)   Stop

If we look at the loop in steps (4) through (7), we see that the loop is *repeated* thirteen times. We also see that *each time* the loop repeats, the data item NUMBER is first added into the sum and then increased by 2. Rewriting the algorithm we get:

     (1)   Set SUM to be 0
     (2)   Set NUMBER to be 2
     (3)   LOOP with COUNT going from 1 to 13
          (3.1)   Add NUMBER into SUM
          (3.2)   Add 2 to NUMBER
     (4)   Print "THE SUM OF THE FIRST THIRTEEN INTEGERS IS" and SUM
     (5)   Stop

Notice that in this case there are two activities to be performed within the loop. Steps (3.1) and (3.2) are a *simple* structure that happens to be *inside* a loop structure. Also notice that the data item COUNT is *only* used in the control statement for the loop. (Here, since COUNT is meant to go up by steps of 1, we just leave the "in steps of" message off. Whenever the step message is omitted, you can assume that the step size is 1.)

PRACTICE

1. Trace the last algorithm to see if it works correctly.

2. Write LOOP statements for the following control conditions:
   a. To print out the first 100 integers.
   b. To print out the odd numbers from 11 to 53.
   c. To count to 100 by tens.
   d. To count backward from 10 to 1.

3. Design an algorithm for this problem:

   Write a program to print out a table of squares and square roots for the integers from 1 to 10.

   Sample output:

NUMBER	SQUARE	SQUARE ROOT
1	1	1.00
2	4	1.42
3	9	1.73
4	16	2.00
•	•	•
•	•	•
•	•	•

1. (The answer can be found in Chapter 10.)

9
SYNTAX:
DO LOOPS

DEFINITIONS

Loop

A set of FORTRAN statements which are to be repeated one or more times.

DO

The FORTRAN instruction for executing loops. DO comes at the beginning of the loop; CONTINUE is often used to mark the end of the loop.

CONTINUE

The FORTRAN instruction that is used to mark a particular location in a program. Often used to mark the ends of DO loops.

FORTRAN LOOPS

The simplest way to show how the DO instruction is used to set up loops is to translate one of the algorithms we developed in the last chapter into FORTRAN. If you remember, the algorithm for summing the numbers from 1 to 10 looked like this:

(1) Set SUM to be 0
(2) LOOP with COUNT going from 1 to 10
     (2.1) Add COUNT into SUM
(3) Print "THE SUM IS" and SUM
(4) Stop

To translate this into FORTRAN code, we will need two variable names.

DATA ITEM	VARIABLE NAME
SUM	SUM
COUNT	COUNT

The translation will look like this:

STEP	REFERENCE		FORTRAN CODE
(1)	1		SUM=0
(2)	2		DO 10 COUNT=1,10,1
(2.1)	3		SUM=SUM+COUNT
(2)	4	10	CONTINUE
(3)	5		PRINT *,'THE SUM IS',SUM
(4)	6		END

Notice that step (2) in the algorithm requires *two* lines in the program. The DO statement marks the beginning of the loop. The CONTINUE statement marks the end of the loop. SUM=SUM+COUNT is the instruction which is to be repeated.

The DO is a code that tells the computer that this is to be a loop. COUNT=1,10,1 is the *control statement*. In this case the control statement tells the computer to initialize the variable COUNT to 1 the first time the loop is executed, and to finish the loop as soon as the value of COUNT is bigger than 20. The last value, 1, is the "step-size" value that tells the computer to increase COUNT by 1 each time the line is repeated.

The CONTINUE line tells the computer that it has reached the end of the loop. When the CONTINUE is executed, the computer automatically goes back to the DO statement at the beginning of the loop and continues from there.

If we trace through the execution of the program, we can see the order in which the instructions will be executed.

REFERENCE LINE	SUM	COUNT	PRINTOUT
1	0	—	—
2	0	1	—
3	1	1	—
4	1	1	—
2	1	2	—
3	3	2	—
4	3	2	—
2	3	3	—
3	6	3	—
4	6	3	—
2	6	4	—
•	•	•	•
•	•	•	•
•	•	•	•
2	45	10	—
3	55	10	—
4	55	10	—
2	55	11	—
5	55	11	THE SUM IS 55
6	(STOP)		

You can see that the CONTINUE line doesn't really *do* anything. Its only job is to act as a place marker to let the computer know when it's reached the end of the loop. If the CONTINUE line wasn't there, the computer wouldn't know when to jump back to the top of the loop and repeat. It is very important in setting up DO loops that the CONTINUE statement be the very *last* statement in the loop. If you put the CONTINUE statement in the wrong place, the computer will generate incorrect answers.

The general form of the DO statement is:

DO line number A = B , C , D

- The *line number* is the label number of the statement that marks the end of the loop. The numbered line does not *have* to be a CONTINUE instruction, but CONTINUE is usually the best choice.
- A is the *counter*. It is always *initialized* (set equal to) to B when the DO statement is executed for the first time.
- C is the *end-of-loop test value*. *Each* time the DO statement is executed, the value of A is tested against the value of C. As soon as A *exceeds* C, the loop is terminated.
- D is the *step size*. Each time the numbered statement is executed, the value of D is added to the value of A and control is returned to the DO statement.

In the DO statement shown above, A must be a FORTRAN variable name. Any of B, C, and D may be either variables or constants. If D is equal to 1, then the step section may be omitted. That is, if no step size is given, FORTRAN assumes it to be 1.

As another example, let's look again at the algorithm for summing even numbers that we developed in Chapter 8.

PROBLEM   Write a program to print out the sum of the even numbers from 24 to 72.

ALGORITHM (1) Set SUM to be 0
           (2) LOOP with NUMBER going from 24 to 72 in steps of 2
                (2.1) Add NUMBER into SUM
           (3) Print "THE SUM IS" and SUM
           (4) Stop

The program looks like this:

STEP	REFERENCE	FORTRAN CODE
(1)	1	SUM=0
(2)	2	DO 10 N=24,72,2
(2.1)	3	SUM=SUM+N
(2)	4	10 CONTINUE
(3)	5	PRINT *, 'THE SUM IS',SUM
(4)	6	END

Again, you can see that the loop in step (2) translates into two lines, 20 and 40, in the program. We can check the output of the program by tracing through the instructions by hand:

REFERENCE LINE	SUM	N
1	0	—
2	0	24
3	24	24
4	24	24
2	24	26
3	50	26
4	50	26
2	50	28
3	78	28
•	•	•
•	•	•
•	•	•

You can see that each time line 2 is executed, the value of the variable N goes up by 2. Then, as long as N is not bigger than 72, the program will execute lines 3 and 4 and then repeat line 2. As soon as the value of N exceeds 72 at line 2, the computer will finish the loop and go on to lines 5 and 6.

USING DO

We have already seen how the DO instruction can be used for *counting*. This particular form of the loop:

```
L = 30
DO  100  COUNT = 1 , L
```

┌─────────────┐
│ Any set of │
│ FORTRAN   │
│ instructions│
└─────────────┘

```
100  CONTINUE
```

will repeat the set of FORTRAN instructions 30 times. Changing the value of L will change the upper limit of the count and, therefore, change the number of times the loop will be repeated. This is one of the most useful forms of the DO, and you will see it used over and over again in the coming chapters.

It is useful to notice that there are no limits on the *step size* in a DO loop. This routine, for example, counts from 1 to 2 in steps of 0.01:

```
DO 400 R=1,2,.01
```

Instructions to be repeated

```
400 CONTINUE
```

Notice that although the counter R begins at 1 and ends at 2, the loop will be repeated 100 times. R will take on the values 1.00, 1.01, 1.02, 1.03, and so on.

If the step size is *negative*, the loop will count *backward*. For example, this routine:

```
DO 93 J=10,1,-1
PRINT*, J
93 CONTINUE
END
```

will print out the numbers 10, 9, 8, · · · 3, 2, 1. In this case J is *initialized* to 10. Then the value of J is tested to see if it is *less than* 1. If it is not, then the loop is executed.

When the DO line is executed again, −1 is added to the value of J. This has the effect of subtracting 1 from J, so the value of J gets smaller each time through. When the value of J is *smaller* than the *end test*, 1, the loop exits.

More generally:

```
DO 200 A=B,C,D
```

Instructions to be repeated

```
200 CONTINUE
```

- If D is positive, then the loop ends when the value of A is greater than the value of D.
- If D is negative, then the loop ends when the value of A is less than the value of D.
- If D is zero, the loop never ends.

Loops may be put inside of one another, or *nested*. When doing this you need to be sure that the second loop is completely inside the first. This, for example, is correct:

REFERENCE

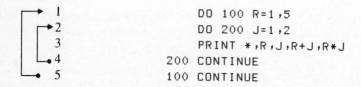

```
              DO 100 R=1,5
              DO 200 J=1,2
              PRINT *,R,J,R+J,R*J
          200 CONTINUE
          100 CONTINUE
```

Notice that the J loop is *inside* of the R loop. This example is incorrect:

REFERENCE

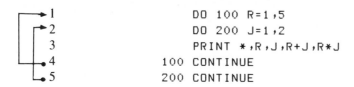

```
 1              DO 100 R=1,5
 2              DO 200 J=1,2
 3              PRINT *,R,J,R+J,R*J
 4         100 CONTINUE
 5         200 CONTINUE
```

If you try to run this, the computer will print an error message. You can always check your nested loops by connecting the DOs and CONTINUEs with lines as in these examples. If the lines cross, the loops are out of order.

If we were to trace the first example shown above, we would get:

REFERENCE	R	J	R+J	R*J
1	1	—	—	—
2	1	1	—	—
3	1	1	2	1
4	1	1	—	—
2	1	2	—	—
3	1	2	3	2
4	1	2	—	—
2	1	3	—	—
5	1	3	—	—
1	2	3	—	—
2	2	1	—	—
3	2	1	3	2
4	2	1	—	—
2	2	2	—	—
3	2	2	4	4
		•		
		•		
		•		
		And so on		

If you continue this to its end, you will see that the R loop is *repeated* 5 times. Since the J loop *repeats* the PRINT* statement twice, the PRINT* line is repeated 10 times. In using nested loops, you need to be careful to estimate the total number of executions you are requesting. This routine, for example:

```
           DO 10 A=1,100
           DO 20 B=1,100
           DO 30 C=1,100
           S=A+B+C
    30     CONTINUE
    20     CONTINUE
    10     CONTINUE
           PRINT *,S
           END
```

will cause S = A + B + C to be executed 1,000,000 times. On most computers this will take an exceptionally long time to run. Loops such as this should be avoided unless you have a very good reason for using them.

PRACTICE

1. Code and test out the FORTRAN program that goes with this algorithm.

ALGORITHM   Sum the first thirteen even numbers.

      (1)   Set SUM to be 0
      (2)   Set NUMBER to be 2
      (3)   LOOP with COUNT going from 1 to 13
           (3.1)   Add NUMBER into SUM
           (3.2)   Add 2 to NUMBER
      (4)   Print "SUM OF THE FIRST THIRTEEN INTEGERS IS" and SUM
      (5)   Stop

2. Run this program with the values given below. Each time, explain why you get the printout that you do.

```
          A = 1
          B = 5
          C = 1
          DO 100 Q=A,B,C
          PRINT *,Q
    100   CONTINUE
          PRINT
          PRINT *,'LAST Q IS',Q
     90   END
```

Change A, B, and C and run the program again.

a. A = 1, B = 5, C = 3
b. A = 0, B = 6, C = 3
c. A = -4, B = 2, C = 1
d. A = -10, B = 10, C = 5
e. A = 2.5, B = 4, C = .2
f. A = 10, B = 1, C = -1

3. Run this program. Why does it print out what it does?

```
        DO 10 N=1,5
        PRINT *,'N IS',N
        DO 20 X=1,3
        PRINT *,'X IS',X
   20   CONTINUE
   10   CONTINUE
        END
```

10
USING THE COMPUTER: A SAMPLE PROBLEM

PROBLEM   Write a program to print out a table of squares, cubes, and roots for the first ten integers.

SAMPLE OUTPUT NUMBER	SQUARE	CUBE	SQUARE ROOT	CUBE ROOT
1	1	1	1.00	1.00
2	4	8	1.42	1.26
3	9	27	1.73	1.45
4	16	64	2.00	1.59
.	.	.	.	.
.	.	.	.	.
.	.	.	.	.

PURPOSE   Produce a table of squares, cubes, and roots.

In looking at the text and sample output of this problem, there are a number of things that we can see that will help us out with the solution.

First of all, we can see that for each value in the column NUMBER, we need to compute four other values—a square, a cube, a square root, and a cube root. Also, since the problem says to compute these for each of the numbers from 1 to 10, we realize that we'll have to *repeat* the set of computations ten times.

We see that *each* time we do a set of computations, the result will have to be printed. This is different from the previous problems where we only printed the final sum.

Finally, we notice that the *headings*—NUMBER, SQUARE, CUBE, and so on—need to be printed out first, at the top of each column of numbers.

We can summarize this information in a sort of *pseudoalgorithm*. (It doesn't have all the exact steps a real algorithm does, but it gives us a general idea of what we want to do.)

- First, print out the headings.
- Next, compute square, cube, square root, and cube root for the number 1 and print those results.
- Next, repeat the computing and printing for numbers 2 through 10.

Now that we have a good first impression as to what we need to do, we can continue analyzing the problem and developing the algorithm.

DATA	First number for use in computations	1
	Last number for use in computations	10
	Headings NUMBER	
	SQUARE	
	CUBE	
	SQUARE ROOT	
	CUBE ROOT	

RULES   Compute square, cube, square root, and cube root for each number

Square	$= \text{number}^2$
Cube	$= \text{number}^3$
Square root	$= \text{number}^{1/2}$
Cube root	$= \text{number}^{1/3}$

Print each set of results for each number.
Print headings once at the top of the output.

If you don't remember how to do powers and roots in FORTRAN, you can look back at Chapter 6. Now, keeping in mind that what we want to do is to print the headings, then repeat a set of computations and printouts, we can start the algorithm.

ALGORITHM

First of all, we need to print the column headings:

(1)   Print headings

We don't *have* to take the time to write out the heading data. When we need it for the actual program, we can look it up in the DATA part of our problem analysis.

Next we need to repeat a set of computations. This will require a loop. Since we repeat the computations using a number that goes from 1 to 10, we'll decide to use that number in the loop control statement.

(2) LOOP with NUMBER going from 1 to 10

For each value of NUMBER, we need to compute the square, cube, square root, and cube root; then we need to print those out.

(2.1) Compute NUMBER^2
(2.2) Compute NUMBER^3
(2.3) Compute NUMBER$^{1/2}$
(2.4) Compute NUMBER$^{1/3}$
(2.5) Print NUMBER and the four computed values

After we've repeated (2.1) and (2.2) 10 times, we'll be finished. So the whole algorithm looks like this:

(1) Print headings
(2) LOOP with NUMBER going from 1 to 10
    (2.1) Compute NUMBER^2
    (2.2) Compute NUMBER^3
    (2.3) Compute NUMBER$^{1/2}$
    (2.4) Compute NUMBER$^{1/3}$
    (2.5) Print NUMBER and the four computed values
(3) Stop

PROGRAM

The FORTRAN translation for this algorithm is relatively easy to do. When we translate step (1), we'll have to remember to look up the exact wording for the headings. Also, we see that we have *five* data items: NUMBER, NUMBER^2, NUMBER^3, NUMBER$^{1/2}$, and NUMBER$^{1/3}$. So we will need five variable names in the program.

DATA ITEM	VARIABLE NAME
NUMBER	NUMB
NUMBER^2	P2
NUMBER^3	P3
NUMBER$^{1/2}$	R1
NUMBER$^{1/3}$	R2

We choose P2 and P3 to refer to the second and third "power" of NUMBER. We choose R2 and R3 to refer to the second and third "root" of NUMBER. We can, of course, choose any variable names we wish, but it's usually a good idea to pick a name that helps us remember what the variable is going to be used for.

STEP	REFER- ENCE	FORTRAN PROGRAM
		TABLE OF SQUARES AND ROOTS
	2	*
	3	* R. W. DILLMAN
	4	* FEBRUARY 1983
	5	*
	6	* NUMB=INTEGER IN RANGE 1-10
	7	* P2,P3=POWERS
	8	* R2,R3=ROOTS
	9	*
	10	INTEGER NUMBER, P2, P3
	11	REAL R2, R3
	12	*
(1)	13	PRINT '(A,T10,A,T20,A,T28,A,T43,A)',
(1)	14	#'NUMBER','SQUARE','CUBE','SQUARE ROOT',
(1)	15	#'CUBE ROOT'
	16	PRINT *
(2)	17	DO 100 NUMB=1,10
(2.1)	18	P2=NUMB**2
(2.2)	19	P3=NUMB**3
(2.3)	20	R2=NUMB**(1.0/2)
(2.4)	21	R3=NUMB**(1.0/3)
(2.5)	22	PRINT '(I6,T10,I6,T20,I6,T28,F6.2,T43,F6.2)'
	23	#,NUMB,P2,P3,R2,R3
(2)	24	100 CONTINUE
(3)	25	END

In lines 13 through 15 we print each column heading as a *string*. (If you don't remember what a string is, go back and look at Chapter 5.) By using the T format code to set the spacing of the column headings, and by using the same tabing codes in the PRINT statement at lines 22 and 23, we keep all of the column values lined up underneath their headings. If you don't remember the use of the T, A, I, and F format codes, you should go back and reread Chapter 5. Line 16 is used to print one blank line after the heading line. If you check the sample output, you'll see that one is needed.

Lines 17 and 24 define the scope of the DO loop. Lines 18 through 23 are repeated for each new value of NUMB. Notice that these lines are a *simple* structure placed inside of a *loop* structure.

PRACTICE

1. Enter and execute this program. (Notice that the heading line is not correct. Fix it.)

2. Change the program so that it prints the square, cube, square root, and cube root for the numbers from 11 to 20.

3. Change the program so that it prints the square, cube, square root, and cube root for the *odd* numbers from 1 to 21.

11
LOGIC: THE IF/THEN/ELSE STRUCTURE

As we saw in Chapter 8, there are only three basic actions you ever take in writing a program. Either you have the computer execute a set of statements in sequence, or you have it repeat a set of statements, or you have it ask a YES/NO question and choose one of two sets of statements to execute based on the answer.

In order to make programming easier, programmers have developed *logical tools* called structures, which represent these three basic actions.

ACTION	LOGICAL STRUCTURE
Execute statements in sequence	Simple
Repeat a set of statements	Loop
Do a YES/NO test	IF/THEN/ELSE

We looked at the simple structure and the loop structure in Chapter 8. Now we're going to investigate the IF/THEN/ELSE structure.

IF/THEN/ELSE

The IF/THEN/ELSE structure is used whenever you want to have the computer make a decision. The structure is given the name IF/THEN/ELSE because computer decisions are always written in the form of questions:

- IF: The answer to this question is "yes."
- THEN: Do this activity.
- ELSE: Do this other, different, activity.

Notice that one or the other of the two activities is performed, but never both of them.

The best way to show how the IF/THEN/ELSE structure works is to develop an algorithm that uses one. Here is a problem that is somewhat different than the ones we've done so far.

PROBLEM   Write a program to print out the count of the negative odd numbers and the positive odd numbers in the set of numbers beginning at −7 and ending at 15.

SAMPLE   `IN THE SET:  -7 to 15 THERE ARE`
OUTPUT   `     4  NEGATIVE ODD NUMBERS`
          `     8  POSITIVE ODD NUMBERS`

PURPOSE   Count the number of negative and positive odd numbers.

DATA   First odd number   −7
          Last odd number   15

RULES   The next odd number can always be found by adding 2 to the last odd number.
          Keep a count of the odd numbers from −7 to −1.
          Keep another count of the odd numbers from 1 to 15.

In looking at the problem, we see that three things stand out as needing to be handled by the algorithm. First, the computer will need to look at all of the odd numbers from −7 to 15. This will require a loop, probably from −7 to 15 in steps of 2. Second, we will need *two* counters—one to count the negative numbers and one to count the positive numbers. Third, the computer will have to be able to *decide* whether a number is negative or positive.

To design the algorithm, then, we will need three data items and two special rules.

DATA ITEM	USED FOR
NUMBER	Loop control
NEGATIVE	Count of the negative numbers
POSITIVE	Count of the positive numbers

SPECIAL   Negative numbers are numbers smaller than zero.
RULES   Positive numbers are numbers equal to or bigger than zero.

Now we can start the algorithm. The first thing we need to do is to initialize the two counters to zero.

    (1) Set NEGATIVE to be 0
    (2) Set POSITIVE to be 0

Then we need to set up the loop.

    (3) LOOP with NUMBER going from −7 to 15 in steps of 2

Inside the loop we need to have the computer look at each number and decide whether to count it as negative or positive.

> (3.1) IF NUMBER is less than 0
> THEN
> (3.11) Add one to NEGATIVE
> ELSE
> (3.12) Add one to POSITIVE

In this step we invent a new convention, the IF/THEN/ELSE instruction. It always takes this form:

- IF: A yes/no question.
- THEN: Do this if answer is "yes."
- ELSE: Do this if answer is "no."

There will *always* be only two different things to be done. *Only one* of the two will actually be done each time; the other will be skipped.

In step (3.1), if the value of NUMBER is smaller than 0, then step (3.11) will be performed, and the loop will continue. If the value of NUMBER is *not* smaller than 0, then step (3.12) will be performed and the loop will continue. Each time the IF/THEN/ELSE is executed, *either* step (3.11) *or* step (3.12) will be performed, but *never both* of them at once.

Adding on the output instructions, we get the whole algorithm:

> (1) Set NEGATIVE to be 0
> (2) Set POSITIVE to be 0
> (3) Loop with NUMBER going from −7 to 15 in steps of 2
> (3.1) IF NUMBER is less than 0
> THEN
> (3.11) Add one to NEGATIVE
> ELSE
> (3.12) Add one to POSITIVE
> (4) PRINT "IN THE SET −7 TO 15 THERE ARE"
> (5) PRINT NEGATIVE, "NEGATIVE ODD NUMBERS"
> (6) PRINT POSITIVE, "POSITIVE ODD NUMBERS"
> (7) Stop

We will see how to code the IF/THEN/ELSE structure into FORTRAN in Chapter 12, but we can check to see if the structure works correctly here.

STEP	NUMBER	NEGATIVE	POSITIVE	ANSWER AT STEP (3.1)
(1)	—	0	0	—
(2)	—	0	0	—
(3)	–7	0	0	—
(3.1)	–7	0	0	YES
(3.11)	–7	1	0	—
(3)	–5	1	0	—
(3.1)	–5	1	0	YES
(3.11)	–5	2	0	—
(3)	–3	2	0	—
(3.1)	–3	2	0	YES
(3.11)	–3	3	0	—
(3)	–1	3	0	—
(3.1)	–1	3	0	YES
(3.11)	–1	4	0	—
(3)	–1	4	0	—
(3.1)	1	4	0	NO
(3.12)	1	4	1	—
(3)	3	4	1	—
(3.1)	3	4	1	NO
(3.12)	3	4	2	—
(3)	5	4	2	—
		•		
		•		
		•		
		And so on		

As you can see, depending on the answer at step (3.1), *either* step (3.11) *or* step (3.12) is performed. Eventually the loop will end and the values of the two counters will be printed out.

COMPLEX LOGIC

You've probably noticed by now that we have the ability to put structures *inside* of one another. This is what allows us to write complicated programs with such a small number of structures. In fact, *any* computer program that can be written can be written with just the three structures we've seen.

Here is a piece of an algorithm that illustrates how the structures can be combined to handle more complex situations. Suppose that as part of solving a problem, the computer at one point must look at a particular data item and do the following:

If the value of the item is less than or equal to zero, print out the value. If the value of the item is greater than zero, add the value into a sum and add 1 to a count. If the sum is greater than 100, print the sum and count and then reset both of those to zero.

SAMPLE   VALUE IS NEGATIVE: -29
OUTPUT   SUM EXCEEDS 100:
             SUM IS   135
             COUNT IS 21

(Remember that this is just a part of a much larger problem. This is why these outputs don't seem to make much sense.) The algorithm for this piece of the processing looks like this:

> (53)   IF ITEM is less than or equal to 0
>   THEN
> (53.1) PRINT "VALUE IS NEGATIVE:",ITEM
>   ELSE
> (53.2) Add ITEM into SUM
> (53.3) Add 1 to COUNT
> (53.4) IF SUM is greater than 100
>   THEN
>   (53.41) PRINT "SUM EXCEEDS 100:"
>   (53.42) PRINT "SUM IS", SUM
>   (53.43) PRINT "COUNT IS", COUNT
>   (53.44) Set SUM to be 0
>   (53.45) Set COUNT to be 0
>   ELSE
>   (53.46) CONTINUE

Notice that the IF/THEN/ELSE structure at step (53) contains another IF/THEN/ELSE structure inside of it at step (53.4). Step (53.4) will only be performed if the value of ITEM is bigger than zero at step (53). Steps (53.41) through (53.45) will be performed only if the value of ITEM is bigger than zero at step (53) *and* the value of SUM is bigger than 100 at step (53.4). The CONTINUE instruction at step (53.46) is another convention. The problem says to perform steps (53.41) through (53.45) if SUM exceeds 100, but if SUM is less than or equal to 100, there isn't anything to do. The computer should just keep going. This is what the CONTINUE instruction tells it to do. So in this case, when step (53.46) was reached, processing would just continue on to step (54).

SUMMARY

Always remember that *any* algorithm that can be done can be done by using the three logical structures. If you teach yourself to think problems through in terms of the structures, you'll find that you'll design algorithms faster and with fewer mistakes. We'll look at the FORTRAN syntax you need to code the IF/THEN/ELSE structure in the next chapter.

PRACTICE

1. Write an algorithm for a loop that goes from 1 to 100. Inside the loop, add the odd numbers into SUM1 and the even numbers into SUM2.

2. Write an algorithm for this problem:

    Compute the sums of the odd numbers and the even numbers in the set of integers starting with A and ending with B. A and B can be any two integers as long as A is even and B is greater than A.

    Sample output:

    ```
    A IS: 10
    B IS: 15
    SUM OF ODD NUMBERS IS: 39
    SUM OF EVEN NUMBERS IS: 36
    ```

3. Write an algorithm that will decide if a number N is even or odd. N must be a positive integer.

    Sample output:

    ```
    THE NUMBER 10 IS EVEN
    ```

    (Chapter 13 gives the answer to this one.)

12
SYNTAX: IF/ENDIF AND IF/THEN/ELSE

DEFINITIONS

GOTO
An instruction that tells the computer to jump to a particular line in the program.

Decision
A point at which the computer has the choice of doing one of two different sets of statements.

Logical Test
Comparing two values to see if they are equal to, greater than, or less than one another.

IF/THEN/ELSE
The FORTRAN statement which has the computer do a logical test in order to make a decision.

CONTINUE
The FORTRAN statement that is most often used as the destination of a GOTO instruction.

GOTO

The GOTO instruction tells the computer to jump to a particular number and continue executing from there. The general form of the GOTO is:

```
GOTO line number
```

When the GOTO is executed, the line number specified becomes the line to be executed next. The computer finds that line, executes it, and continues on from there.

The line number that follows the GOTO must be a line number that exists in the program. Other than that, the GOTO may be used to send the computer to any line the programmer wants.

Although it is not strictly necessary, most FORTRAN programmers agree that it is best to use a CONTINUE line as the *destination* of the GOTO instruction. CONTINUE is a special FORTRAN instruction that doesn't actually do anything when executed. Its use is to act as a place marker at lines that need to be labeled as destinations of instructions like GOTO. The form of CONTINUE is very simple:

line #   CONTINUE

Programmers realize that the programs they write will need to be altered as time goes on, and that programs that use CONTINUE as the destination of GOTOs will be easiest to change. For example, here is an example of a GOTO:

```
        .
        .
        .
        GOTO 230
        .
        .
        .
230 PRINT *,'THE ANSWER IS ',PIX
    END
```

In this case a PRINT statement has been labeled as line number 230. Now suppose that a change has to be made. The programmer has discovered that the value of PIX must be multiplied by 5.83 before it is printed out. To do this, a new line:

PIX=PIX*5.83

must be inserted in front of the PRINT line, and the new line must be the destination of the GOTO. This means that the programmer must insert the new line and also renumber the program to look like this:

```
        .
        .
        .
230 PIX=PIX*5.3
    PRINT *, 'THE ANSWER IS ',PIX
    END
```

If the original program had been written using a CONTINUE at line 230:

```
        .
        .
        .
230 CONTINUE
    PRINT *, 'THE ANSWER IS ',PIX
    END
```

then it would have been much easier to insert the new line:

```
        ·
        ·
        ·
230 CONTINUE
    PIX=PIX*5.83
    PRINT *, 'THE ANSWER IS ',PIX
    END
```

Since even small programs may require many changes before they work correctly, it is worth it to a programmer to take the time to use CONTINUEs wherever they are needed.

The GOTO can occasionally cause problems. Here is an example of a situation called an "infinite loop":

```
10 CONTINUE
   PRINT *,'HI THERE'
   GOTO 10
   END
```

Line 10 is the *destination* of the GOTO statement. In this case the PRINT line will be executed over and over again. (If you run this program, the words HI THERE will print out repeatedly until *you* stop the program. Be sure you *know how* to stop the program before you run it. Look in your *Computer User's Manual* or ask your instructor.)

In large programs infinite loops can be very complex and hard to find and eliminate. Good programmers only use the GOTO instruction as part of a carefully designed loop or IF/THEN/ELSE structure.

IF: THE SIMPLE FORM

The general form of the IF statement is:

IF (*logical expression*) FORTRAN statement

The IF statement is used to make decisions *within* a program. The *logical expression* is tested. If the expression is *true,* the computer executes the statement that follows the THEN. If the expression is *false,* the computer continues with the next statement in line.

EXAMPLE
```
IF (X3 .GT. 0) PRINT *, 'X3=',X3
S=S+X3
PRINT *,S
```

Here, if the value of X3 is greater than zero, the computer will print a message to show that. Whatever the value of X3 is, it will then be added into S and the new value of S will be printed.

In the example shown above, the .GT. tells the computer to test to values to see if one is greater than the other. There are five other *logical operators:*

. EQ.	equal to	
. LT.	less than	
. GT.	greater than	
. NE.	not equal to	
. LE.	less than or equal to	
. GE.	greater than or equal to	

Here is an example of a loop structure:

```
1       K = 0
2    10 CONTINUE
3       K = K + 1
4       IF (K .GT. 10) GOTO 60
5       PRINT *,'K=',K
6       GOTO 10
7    60 CONTINUE
8       END
```

In this program at line 4 if the value of K is greater than 10 (that is, if the logical test is true), then the computer will go to statement number 60, skipping over the PRINT statement. If K is less than or equal to 10, then the PRINT statement will be executed and the computer will execute line 6 and go back to line 2.

   If we trace the execution of the routine, we see that the output is a list of the integers from 1 to 10:

REFERENCE	K	TEST AT LINE 4	PRINTED OUT
1	0	—	—
3	1	—	—
4	1	False	—
5	1	—	1
6	1	—	—
3	2	—	—
4	2	False	—
5	2	—	2
6	2	—	—
3	3	—	—
•	•	•	
•	•	•	
•	•	•	
3	10	—	—
4	10	False	—
5	10	—	10
6	10	—	—
3	11	—	—
4	11	True	—
8 Stop			

Here is another way of doing the same loop:

```
      K = 0
   20 CONTINUE
      K = K + 1
      PRINT *,'K=', K
      IF (K .LE. 10) GOTO 20
      END
```

Here K starts at zero. Then 1 is added to it, and that value is printed out. The IF/THEN test checks to see if K is less than 10. If it is, the computer goes back to statement 20, adds one more to the value of K, writes the new value out, and then does the test again. This continues until K is exactly 10, at which point the last line is executed and the program stops. This also prints a list of the integers from 1 to 10. For practice, do a trace to verify this.

There are often many different ways of organizing a program to get the desired results. For example, the same output could be generated with a DO loop:

```
      DO 100 K=1,10
      PRINT *, K
  100 CONTINUE
```

It is always up to the programmer to choose what he or she thinks is the best way to translate the algorithm.

IF: A MORE POWERFUL FORM

Loops are usually coded in FORTRAN by using the DO instruction, but IF/THEN/ELSE structures are always coded by using the IF/THEN/ELSE instruction. Remember that the IF/THEN/ELSE structure has three parts:

IF X is equal to L9
THEN

| Executed if test is true |

ELSE

| Executed if test is false |

This structure can be translated directly into FORTRAN by using the FORTRAN IF/THEN/ELSE/ENDIF instruction. (To make this instruction easier to talk about, we'll refer to it as the "logical-IF" instruction.) The logical-IF instruction has this general form:

```
IF (logical test)
    THEN
```

This part is executed if the logical test is *true*.

```
ELSE
```

This part is executed if the logical test is *false*.

```
ENDIF
```

The words IF, THEN, ELSE, and ENDIF are required in this form of the IF instruction. The (logical test) part is also required—the logical test itself is written using the same *logical operators* that were described on page 91.

It is important to see that the form of the FORTRAN logical-IF instruction is an exact match of the IF/THEN/ELSE structure that we use to create algorithms. This means that if you use IF/THEN/ELSE structures when you are solving problems and designing algorithms, it will be very easy for you to translate those parts of your algorithms into FORTRAN. As an example of this, we'll translate the algorithm that was developed in Chapter 11.

PROBLEM   Write a program to print out the count of the negative odd numbers and the positive odd numbers in the set beginning at –7 and ending at 15.

ALGORITHM   (1)   Set NEGATIVE to be 0
           (2)   Set POSITIVE to be 0
           (3)   LOOP with NUMBER going from –7 to 15 in steps of 2
                (3.1)   IF NUMBER is less than 0
                      THEN
                      (3.11)   Add 1 to NEGATIVE
                      ELSE
                      (3.12)   Add 1 to POSITIVE
           (4)   Print "IN THE SET –7 TO 15 THERE ARE"
           (5)   Print NEGATIVE, "NEGATIVE ODD NUMBERS"
           (6)   Print POSITIVE, "POSITIVE ODD NUMBERS"
           (7)   Stop

To translate this into a program, we will need three variable names.

DATA ITEM	VARIABLE NAME
NUMBER	NUMBER
NEGATIVE	NEG
POSITIVE	POS

STEP	REFER-ENCE	FORTRAN CODE
	1	`* COUNT ODD NUMBER, -7 TO 15`
	2	`*`
	3	`* R. W. DILLMAN`
	4	`* FEB. 1984`
	5	`*`
	6	`* VARIABLES:`
	7	`*   NUMBER=ODD INTEGER IN RANGE -7,15`
	8	`*   NEG=COUNT OF NEGATIVE NUMBERS`
	9	`*   POS=COUNT OF POSITIVE NUMBERS`
	10	`*`
	11	`      INTEGER NUMBER, NEG, POS`
(1)	12	`      NEG=0`
(2)	13	`      POS=0`
(3)	14	`      DO 100 NUMBER=-7,15,2`
(3.1)	15	`      IF (NUMBER .LT. 0)`
	16	`      THEN`
(3.11)	17	`         NEG=NEG+1`
	18	`      ELSE`
(3.12)	19	`         POS=POS+1`
	20	`      ENDIF`
(3)	21	`  100 CONTINUE`
(4)	22	`      PRINT *, 'IN THE SET -7 TO 15 THERE ARE'`
(5)	23	`      PRINT *, NEG, 'NEGATIVE ODD NUMBERS'`
(6)	24	`      PRINT *, POS, 'POSITIVE ODD NUMBERS'`
(7)	25	`      END`

As is usual, lines 1 through 10 describe the program, the programmer, and the variables to be used. Line 11 defines the variables—in this case they are all integers. Lines 12 and 13 initialize the counters NEG and POS to zero. Lines 14 and 21 define the scope of the loop. NUMBER is the loop variable. It goes from −7 to 15 by twos. At line 15 the loop variable is checked to see if it is less than zero. If it is, then line 17 is executed. If it is not, then line 19 is executed. When the loop ends, the three PRINT instructions are performed, and the program terminates. Compare lines 15 through 20 of this program with step (3) of the algorithm. Do you see how well they match? Trace the program and verify that it works correctly.

PRACTICE

Translate these algorithm sections into FORTRAN. Execute and verify the code.

1. (4) IF Q is less than 0
        THEN
        (4.1) Q=Q+1
        ELSE
        (4.2) Print "VALUE IS",Q

2. (11)   IF NUMBER is not equal to 0
          THEN
          (11.1)   ROOT=DISC/(2*NUMBER)
          (11.2)   PRINT "ROOT IS",ROOT
          ELSE
          (11.3)   PRINT "NO ROOT EXISTS"

3.   (8)   IF VALUE is less than or equal to 100
           THEN
           (8.1)   IF VALUE is greater than 0
                   THEN
                   (8.11)   Add VALUE into SUM
                   (8.12)   Add 1 to COUNT
                   ELSE
                   (8.12)   CONTINUE
           ELSE
           (8.2)   PRINT "LIMIT EXCEEDED"

4.   (9)   IF ITEM is less than TEST
           THEN
           (9.1)   IF ITEM is greater than 0
                   THEN
                   (9.11)   LOOP with I going from 1 to ITEM
                            (9.111)   PRINT I
                   ELSE
                   (9.12)   PRINT "ITEM VALUE NEGATIVE"
           ELSE
           (9.2)   Add 1 to ITEM

5.   Enter the program that was developed at the end of the chapter and execute it. Does the output match the results of your trace?

6.   In that program the output lines could have been written as one long PRINT instruction, like this:

```
PRINT*, 'IN THE SET -7 TO 15 THERE ARE',
#NEGATIVE, 'NEGATIVE ODD NUMBERS AND',
#POSITIVE, 'POSITIVE ODD NUMBERS'
```

How would this change the way the output looks?

7.   Rewrite the output lines using the formatted form of the PRINT instruction.

13
USING THE COMPUTER: A SAMPLE PROBLEM

PROBLEM   The computer will be given a positive, integer number. It should decide whether the number is even or odd and print out "EVEN" or "ODD" depending on the result.

SAMPLE   `THE NUMBER 8 IS EVEN`
OUTPUT   `THE NUMBER 13 IS ODD`

PURPOSE   Decide if a number is even or odd.

DATA   NUMBER—a positive integer

ALGORITHM

If someone were to *give* you a number to look at, you could easily decide whether it was even or odd. For example, when you see the number:

5206

you immediately say *even*. Human beings solve this problem by looking at the last digit of the number. If the last digit is 0, 2, 4, 6, or 8, then the number is even. If the last digit is 1, 3, 5, 7, or 9, then the number is odd.

Thus one possible algorithm looks like this:

(1) Get a value for NUMBER
(2) Set DIGIT equal to the last digit in NUMBER
(3) IF DIGIT is equal to 0, 2, 4, 6 or 8
THEN
(3.1) PRINT "EVEN"
ELSE
(3.2) PRINT "ODD"
(4) Stop

In terms of *logic* this algorithm is perfectly correct. In fact, it describes the way many people actually solve the problem, so we know it will work. We run into trouble, however, when we try to translate step (2) into FORTRAN. There is no FORTRAN instruction that will "get the last digit" of a number. There *is* a fairly complicated arithmetic procedure that produces the last digit, but there's also another algorithm that uses a method that's easier to follow.

Let's just take one number and see what we know about it. Let's take:

13

This is an "odd" number. What do we know about odd numbers?

We know that 1 is the *first* odd number. We know that to get the second odd number we add 2 to the first one. In fact, we know that if we have *any* odd number, we can *always* get the next odd number by adding 2 to the one we have.

How does knowing this help us solve the problem? Well, except for the number 1, *every* odd number has another odd number that came before it. Not only that, but we can *find* the earlier odd number by *subtracting* 2 from the one we have. For example, 13 − 2 gives us 11, and 11 is the odd number that came before 13.

This is a useful idea. It's useful because if we *repeat* the process long enough:

```
13 − 2 is 11
11 − 2 is  9
 9 − 2 is  7
 8 − 2 is  5
 5 − 2 is  3
 3 − 2 is  1
```

we *always* end up with the first odd number, 1. It's even more useful when we realize that we can do the same thing with even numbers.

Of course, the first *even* number is 2, so the result is a little bit different. For example, suppose we have the number 12:

12 − 2 is 10
10 − 2 is 8
8 − 2 is 6
6 − 2 is 4
4 − 2 is 2

We see that although the final result is 2 instead of 1, the process is the same. In fact, we can summarize the process as a rule.

If you have a positive integer number, and you subtract 2 from it and continue to subtract 2 from the result, eventually the result will be *either* a 1 *or* a 2. If the final result is 1, then the original number was odd. If the final result is 2, then the original number was even.

This is the kind of thing we can do with loops and IF/THEN/ELSE tests. If we put it into algorithm form, we get:

(1)   Get a value for NUMBER
(2)   Set DIGIT equal to NUMBER
(3)   LOOP FOREVER
     (3.1)   IF DIGIT is less than or equal to 2
         THEN
         (3.11) EXIT LOOP
         ELSE
         (3.12) Subtract 2 from DIGIT
(4)   IF DIGIT is equal to 1
     THEN
     (4.1)   Set ANSWER equal to "ODD"
     ELSE
     (4.2)   Set ANSWER equal to "EVEN"
(5)   Print "THE NUMBER", NUMBER, "IS", ANSWER
(6)   Stop

Step (1) requests a value for the data item NUMBER. Since this algorithm must work for all possible odd or even numbers, we cannot specify a particular value. In step (2) we store the value of NUMBER into DIGIT. We are doing the "odd or even" question by repeatedly subtracting 2 from the original value. Doing this will destroy the value, so we copy it into a "temporary" data item for use in the processing loop.

Step (3) introduces a new loop instruction. Since we don't know exactly how many times we will have to repeat the subtraction process, we can't specify an exact counter in the loop control statement. By saying FOREVER, we mean, "Keep repeating this until we tell you to stop." Step (3.11) is a new instruction that does the stopping. When EXIT

LOOP is performed, the loop is terminated and the next available statement *outside* the loop is executed. In this case that will be step (4).

The IF test at step (3.1) checks the value of DIGIT. If DIGIT is a 1 or a 2, then we have the answer; step (3.11) will be performed, and the loop will end. If DIGIT is still bigger than 2, the 2 will be substracted from it at step (3.12), and the loop will repeat.

The IF/THEN/ELSE at step (4) sets the *string* data item ANSWER equal to "even" or "odd," depending on the result of the subtraction loop. (If you don't remember the FORTRAN syntax for string variables, look back at Chapter 5.) Step (5) prints the final results.

Let's check out the algorithm by giving it the number 6:

STEP	NUMBER	DIGIT	ANSWER AT STEP (3.1)	ANSWER AT STEP 4	ANSWER
(1)	6	—	—	—	—
(2)	6	6	—	—	—
(3)	6	6	—	—	—
(3.1)	6	6	NO	—	—
(3.12)	6	4	—	—	—
(3)	6	4	—	—	—
(3.1)	6	4	NO	—	—
(3.12)	6	2	—	—	—
(3)	6	2	—	—	—
(3.1)	6	2	YES	—	—
(3.11)	6	2	—	—	—
(4)	6	2	—	NO	—
(4.2)	6	2	—	—	EVEN
(5)	(Printout)				
(6)	(Stop)				

We can see that it works for even numbers. For practice, verify that it works for odd numbers by checking it out with the number 9.

PROGRAM

We will use NUMBER for NUMBER and DIGIT for DIGIT. Since it is impossible to create an "endless" loop with the FORTRAN DO instruction, we will instead set up a loop with a *very* large counter. The EXIT LOOP at step (3.11) will be handled by a GOTO instruction. We will choose ANSWER as the string variable.

STEP	REFER- ENCE	FORTRAN CODE
	1	* DECIDE IF A NUMBER IS EVEN OR ODD
	2	*
	3	* R. W. DILLMAN
	4	* FEB. 1983
	5	CHARACTER*4 ANSWER
	6	INTEGER NUMBER, DIGIT, COUNT
(1)	7	NUMBER= ?
(2)	8	DIGIT=NUMBER
(3)	9	DO 100 COUNT=1, 10000
(3.1)	10	IF (DIGIT .LE. 2)
	11	THEN
(3.11)	12	GOTO 110
	13	ELSE
(3.12)	14	DIGIT=DIGIT-2
	15	ENDIF
(3)	16	100 CONTINUE
(3.11)	17	110 CONTINUE
(4)	18	IF (DIGIT .EQ. 1)
	19	THEN
(4.1)	20	ANSWER='ODD'
	22	ELSE
(4.2)	22	ANSWER='EVEN'
	23	ENDIF
(5)	24	PRINT *, 'THE NUMBER ',NUMBER, ' IS ', ANSWER
(6)	25	END

We didn't put in a value for NUMBER at line 7. A value will have to be supplied each time the program is to be run. This is an awkward thing to do, and in the next chapter we'll see a FORTRAN instruction that gives an easier way to do it.

The loop at lines 9 through 13 will repeat up to 10,000 times. If this isn't enough, the limit can be made bigger. Notice that the THEN part of the IF test at lines 10 through 14 performs the EXIT LOOP part of the algorithm by jumping out of the loop to a CONTINUE statement at line 17. It is important to see that:

```
100 CONTINUE
```

is the last line of the DO loop. This means that:

```
110 CONTINUE
```

is outside of the loop. (We put it there on purpose to provide an exit.)

PRACTICE

1. Type the program into the computer and verify that it works by executing it with the following values of NUMBER.
   a. NUMBER = 3
   b. NUMBER = 12
   c. NUMBER = 61
   d. NUMBER = 3016

2. Execute the program with each of these values of NUMBER:
   a. NUMBER = 0
   b. NUMBER = -1
   c. NUMBER = 5,3

   What happens in each case? These are not valid inputs to this program. Use an IF/THEN/ELSE structure to test to see if NUMBER is valid. If NUMBER is not valid, the program should print an error message.

3. Develop a *different* algorithm for solving the program. Prove that it works.

14
SYNTAX: READ AND DATA

DEFINITIONS

Input
: The act of entering data into the computer terminal at the request of a program.

READ *
: The FORTRAN instruction that tells the computer to ask for input.

DATA
: A way of doing input from values stored inside the program itself.

Parameter
: A variable name whose value is set once at the beginning of a program and may not change during execution.

READ*

READ* tells the computer to do input at the terminal. The general form is:

```
READ*, variable, variable, . . .
```

When the READ* statement is executed, the computer pauses until you enter the data that it is waiting for. You must type in one piece of data for each variable name in the READ* statement. If you enter more than one piece of data, they must be separated by commas:

```
READ *, TEMP12
```

When this instruction is executed, the computer will pause. At that point you must type in a number. The number you enter will be stored in the variable TEMP12. If, for example, you type in the number 37.6, the value of TEMP12 will become 37.6.

Unless the computer is in the middle of printing something (in which case the pause will be obvious), there is no way for the person using the computer to know *exactly when* the computer reaches a READ* statement. To eliminate this problem, good programmers always use a PRINT* line to *label* their input statements.

```
PRINT *,'ENTER TEMPERATURE FOR DAY 12'
READ *, TEMP12
```

At the terminal:

```
ENTER TEMPERATURE FOR DAY 12
37.6
```

Now the person using the program knows exactly which piece of data to enter and when.

The READ* instruction can be used to enter both numeric and character data. One READ* instruction may input more than one piece of data.

```
REAL MAXTEM
CHARACTER*10 DAY
PRINT *,'ENTER DAY, MAXIMUM TEMPERATURE'
READ *, DAY, MAXTEM
```

At the terminal:

```
ENTER DAY, MAXIMUM TEMPERATURE
'WEDNESDAY', 78.3
```

Here the string 'WEDNESDAY' will be stored into the variable DAY, and 78.3 will be stored into the variable MAXTEM. Notice that strings have to be enclosed in quotes when they are being input from the terminal.

CONTROLLING PROGRAMS WITH INPUT

The READ* statement can be used to control a program while the program is executing. For an example, let's look back at the program for deciding whether a number is odd or even (Chapter 13).

REFER- ENCE	FORTRAN CODE

```
1    * DECIDE IF A NUMBER IS ODD OR EVEN
2    *
3    * R. W. DILLMAN
4    * FEB. 1983
5        CHARACTER*4 ANSWER
6        INTEGER NUMBER, DIGIT, COUNT
7        NUMBER= ?
8        DIGIT=NUMBER
9        DO 100 COUNT=1,10000
10          IF (DIGIT .LE. 2)
11          THEN
12            GOTO 110
13          ELSE
14            DIGIT=DIGIT-2
15          ENDIF
16   100 CONTINUE
17   110 CONTINUE
18       IF (DIGIT .EQ. 1)
19         THEN
20           ANSWER='ODD'
21         ELSE
22           ANSWER='EVEN'
23         ENDIF
24       PRINT *, 'THE NUMBER ', NUMBER,'IS ', ANSWER
25       END
```

This program cannot work unless a value is assigned to NUMBER at line 7. This is easy enough to do by retyping the line, for example:

```
NUMBER=651
```

However, the fact that the line must be retyped each time the program is to be run makes the program cumbersome to use. By replacing line 7 with:

```
READ *, NUMBER
```

values can be assigned to NUMBER while the program is running. This makes the program much easier to use.

Adding a PRINT line to label the input, we set:

```
PRINT *, 'ENTER A NUMBER'
READ *, NUMBER
```

and the program will now have this output:

```
RUN
ENTER A NUMBER
12
THE NUMBER 12 IS EVEN
```

We can see that since the number 12 is now an input, it is visible on the screen. This means that we no longer need to print the 12 as part of the output at line 22. So by changing lines 7 and 22 and adding one PRINT line, we set the final version of the program.

REFERENCE	FORTRAN CODE
1	* DECIDE IF A NUMBER IS ODD OR EVEN
2	*
3	* R. W. DILLMAN
4	* FEB. 1983
5	CHARACTER*4 ANSWER
6	INTEGER NUMBER, DIGIT, COUNT
7a	PRINT *, 'ENTER A NUMBER'
7b	READ *, NUMBER
8	DIGIT=NUMBER
9	DO 100 COUNT=1,10000
10	IF (DIGIT .LE. 2)
11	THEN
12	GO TO 110
13	ELSE
14	DIGIT=DIGIT-2
15	ENDIF
16	100 CONTINUE
17	110 CONTINUE
18	IF (DIGIT .EQ. 1)
19	THEN
20	ANSWER='ODD'
21	ELSE
22	ANSWER='EVEN'
23	ENDIF
24	PRINT *, 'THE NUMBER IS ', ANSWER
25	END

TWO IMPORTANT THINGS TO REMEMBER ABOUT INPUT/OUTPUT OPERATIONS

1. Always label your output.

```
Q=9.2
PRINT*, 'THE TOTAL IS',Q
```

At the terminal:

```
THE TOTAL IS 9.2
```

2. Always label your input.

```
PRINT *,'TYPE IN AN ODD NUMBER:'
READ *, J
```

At the terminal:

```
TYPE IN AN ODD NUMBER:
```

PRACTICE

1.
```
        INTEGER A,B,C,D
        PRINT *,'ENTER THREE VALUES'
        READ*, B,C,D
        DO 100 A=B,C,D
        PRINT *,A,B,C,D
100 CONTINUE
        PRINT *,'FINISHED. A=',A
        END
```

Run this program with the following inputs. Make sure you understand why the outputs happen the way they do.

a. 1, 5, 1
b. 1, 10, 2
c. 0, 9, 3
d. 5, 5, 1
e. 5, 1, 1
f. 5, 1, −1
g. 5, −5, −2

2. Enter, execute, and verify the "odd/even" program. Test it for these inputs.

    a. 1
    b. 18
    c. 0
    d. 10.93
    e. −6
    f. −5

3.
```
           READ *, A
        20 CONTINUE
           READ *, B
           X=A-B
           IF (X .LT. 0) GOTO 70
           READ *, C
           IF (C .EQ. 0) GOTO 100
        70 CONTINUE
           READ *, D
           A=A+D
           GOTO 20
       100 CONTINUE
           END
```

    a. Enter and execute this program. How do you make the program stop?

    b. Supply PRINT statements to print labels for each READ statement. Why should the READ *,C statement be labeled differently from the others?

DATA

The DATA statement is similar to the READ statement in that it also causes the computer to store data into variable names. The difference is that the DATA statement obtains its data from statements within the program rather than from an input device.

EXAMPLE   DATA ALPHA/3.6/,X/2/,WORD/'FROG'/

In this case 3.6 is stored into ALPHA, 2 is stored into X, and 'FROG' is stored into WORD.

It is important to see that the DATA statement does not *assign* data to a variable in the sense that the assignment operator (=) does. Rather, the DATA statement *initializes* the variable to a particular value.

Important: DATA statements do not execute.

Instead, DATA statements are evaluated by the computer during the time it is checking the program for syntax errors. This means that DATA statements can only be used to give variables initial values at the very *beginning* of a run. DATA statements *cannot* be used to *change* the value of a variable *during* a run.

PRACTICE

4. Run this program. Make sure you understand why you see the output you do. Do a trace if necessary.

```
      INTEGER A,B,C,J,K,N
      DATA A/-3/, B/8/, C/2/, N/2/
      DO 60 K=1,N
      DO 50 J=A,B,C
      PRINT *, J
   50 CONTINUE
   60 CONTINUE
      END
```

5. Explain why it is not necessary to label DATA statements.

PARAMETERS

There are two problems, often encountered by computer programmers, whose bad effects can be easily reduced by the use of a special FORTRAN instruction called PARAMETER.

The first case involves poorly specified data. It may be that the data given in a problem statement is not correct. Eventually, of course, the program will be tested, and the bad data will be located. If the bad data item was only used once, little time will be lost in making the correction. However, if the bad data item was used many times in the program, it may take a large effort to complete the correction. For example, suppose a problem statement specified $10,500 in sales as the point at which the percentage of a salesperson's commission changed from 2 to 5%. And suppose that the number 10500 was used eight different places in a 2000-line program. If the limit was *really* supposed to be $15,500, each of those eight uses would have to be tracked down and altered.

A second, similar problem involves programmer error. Suppose, for example, the number 21.57 is used at 15 different places in a program. If, in one of the lines that use the number, the programmer accidentally types 31.57, the program output will be incorrect. As before, the loss in this situation is the amount of time it will take to track down and correct the error.

The effect of these problems can be greatly reduced by always using *parameters* in place of constant values. A parameter is a variable name which contains a value that is not ever *expected* to change. (The problem, as we have seen, is that values which are not expected to change sometimes *do* change.) The value is assigned to the parameter at the beginning of the program, and then the parameter is used whenever that value is needed later in the program. For example:

Without Parameter

```
K9=21.57*B9+2
       .
       .
       .
F=J/B9-(K*21.57)
       .
       .
       .
IF (T3 .NE. K+21.57) GOTO 890
DO 2010 F3=T1,T2,21.47
       .
       .
       .
L1=K+B9*21.57
L2=K2+B9*21.57
       .
       .
       .
IF (E3 .EQ. K-21.57) GOTO 3290
       .
       .
       .
```

With Parameter

```
PARAMETER  (P=21.57)
            .
            .
            .
K9=P*B9+2
            .
            .
            .
F=J/B9-(K*P)
            .
            .
            .
IF (T3 .NE. K+P) GOTO 890
            .
            .
            .
DO 2010 F3=T1,T2,P
            .
            .
            .
L1=K+B9*P
L2=K2+B9*P
            .
            .
            .
IF (E3 .EQ. K-P) GOTO 3290
            .
            .
            .
```

Notice that an error in the first example (at DO 2010 F3=...) is avoided in the second. Also notice that if the value 21.57 was found to be incorrect, *seven* lines would have to be retyped in the first example. In the second, only one line would need to be retyped.

Good programmers design parameters into their algorithms and use the PARAMETER instruction to initialze the parameter variables at the beginning of their programs. This involves a little extra work, but often saves them a lot of extra work later on.

DATA, READ, AND ASSIGNMENT

We now have three different ways of storing values into variable names:

METHOD	EXAMPLE
Assignment	`X=230`
READ	`PRINT *,'ENTER V VALUE'`
	`READ *,X`
DATA	`DATA X/230/`

Although each of these instructions produces the same result, it is important to see that the activities are performed in different ways. Here is a brief guide to the use of the three instructions.

The *assignment* instruction makes the data value a part of the program. Because of this, the data value cannot be *changed* without editing the program itself. This is an inefficient way to program. Assignment should be used only with variable data.

The READ instruction accesses data values that are not a part of the program, but are given *to* the program while it is executing. The great advantage of READ is that it allows variables within the program to take on *different* values *each* time the program is executed *without* the program having to be changed. There is a disadvantage in the use of READ, however, in that when the computer executes a READ instruction, it must *wait* for the data to be entered. Thus READ is by far the slowest of the three instructions. READ should *only* be used for data that is expected to change every time the program is rerun. It should not be used in place of assignment or DATA.

Like the assignment instruction, the DATA instruction uses data values which are part of the program. There are two major advantages to using DATA. First, because the data is collected into easily identified DATA lines, it is easy to enter and alter. Second, DATA allows multiple data values to be assigned in a single line of code. DATA should be used to assign data values that are expected to change over the lifetime of a program, but are not expected to change each time the program is run.

Finally, the PARAMETER statement is used to associate constant data items with names. Data stored in PARAMETER names may not be altered during the execution of the program. Most, if not all, constants should be set up as PARAMETERS.

CODE	COMMENTS

```
* COMPUTE SUMS OF AREAS OF CIRCLES
*
      REAL PI, AREA, RADIUS, TOTAL
      INTEGER MAXCIR
      CHARACTER FORM*14
*
      PARAMETER (PI=3.1417)
*
      PARAMETER (MAXCIR=20)
*
*
*
*
*
      PARAMETER (FORM='(A,I2,A,F10.4)')
*
*
*
*
*
      DATA TOTAL/0.0/
*
*
      DO 100 I=1, MAXCIR
      READ *, RADIUS
*
*
*
      IF (RADIUS .EQ. 0) GOTO 110
*
*
      AREA=PI*RADIUS**2
*
*
*
*
*
      TOTAL=TOTAL+AREA
*
*
  100 CONTINUE
  110 CONTINUE
*
      PRINT FORM, 'NUMBER OF CIRCLES ',
      I-1,'TOTAL AREA ', TOTAL
*
*
*
*
*
      END
```

Pi is a numeric constant.

MAXCIR is the maximum number of circles to be processed.

FORM supplies the format codes for the PRINT instructions near the end of the program. (Chapter 33 discusses formatted output.)

TOTAL is initialized to zero. Its value will change during execution.

A new value of RADIUS must be input for each circle whose area is to be computed. Zero radius is used as the end-of-data test.

Compute the area of this circle and assign it to the variable AREA. Notice that the constant PI is used here.

Keep total of computed areas.

FORM is a character constant that contains the format string for the PRINT statement.

PRACTICE

1. Enter this program and run it. Make the following improvements.

    a. Add a PRINT statement to supply a label for the READ. Use the form PRINT *, LABEL where LABEL is a character parameter. In your opinion is this a good way to do labels? Why or why not?

    b. The end-of-data marker is a constant. Change the IF line so that a parameter is used instead of the number 0.

    c. The number of circles entered is computed as I - 1 in the PRINT line. Replace I - 1 with a variable, COUNT, whose value is computed just after exiting from the loop. Why is this an improvement?

    d. In the line AREA = PI * RADIUS ** 2, is it *not* an improvement to replace the 2 with a parameter name. Why not?

2. Write programs to compute one or more of the following. Pay strict attention to your use of variables and parameters.

    a. Given their radii, compute the total circumference of a set of circles.

    b. Given a set of Cartesian points, input as ordered pairs, compute the total distance from the first point input to the last.

    c. Given a set of three points as in item b, compute the perimeter and area of the triangle formed.

    d. Given a set of points as in item c, establish whether the triangle formed is equilateral, isosceles, or obtuse.

15
USING THE COMPUTER: A SAMPLE PROBLEM

PROBLEM A teacher who has 30 students in his class wants a computer program to compute the average score on a test he has given. The highest possible score is 100. The lowest possible score is 0. He plans to use the program each time he gives a test.

SAMPLE
OUTPUT

```
ENTER TEST SCORES, USE -1 TO EXIT
90
72
83
-1
THE AVERAGE OF 3 SCORES IS 81.67
```

PURPOSE Compute average of a set of numbers.

The first thing we notice about this problem is that we will have to have the computer compute an *average*. An average is simply the *sum* of a set of numbers *divided by* the *count* of the set. For example, the sum of the set 3, 5, 7 is 15, and the count is 3. So the average is equal to 15 divided by 3, or 5.

Obviously, then, among our data items we will need a sum, a count, and an average.

DATA
SUM	Sum of test scores
COUNT	Count of test scores
AVERAGE	Average of test scores

Since it is test scores that are being summed, we will need a data item to store the individual scores when they are typed in from the terminal. We will also need a data item called "end of data."

The problem says there are 30 students in the class, so the program will need to handle a *maximum* of 30 test scores. But the problem also says that the teacher plans to use this program each time he gives a test. Since there are bound to be some students who

114

are absent, the program should be able to handle *fewer* than 30 scores. When we look at the sample output, we see that the test scores are typed in one at a time. We also see that −1 is typed to tell the computer that there are no more scores to be entered.

In this case −1 is the end-of-data marker. −1 is *not* a test score. It will *not* be summed or counted. Its *only* purpose is to serve as a kind of code to mark the end of the input data. With this we can write out the list of data items.

DATA   SCORE   Input test score
COUNT   Count of scores
SUM   Sum of scores
AVERAGE Average of scores
EOD   End-of-data market (−1)
MAXNUM   Maximum number of scores (30)
BIGGEST   Biggest possible score (100)
SMALLEST Smallest possible score (0)

We need BIGGEST and SMALLEST because we need to check each score as it is typed in to see if it's valid. The program should not accept illegal scores.

RULES   AVERAGE = SUM/COUNT

No more than MAXNUM scores should be accepted.
EOD is not a score. When it is input, there are no more scores to be entered.
Any score that is bigger than BIGGEST or smaller than SMALLEST should be rejected and the message "illegal score" printed out.

ALGORITHM

We can summarize the problem like this:

1. Initialize data items.
2. Enter scores. Sum them and count them. When EOD is entered, go to step 3.
3. Compute AVERAGE = SUM/COUNT.
4. Print results.

The first part is easy. We just set up our data items.

(1) Set SUM to be 0
(2) Set COUNT to be 0
(3) Set MAXNUM to be 30
(4) Set BIGGEST to be 100
(5) Set SMALLEST to be 0
(6) Set EOD to be −1

The second part is a loop that goes from 1 to MAXNUM. SCORE will be input each time through the loop. After the input, SCORE will have to be checked to see if it is equal to EOD, and to see if it is a valid score.

```
(7)    LOOP from 1 to MAXNUM
       (7.1)   INPUT SCORE
       (7.2)   IF SCORE is equal to EOD then EXIT LOOP
       (7.3)   IF SCORE is not bigger than BIGGEST and SCORE is not
               smaller than SMALLEST
               THEN
               (7.31)   Add SCORE to SUM
               (7.32)   Add 1 to COUNT
               ELSE
               (7.33)   Print "ILLEGAL SCORE"
```

This is a fairly complex piece of algorithm. Step (7) sets up a loop that repeats up to MAXNUM times. Notice that MAXNUM (as well as EOD, BIGGEST, and SMALLEST) is a *parameter* just as we discussed in Chapter 14. In this case MAXNUM is 30, but it could be reset to any number in order to change the upper limit on the number of test scores.

Step (7.2) inputs the score from the terminal. Step (7.1) assumes that when the algorithm is translated, the programmer will supply a label for the input instruction. Step (7.2) tests to see if the input is the end-of-data marker. If it is, the loop is finished and step (8) is performed next. Notice that step (7.2) is not a complete IF/THEN/ELSE structure—the "else" part is missing. Very often programmers abbreviate the *particular* structure:

```
IF      condition
THEN
        single activity
ELSE
        CONTINUE
```

this way:

```
IF      condition THEN single activity
```

with the assumption that if the condition is false, the algorithm automatically continues on.

Step (7.3) shows another different kind of IF/THEN/ELSE. In this case it is the logical condition that has changed. In this problem we want to print an error message if SCORE is bigger than BIGGEST *or* if SCORE is smaller than SMALLEST. We could have written this as a nested IF test:

```
(7.3)    IF SCORE is not bigger than BIGGEST
         THEN
         (7.31)   IF SCORE is not smaller than SMALLEST
                  THEN
                  (7.311)   Add SCORE to sum
                  (7.312)   Add 1 to COUNT
                  ELSE
                  (7.313) Print "ILLEGAL SCORE"
         ELSE
         (7.32)   Print "ILLEGAL SCORE"
```

By tracing through this, you can see that the effect is the same as in our algorithm. This approach is more complicated, however, and the use of the "AND" in the IF test makes things easier to understand. There are two forms of this type of logical operator:

> IF   condition #1
> OR   condition #2
> THEN
>   activity A (One or both are true)
> ELSE
>   activity B (Both are false)

Here, if *either* condition 1 or condition 2 is true, or if *both* are true, then activity A is performed. If both conditions are false, then activity B is performed.

> IF   condition #1
> AND condition #2
> THEN
>   activity A (Both are true)
> ELSE
>   activity B (One or both are false)

With the "AND" operator, *both* conditions must be true for the THEN part of the IF/THEN/ELSE to be performed. If either condition or both conditions are false, the ELSE part will be executed. In *our* algorithm, if SCORE is *not* bigger than BIGGEST, *and* not smaller than SMALLEST, then we want to add it to the sum.

We can now complete the algorithm.

(1)   Set SUM to be 0
(2)   Set COUNT to be 0
(3)   Set MAXNUM to be 30
(4)   Set BIGGEST to be 100
(5)   Set SMALLEST to be 0
(6)   Set EOD to be -1
(7)   LOOP from 1 to MAXNUM
     (7.1)   INPUT SCORE
     (7.2)   IF SCORE is equal to EOD THEN EXIT LOOP
     (7.3)   IF SCORE is not bigger than BIGGEST
            AND SCORE is not smaller than SMALLEST
            THEN
            (7.31)   Add SCORE to SUM
            (7.32)   Add 1 to COUNT
            ELSE
            (7.33)   PRINT "ILLEGAL SCORE"
(8)   Set AVERAGE equal to SUM/COUNT
(9)   Print "THE AVERAGE OF",COUNT,"SCORES IS", AVERAGE
(10) Stop

As always, our next step is to check the algorithm to see that it works correctly. We'll use this set of input data. Notice that 185 is an illegal value.

$$70, 185, 92, -1$$

STEP	SCORE	SUM	COUNT	AVERAGE	ANSWER AT STEP (7.2)	ANSWERS AT STEP (7.3)	
(1)	—	0	—	—	—	—	—
(2)	—	0	0	—	—	—	—
(3)	Through (6): To save space, we've left the parameters off this chart.						
(7)	Loop 1						
(7.1)	70	0	0	—	—	—	—
(7.2)	70	0	0	—	NO	—	—
(7.3)	70	0	0	—	—	YES	YES

Both of the conditions are true at step (7.3), so the THEN part of the IF/THEN/ELSE is performed.

STEP	SCORE	SUM	COUNT	AVERAGE	ANSWER AT STEP (7.2)	ANSWERS AT STEP (7.3)	
(7.31)	70	70	—	—	—	—	—
(7.32)	70	70	1	—	—	—	—
(7)	Loop 2						
(7.1)	185	70	1	—	—	—	—
(7.2)	185	70	1	—	NO	—	—
(7.3)	185	70	1	—	—	NO	—
(7.33)	Prints "ILLEGAL SCORE"						
(7)	Loop 3						
(7.1)	92	70	1	—	—	—	—
(7.2)	92	70	1	—	NO	—	—
(7.3)	92	70	1	—	—	YES	YES
(7.31)	92	162	—	—	—	—	—
(7.32)	92	162	2	—	—	—	—
(7)	Loop 4						
(7.1)	-1	162	2	—	—	—	—
(7.2)	-1	162	2	—	YES	—	—

Step (7.2) has found the end-of-data market. Now we go on to step (8).

STEP	SCORE	SUM	COUNT	AVERAGE			
(8)	-1	162	2	81	—	—	—
(9)	Prints THE AVERAGE OF , 2, SCORES IS, 81						
(10)	Stops						

PROGRAM

DATA ITEM	VARIABLE NAME
SUM	SUM
COUNT	COUNT
MAXNUM	MAXNUM
BIGGEST	BIGGST
SMALLEST	SMALST
EOD	EOD
AVERAGE	AVERG
SCORE	SCORE

STEP	REFERENCE	FORTRAN CODE
	1	* COMPUTE AVERAGE OF TEST SCORES
	2	*
	3	* R. W. DILLMAN
	4	* FEB. 1984
	5	*
	6	* VARIABLES
	7	* COUNT=COUNT OF INPUTS
	8	* SUM=SUM OF INPUTS, AVERG=SUM/COUNT
	9	* SCORE=VALUE OF CURRENT INPUT
	10	* MAXNUM=MAXIMUM NUMBER OF INPUTS
	11	* BIGGST=LARGEST POSSIBLE INPUT
	12	* SMALST=SMALLEST POSSIBLE INPUT
	13	* EOD=END-OF-DATA MARKER
	14	*
	15	INTEGER COUNT, MAXNUM
	16	REAL SUM, BIGGST, SMALST, AVERAGE, EOD, SCORE
(1)	17	PARAMETER (MAXNUM=30, BIGGST=100, SMALST=0)
•	18	PARAMETER (EOD=-1)
•	19	SUM=0
(6)	20	COUNT=0
(7.1)	21	PRINT *, 'ENTER SCORES, USE -1 TO EXIT'
(7)	22	DO 100 I=1,MAXNUM
(7.1)	23	READ *, SCORE
(7.2)	24	IF (SCORE .EQ. EOD) GOTO 199
(7.3)	25	IF ((SCORE .LE. BIGGST) .AND. (SCORE .GE. SMALST))
(7.31)	26	THEN
(7.31)	27	SUM=SUM+SCORE
(7.32)	28	COUNT=COUNT+1
	29	ELSE
(7.33)	30	PRINT *, 'ILLEGAL SCORE'
	31	ENDIF
(7)	32	100 CONTINUE
	33	199 CONTINUE
(8)	34	AVERG=SUM/COUNT
(9)	35	PRINT *, 'THE AVERAGE OF ',COUNT, ' SCORES IS ',# AVERG
(10)	36	END

Line 24 checks the input value and jumps out of the loop if the input is −1. Line 25 checks the input to make sure it is in the range 0 to 100. If it is not, then line 30 is executed, and an error message is printed. Notice that the input is only added into the sum and counted (lines 27 and 28) after it has been checked for correctness. At line 32, statement number 100 is the end-of-loop marker. At line 33, statement number 199 is the destination of the loop exit test in line 24.

PRACTICE

1. Enter, execute, and verify this program. When testing it, be sure to give it some illegal scores.

2. Change the program so that it will accept a maximum of 50 test scores. Change it so that the biggest score it will accept is 200.

3. Why is -1 a good choice for the end-of-data marker? Why not choose -237? Why not choose 101?

16
LOGIC: PROGRAM ORGANIZATION AND DISPLAY

DEFINITIONS

Algorithm
: A set of steps that gives an exact procedure for the solution of a problem.

Flowchart
: A way of representing the steps in an algorithm with specially coded symbols.

Pseudocode
: A way of representing the steps in an algorithm with a special kind of "language."

Structures
: The name given to the three logical forms with which all algorithms can be constructed.

Structured Programming
: An approach to programming which uses *only* the logical structures.

Software
: Programs.

Comments
: Notes written *inside* a program to help explain the code to other programmers.

Documentation
: Information written *outside* the program to show users how to operate the program.

Style
: The art of writing programs that are easy for *people* to read.

We will start with a very simple statement:

A person who cannot write computer programs that work correctly is not a computer programmer.

This statement is so obvious that it probably sounds kind of dumb to you, but it turns out to be very important. In this chapter we're going to be discussing the difference between "good" programmers and "bad" programmers. Before we do this, you should understand that there are some things that *all* programmers, both good and bad, can do.

In the same way that plumbers know how to fix leaky pipes, mechanics know how to repair engines, and secretaries know how to type, programmers know how to design algorithms and code programs. And just as there are people who are not plumbers, mechanics, or secretaries but who know a little bit about fixing leaks, adjusting engines, and typing letters, there are people who are not programmers who know a little bit about programming.

To be called a "programmer," even at a beginning level, a person *must* be able to do the following:

1. Read a problem statement and:
   a. Organize the *data* given in the problem.
   b. Organize the *rules* given in the problem.
   c. Decide if the data and rules are complete enough to allow the problem to be solved.
2. Design and test an algorithm which will show how to solve the problem.
3. Translate the algorithm into a computer language.
4. Enter, debug, and test the program.
5. Comment and document the program.

"Good" programmers perform these tasks quickly and efficiently with a minimum of errors. In this chapter we will be looking at some "good" programming techniques.

If you plan to write programs *only* for your own personal use, and never plan to write programs as part of your job, then this material may not be of great importance to you. If, however, you plan at some point to be involved in professional programming, then you should pay very close attention to this chapter. The "best" programmers are the programmers who are best able to use these techniques. The techniques aren't difficult to understand or to apply. There is no reason why you shouldn't make them a part of every program you write.

COMMERCIAL PROGRAMMING

Professionally written programs are often divided into two categories: *business* and *scientific*. Scientific programs are generally taken to be more mathematically oriented and are used in scientific research and development. Business programs are usually oriented toward "data processing." Data processing involves the collection, evaluation, and display of information for use by a business.

The business and scientific categories are relatively old terms. Some of the newer computer applications (such as computer games, animated graphics, computer-aided instruction, robotics) fit into both categories. With this in mind, and because the requirements of a "good" program are the same regardless of its application, we will lump all of the various applications into one category: *commercial* programming.

Commercial programming is programming which is done by professional programmers for pay. (The category excludes home computer hobbyists whose programs are meant for their own use and will never be seen by other programmers.) Here are some facts about commercial programming.

Commercial programs are *large*. They often contain thousands, and sometimes hundreds of thousands, of lines of code. Because of this it is unusual for a commercial programmer to design and code an entire program. Programmers often work in groups. Each programmer does a piece of the problem, and the pieces are fitted together later to get the whole program. In cases like this, each programmer must understand what all the other programmers are doing; otherwise the final pieces would never fit together.

Commercial programs are *expensive*. The company must pay for computer time to test the programs as well as pay the programmers' salaries. The longer it takes to develop the program, the more it costs the company. As far as companies are concerned, good programmers are those who solve problems consistently and with a minimum of errors.

A word about *errors*. Syntax and typing errors in a program are relatively easy to locate and correct. The computer helps out with these kinds of errors by printing error messages. But logical errors, places where the program has been designed incorrectly, are often very difficult to track down. The difficulty comes from the fact that while the programmer knows that the output is wrong, he or she doesn't know *why* it's wrong. Since the computer only does what it is told to do, it can't give much help with this kind of problem.

The best way to avoid logical errors is to develop and check out an *algorithm* for *every* program you write. Beginning programmers often skip the algorithm and go directly to writing the code. They can get away with that for awhile because the beginning problems are very simple. As the problems get more complex, however, they will reach a point where they won't be able to sit down and work out the solution in your head. If they persist in writing in FORTRAN without doing the algorithms first, they will find that their programs will contain more and more logical errors. While they waste time tracking down errors and rewriting codes, the programmers who use algorithms will be going on to the next problem. In the long run, it is the ability to analyze problems, organize data, and develop algorithms that separates the successful programmers from the unsuccessful ones.

Commercial programs also have *long lifetimes*. Once a company has a program working, it may continue to use that program as long as it owns the computer that the program runs on. In fact, it is not unusual for a company buying a new computer to transfer some of its old programs to it.

However, although the program as a whole will last a long time, *parts* of it will change frequently. As the company grows and changes, it will require adjustments in its programs. Making these day-to-day changes in existing software is called *maintenance programming*.

There are *more* commercial programmers doing *maintenance* programming than there are developing *new* programs. This is important because maintenance represents a large part of a company's programming costs, companies are always looking for ways to make maintenance easier and more efficient. Here is an example.

PROBLEM   A company's payroll program is based on the present nine-digit Social Security number. The government has announced that because it is running out of numbers, all Social Security numbers issued after January 1 of next year will have two additional digits added to the front. In all existing numbers the new digits will be treated as 00. Your job is to adjust the program to handle the new numbering system.

Suppose you've just been hired by this company and the job is handed to you. Where do you start?

Well, first you might ask for a listing. The printer runs it off and somebody delivers it to your office. It's 6000 lines of code, 100 pages with 60 lines to a page. You thumb through it, page after page of FORTRAN—full of IF tests and GOTOs and variable names that don't mean anything to you. So you think for a moment, and decide to go look up the algorithms from which the FORTRAN was coded.

In the computer room they tell you that the program was written ten years ago and that in those days they didn't keep the algorithms around after the program was tested and working. They also tell you that some other changes have been made over the years, but no one is really sure exactly what they were. The data processing director does have a packet of reports and memos (40 pages, xeroxed) that tell how to *use* the program. It doesn't contain any information on how the code itself is constructed, but she has it copied for you just in case it will help.

Back in your office you read over the packet. At the front of the report are the names of the five programmers who designed the original program. You decide that even though it's been ten years, they ought to remember enough to be able to give you *some* help in figuring out how the program works. So you head for the personnel office to check on where to find them.

Unfortunately it has been ten years. Three of the programmers have taken new jobs with other companies, one has been promoted to a managerial position with the company's Australian division, and one has retired. So you're on your own—and you have a large problem. If you make changes in the current program, and if those changes produce any kind of errors, then the company's payroll will come out wrong and you'll be in trouble.

You only have one alternative. That's to go through the program, line by line, and reconstruct the algorithm. Only after you are absolutely sure that you understand everything about how the programs works will you be able to make your changes.

None of this is your fault. You could be the best programmer in the country, but because the programmers who worked *before* you didn't keep good records, a two-week job has turned into a three-month job. The extra ten weeks of salary to you is the price the company will have to pay for not hiring "good" programmers in the first place.

Modern companies understand this. They have evolved a set of standards for evaluating programs:

1. A "good" program does exactly what the problem statement says it should do—no more, no less. It produces output in exactly the form that was specified.
2. A "good" program is easy to use. Its printouts are clear and understandable. It comes with documentation that explains what it is for and gives instructions for its use in language that nonprogrammers can understand.
3. A "good" program is easy to change. It is written in a simple, easy-to-follow style, and the code contains comments that are sufficient to explain the workings to another programmer. The original algorithms are written out and updated whenever changes occur.

"Good" programmers are programmers who produce "good" programs. There are only these three questions that will be asked when people evaluate your programming:

1. Does it work?
2. Is it easy to use?
3. Will it be easy for another programmer to change it?

If the answers to these three questions are "yes," then you'll be writing good programs.

We have already seen a few programming techniques that contribute to good programming. Designing algorithms, using logical structures, and using parameters all help. In the rest of this chapter we will look at some additional useful techniques.

STRUCTURED PROGRAMMING

Structured programming is an approach to problem analysis, algorithm design, and program coding in which the programmer decides to use *only* the logical structures. The structures themselves are *logical* tools. They are not part of the computer language, but rather are part of the way the programmer *uses* the language.

There are two good, strong reasons for using structured programming. First, if you get in the habit of *always* analyzing and coding your problems with the same techniques, you'll find that parts of the problem-solving process will become automatic to you. Your analysis, design, and coding will go faster, and you'll tend to make fewer errors.

Second, if all programmers were to use structured techniques, then it would be much easier for one programmer to read another programmer's work. As we've seen, that's one of the main goals of commercial programming. It's possible that in the future some new, better approach to programming will develop, but for now, most good programmers use structured programming techniques.

Programmers who use structured programming techniques approach the problems they have to solve with the structures in mind. When analyzing the problem, they try to identify activities that will need to be repeated, activities that will require IF/THEN/ ELSE tests, and activities that will occur in simple sequences. They then use this information to develop algorithms in which *every* activity to be performed is part of a structure. Finally, when they translate the algorithm into a computer language, they make sure that the structures are not lost.

Since the structures are *logical* devices, they can be programmed in *any* general-purpose programming language. There are *some* languages, however, which are more suited to structured code. COBOL, FORTRAN 77, PL/I, and Pascal allow structured coding to be done easily. In FORTRAN IV, BASIC, APL, and many of the specialized languages such as LISP or SNOBOL, structured code is much more difficult to construct.

There are two major versions of FORTRAN available on today's computers. The older version, called FORTRAN IV, lacks many of the structured programming features of FORTRAN 77. In particular, FORTRAN IV does not allow the ELSE/ENDIF part of the IF instruction. As an example, this algorithm:

> (5) IF KTEST is not equal to ALIGN
>   THEN
>   (5.1)   Add KTEST to SUM
>   (5.2)   Add 1 to COUNT
>   ELSE
>   (5.3)   Print "SEQUENCE INVALID"
> (6)

would be translated into FORTRAN IV as follows:

```
        IF (KTEST .EQ. ALIGN) GOTO 500
           SUM=SUM+KTEST
           COUNT=COUNT+1
           GOTO 510
   500  CONTINUE
           PRINT *, 'SEQUENCE INVALID'
   510  CONTINUE
```

Because FORTRAN IV does not provide the ELSE/ENDIF instruction, programmers must translate IF/THEN/ELSE structures by using GOTO and CONTINUE statements. This makes the translation process more difficult, and also reduces the readability of the programs. (Notice, for example, that because of the way the logic operates, .EQ. must be used in the IF test instead of .NE.) In FORTRAN 77 the same algorithm would be translated like this:

```
IF (KTEST .NE. ALIGN)
   THEN
      SUM=SUM+KTEST
      COUNT=COUNT+1
   ELSE
      PRINT *, 'SEQUENCE INVALID'
ENDIF
```

You can see that the absence of the GOTOs and CONTINUEs makes the logic of this program much easier to follow.

REPRESENTING ALGORITHMS

An algorithm is useless unless it can be written down and later translated into computer code. We have been writing algorithms in an English-oriented step-by-step form because we think it's the easiest form for beginning programmers to read. There are a number of other ways to write algorithms down, however, and there are two in particular that are very widely used.

Before we show them to you, though, we need to make an important point. It is totally unimportant as to *which* of these forms you decide to use. Good programmers tend to be able to use all three, but mostly they use the one with which they are most comfortable. You should try the new methods out and see which one you like best. The *most* important thing is that you take the time to write down your algorithms. *How* you choose to write them down doesn't really matter too much.

First we'll write down an algorithm using the English step-by-step form, and then we'll do the same one in pseudocode and by flowchart.

    (1)   Set SUM to be 0
    (2)   Set COUNT to be 0
    (3)   Set EOD to be −1
    (4)   LOOP from 1 to 100
    (5)   Get a value for NUMBER
    (6)   IF NUMBER is equal to EOD
           THEN
           (6.1)   EXIT LOOP
           ELSE
           (6.2)   Add NUMBER into SUM
           (6.3)   Add 1 to COUNT
    (7)   Compute AVERAGE=SUM/COUNT
    (8)   Print "AVERAGE IS", AVERAGE
    (9)   Stop

You recognize this as the algorithm for computing the average of a set of numbers. It's a good example because it makes use of all three of the structures. Here's the same algorithm in *pseudocode:*

```
         SUM, COUNT=0
         EOD=-1
A:  LOOP (1,100)
         INPUT NUMBER
B:       IF NUMBER=EOD
         THEN
            EXIT LOOP A
         ELSE
            SUM=SUM+NUMBER
            COUNT=COUNT+1
         ENDIF B
         ENDLOOP A
         AVERAGE=SUM/COUNT
         PRINT "AVERAGE IS", AVERAGE
         STOP
```

Compare this with the first algorithm. You will notice that they're very much alike.

To use *pseudocode* means to write the algorithm in a form that is similar to programming language code. There are two major advantages to using pseudocode.

First, by eliminating excess English, and by giving labels only to the beginning lines of loops and IF/THEN/ELSE, the algorithm can be written in a much shorter form. If you're comfortable with it, you can write algorithms more quickly with pseudocode than with the English approach.

Notice that if you're using the logical structures, you only *need* to label the beginning line of the loop and IF/THEN/ELSE structures. This is so because the only way to perform a structure is to start with its first line.

Similarly, the only way to leave a structure is to exit through its last line. Pseudocode users often employ ENDIF and ENDLOOP lines to mark the ends of those structures. This isn't strictly necessary, but it makes the pseudocode easier to read.

The second advantage is that since pseudocode looks very much like programming language code, it can often be translated faster than the English-type algorithm.

It is *important* to see that pseudocode is *not* programming language code. The difference is that pseudocode cannot be fed to the computer and executed. Because of this, the programmer does not have to worry about strict syntax rules while writing down the algorithm. This leaves him or her free to concentrate on the *logic* of the solution, and that, of course, is the whole purpose of doing algorithms in the first place.

The main disadvantage of pseudocodes that they are *personal* tools. That is, a programmer who uses pseudocode invents a code to suit his or her particular approach to programming. Because of this, it can be difficult for one programmer to read another programmer's algorithms. If you decide to do most of your algorithms in pseudocode, you should make up a simple code, sufficient to represent the logical structures and the basic activities that the computer will have to perform. The more complicated you make your code, the harder it will be to use, and the more difficult it will be for others to understand.

FLOWCHARTS

The next approach to representing algorithms is called a *flowchart:*

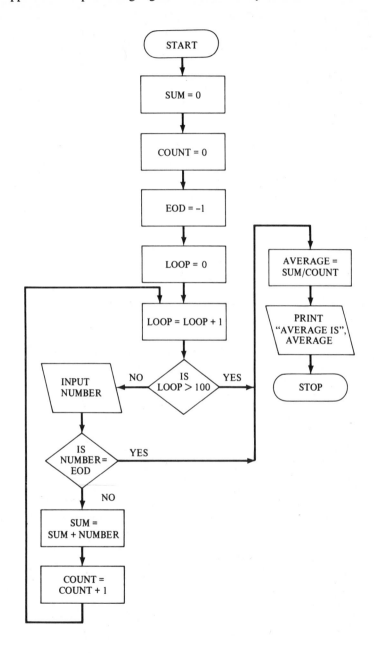

In a flowchart, each activity to be performed is written inside a box. The boxes are connected by arrows that show the sequence in which the activities will be performed. Because the logical "flow" is so easy to follow, flowcharts are very easy to translate into computer language.

The *shape* of the boxes in a flowchart is important; it tells you what type of activity is to be performed. There are a large number of flowchart symbols; we will show only the basic ones.

SYMBOL	NAME	DESCRIPTION
▭	PROCESS	Perform an arithmetic or assignment operation.
▱	INPUT/OUTPUT	Perform an I/O operation.
YES ◇ NO	DECISION	Ask a yes/no question; then follow the branch of the arrow with the answer.
▢	TERMINAL	Start or stop the flowchart.
↓	ARROW	Indicates direction of "flow." Except for DECISION (which has two), no box may have more than one arrow leaving it.

As you can see from the example, flowcharts make it very easy for the programmer to follow the step-by-step sequencing of the steps in the algorithm. But if you look at the example and try to pick out the logical structures, you will see the major disadvantage of flowcharts.

Flowcharts emphasize flow, not form. It is more difficult to represent the structures in flowchart symbols than it is to represent them in pseudocode. Of course, since the structures are just logical constructs, they *can* be represented as:

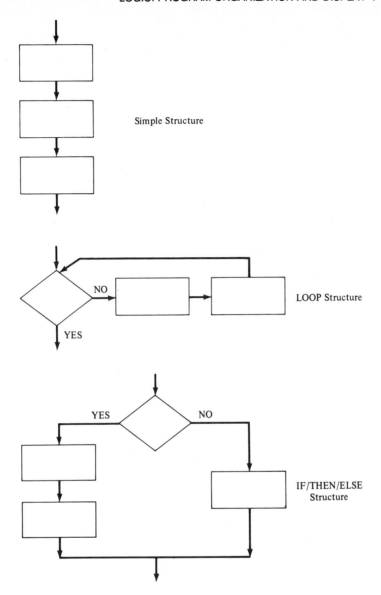

Simple Structure

LOOP Structure

IF/THEN/ELSE
Structure

Thus the problem is not that the structures can't be written down in flowchart symbols, but, rather, that it is hard to read the flowchart and pick out the structures right away.

There are two other major disadvantages of flowcharting as a way of representing algorithms. One is that a large amount of programmer time must be used just in selecting and drawing the symbols. The second is that it is relatively more difficult to make changes in flowchart symbols than in pseudocode. It is not unusual to see half-finished designs that look like this:

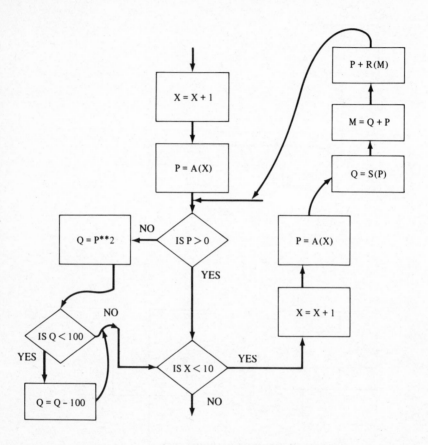

Even if the structure was being maintained at first, it is lost in the confusion of the corrections.

The major advantage of the flowchart symbols is that they are *standardized*. This means that there is only one set of symbols, so once you know how to flowchart, you can understand *any* flowchart you see. Because of this, program logic is often *maintained* in flowchart form. This means that once the program is tested and working, a flowchart of it is made and kept for later reference.

There are a number of books on flowcharting, and if you're attracted to this approach, you should do some more reading on the subject. It's probably to your advantage to be able to write *both* pseudocode and flowcharts, but you should choose one way to write *your* algorithms and stick with it.

PROGRAM COMMENTS

If you look on page 5, at the very first program we showed you, you'll see that the first two lines of that program use the FORTRAN statement *. Those two lines are called *comment* lines, and * is the FORTRAN instruction used for inserting comments into a program.

A comment is a line of text which is put into a program to explain what the program code is doing. Comment lines *do not execute*. The computer ignores them. Comment lines are written by programmers for other programmers to read.

There are no standard rules for what the comments should say, exactly. In general, the comments are there to help someone else understand your code. Therefore, you should try to write comments that are helpful. Most programmers agree that *at least* the following should be included:

At the beginning:

- The programmer's name
- The date the program was finished
- The purpose of the program and the program name
- A brief description of each of the major variable names

Within the program code:

- Spacing to show the major structures, especially loop structures
- Brief explanations of unusual or complex logic

A program with too *few* comments and one with too *many* comments are equally bad. Both are unreadable.

We suggest that you start *every* program you do with the following:

```
* PROGRAM NAME: ODDAVG
* PURPOSE: COMPUTE THE AVERAGE OF ODD NUMBERS
*
* PROGRAMMER: SUSAN P. SMITH
* DATE: SEPT. 1984
*
* VARIABLES:
*   NUMB=INPUT VALUE
*   SUM=SUM OF INPUTS
*   COUNT=COUNT OF THE INPUTS
*   AVERG=SUM/COUNT
              .
              .
              .
         And so on
```

If this seems too much bother, just remember that in many companies this much commenting is an *absolute* requirement. Programs without comments are not accepted, and programmers who fail to write comments are not promoted. An example of a well-commented program is shown in Chapter 17.

PROGRAM DOCUMENTATION

Just as "comments" refers to information about the program stored *inside* the program, "documentation" refers to information about the program stored *outside* the program. Documentation is used for two things. Its main purpose is to explain what the program is for and how to use it. This information is often called *user* documentation.

"Documentation" is also used to describe the copy of the algorithm and other explanatory information written for other programmers (not necessarily users) to read. Every company will have its own set of rules for producing documentation, but the following are generally accepted as the minimum that is needed.

Programmer documentation:

- A complete listing of the *current* version of the program code
- A copy of the original problem statement with any subsequent additions and/or corrections
- A copy of the algorithm that fits the *current* version of the program
- A list of the data items with a description of each item and the variable name which represents the item in the program

The algorithm should include explanations that tell what the major activities are. Any unusual or complex logic should be explained in detail.

User documentation:

- A general description of the program's purpose and function
- Clear, easy-to-follow, *complete* instructions for using the program

Instructions should be written with the assumption that the user is not a programmer.

17
USING THE COMPUTER: A SAMPLE PROBLEM

Presented here, in commented and documented form, is the program that was developed in Chapter 15.

PROGRAM

REFERENCE	FORTRAN CODE
1	`* AVGSCR -- COMPUTE AVERAGE OF TEST SCORES`
2	`*`
3	`* R. W. DILLMAN`
4	`* FEB. 1984`
5	`*`
6	`*         VARIABLES`
7	`* COUNT=(COUNT OF INPUTS)`
8	`* SUM=(SUM OF INPUTS), AVERG=(SUM/COUNT)`
9	`* SCORE=(VALUE OF CURRENT INPUT)`
10	`* MAXNUM=(MAXIMUM NUMBER OF INPUTS)`
11	`* BIGGST=(LARGEST POSSIBLE INPUT)`
12	`* SMALST=(SMALLEST POSSIBLE INPUT)`
13	`* EOD=(END-OF-DATA MARKER)`
14	`*`
15	`* *** INITIALIZE *************************************`
16	`*`
17	`      INTEGER COUNT, MAXNUM`
18	`      REAL SUM, BIGGST, SMALST, AVERG, EOD, SCORE`
19	`      PARAMETER (MAXNUM=30, BIGGST=100, SMALST=0)`

(continued)

135

REFERENCE	FORTRAN CODE

```
20          PARAMETER (EOD=-1)
21          SUM=0
22          COUNT=0
23    *
24    *** INPUT TEST SCORES -- COMPUTE SUM AND COUNT ***
25    *
26          PRINT *, 'ENTER SCORES, USE -1 TO EXIT'
27          DO 100 I=1,MAXNUM
28            READ *, SCORE
29            IF (SCORE .EQ. EOD) GOTO 199
30    *
31    *     CHECK IF SCORE IS OUTSIDE LEGAL RANGE
32    *
33            IF ((SCORE .LE. BIGGST) .AND.
         #       (SCORE .GE. SMALST))
34              THEN
35                SUM=SUM+SCORE
36                COUNT=COUNT+1
37              ELSE
38                PRINT *, 'ILLEGAL SCORE'
39              ENDIF
40    100 CONTINUE
41    199 CONTINUE
42    *
43    *** COMPUTE AVERAGE AND DO OUTPUT ********************
44    *
45          AVERG=SUM/COUNT
46    *
47          PRINT *, 'THE AVERAGE OF ', COUNT, ' SCORES IS',
         #AVERG
48   END
```

The comments in lines 1 through 5 identify the program and the programmer. Those in lines 6 through 13 identify the variables and parameters to be used. Comments at lines 15, 24, and 43 identify major sections of the program. The comment line at 31 describes the purpose of the somewhat complicated IF test used at line 33. The one at line 46 is just to provide spacing between lines 45 and 47.

The purpose of comment lines is to make the program more readable. Comments should be used to identify, to explain, and to separate. Comments are not an end in themselves. Too many are as bad as, or worse than, not enough.

USER DOCUMENTATION

PROGRAM   TSAVRG
NAME

PURPOSE   Compute the average of a set of test scores.

SAMPLE RUN
```
ENTER TEST SCORES, USE -1 TO EXIT
90
65
107
ILLEGAL SCORE
80
77
-12
ILLEGAL SCORE
84
-1

THE AVERAGE OF 5 SCORES IS 79.20
```

INPUT   At input, enter one score. Score must be greater than or equal to zero; less than or equal to 100.
A maximum of 30 scores may be entered. When you have no more scores to enter, enter -1. Computer will then compute and print the average of the entered scores.

ERROR   ILLEGAL SCORE—This means that the score entered was less than
MESSAGES   zero or greater than 100. Illegal scores are rejected; they are not averaged.

ACTION   Continue to enter data.
TO TAKE

PROGRAMMER DOCUMENTATION

PROGRAM   TSAVG
NAME

PROGRAMMER R. DILLMAN

DATE   AUGUST 1984

PROBLEM   A teacher who has 30 students in the class wants a computer program to
              compute the average score on a test. The highest possible score is 100.
              The lowest possible score is 0. The teacher plans to use the program
              whenever a test is given.

SAMPLE   ENTER TEST SCORES, USE -1 TO EXIT
OUTPUT   80
              70
              109
              ILLEGAL SCORE
              -12
              ILLEGAL SCORE
              90
              77
              -1

              THE AVERAGE OF 4 SCORES IS 79.22

DATA ITEM	VARIABLE NAME	DESCRIPTION
SCORE	SCORE	Input test score
COUNT	COUNT	Count of scores
SUM	SUM	Sum of scores
AVERAGE	AVERG	Average
MAXNUM	MAXNUM	Maximum number of scores (30)
BIGGEST	BIGGST	Biggest possible score (100)
SMALLEST	SMALST	Smallest possible score (0)
EOD	EOD	End-of-data test (-1)

RULES   1.   AVERAGE = SUM/COUNT

              2.   Accept no more than MAXNUM scores.

              3.   If SCORE>BIGGEST or SCORE<SMALLEST, print
                   "ILLEGAL SCORE" message and reject input.

ALGORITHM

FLOWCHART	DESCRIPTION

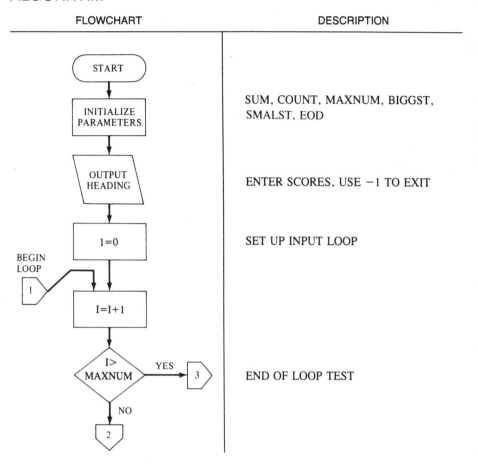

SUM, COUNT, MAXNUM, BIGGST, SMALST, EOD

ENTER SCORES, USE −1 TO EXIT

SET UP INPUT LOOP

END OF LOOP TEST

(*Note:* The ⟩2⟩ flowchart symbol is used when the chart carries over to a new page.)

FLOWCHART   DESCRIPTION

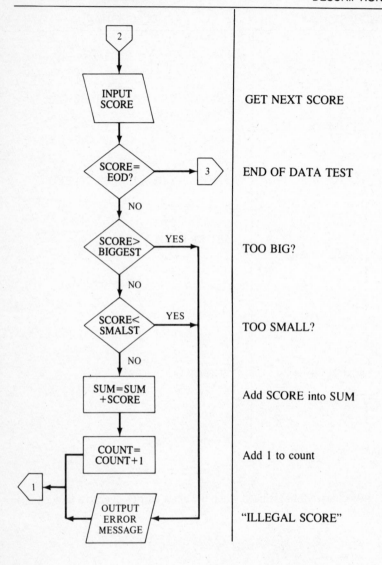

GET NEXT SCORE

END OF DATA TEST

TOO BIG?

TOO SMALL?

Add SCORE into SUM

Add 1 to count

"ILLEGAL SCORE"

FLOWCHART	DESCRIPTION

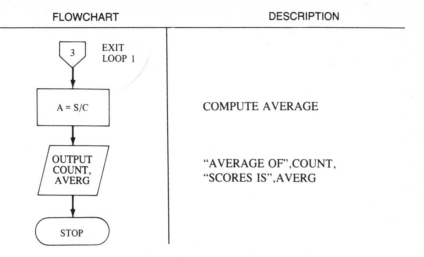

COMPUTE AVERAGE

"AVERAGE OF",COUNT,
"SCORES IS",AVERG

The flowchart was prepared *after* the program had been coded and tested. Its purpose is to show the sequencing of the program's logic, and to provide helpful comments on the purpose of individual instructions. (The "BEGIN LOOP" and "EXIT LOOP" are not standard flowcharting symbols. We add them to help show the structure.) The flowchart is used along with the tables of sample output, data items, and rules, and with a listing of the program. With this information, a competent FORTRAN programmer should be able to understand this program and to make changes if necessary.

PRACTICE

These are not trivial problems. They may require some changing of the logical design. You may want to review Chapter 15 as you begin.

1. In testing this program, a flaw has been discovered. When an illegal score is entered, the score is rejected as required. At that point, however, the loop counter has already been incremented. So although the illegal score isn't counted for the average, it is counted toward the MAXNUM (maximum number) of inputs. This means, for example, that if you type in five illegal scores, you can only type a maximum of 25 legal scores. Fix the program so that you can always type in MAXNUM legal scores, no matter how many illegal scores you enter.

2. After using the program for awhile, the teacher complains that if he accidentally mistypes a score, the computer won't let him fix it. For example, if the test score is 88, and he mistypes it as 89, there is no way he can correct his mistake.
    Adjust the program to allow a new special entry, -2, which will erase the previous entry.

SAMPLE
```
        89
        -2
        SCORE VALUE 89 ERASED
        88
          ¹
          ¹
          ¹
```

The effect of −2 is to subtract the value of the previous entry from the sum, and subtract 1 from the count.

Notice that in the current program, if −1 is the very *first* entry, the output is meaningless but no error occurs. Be sure that −2 as the first entry produces no errors.

3. After making and testing the changes in question 2, comment and document the new part of the program. If you changed the way the current program worked, be sure to update the flowchart to show the new logic.

4. Compare one of your old homework programs with the sample program on page 135. Does your program have good comments and documentation? If not, fix it so that it does.

SUMMARY
FOR PART II

To write computer programs well, you must be able to apply two *different* kinds of skills.

The first skill is called "logic design." To do design you must be able to read and understand the problem, and then to develop an algorithm that will solve the problem.

The second skill is called "program coding and testing." To do coding you must be able to translate an algorithm into a computer language, enter the program into a computer, and verify that it executes correctly.

In doing logic design you should keep in mind that programming problems are concerned with the manipulation of data. Because of this, it is important that you *organize* the information the problem statement gives you about the inputs and outputs of the problem. It is also important that you be careful to *define* the data items that the algorithm is to use. Careful definition of the data items will make it easier for you to select the proper *variable names* when it comes time to translate the algorithm into a program.

In doing the design you should also remember that most programming problems can be solved by using combinations of the IF/THEN/ELSE and LOOP structures. You should try to think through the problems in terms of these structures. Algorithms should be written out, usually in flowchart form or with pseudocode, and *traced*. Only after the trace is complete should you begin to translate the algorithm into a program.

In coding the program your objective is to find a set of computer language instructions that will allow the computer to execute the algorithm. If you have developed and traced a complete, structured algorithm, the coding should be fairly easy to do. You should not expect to be able to *remember* FORTRAN syntax in all of its complexity. Even the most experienced programmers spend time reading (and rereading) the computer reference manuals as they work. Knowing how to find things quickly in the manuals is another important skill in computer programming.

Once a program has been entered into the computer and debugged—that is, once you have managed to run it all the way through *once* correctly—it must be *tested* and *documented*. To test a program you should give it various kinds of different data, including erroneous or invalid data. Your objective is to locate situations where the program doesn't work correctly and to fix them. To document the program you should add comments to the code to explain the *logic* of the program. You should also look at the places where the program requests inputs or prints outputs to make sure that the program is easy to use and that its output is understandable.

PROGRAMMING PROBLEMS

The following set of problems is designed to give you practice in logic design and program coding. Some of the programs may seem simple enough that you can code them directly without worrying about doing a design. **Don't do this.** The purpose of the easy problems is to let you *practice* design; the problems will get much harder as we go on.

Most of the problems have follow-ons that ask you to add to or make changes in the original program. You should do as many of these as you can. There are very few *entirely new* programs written in the world each year. Most professional programmers spend their time making changes to, or fixing mistakes in, existing programs. Yet follow-on programming is difficult to do well. It can only be learned through practice.

1.0

PROBLEM
STATEMENT

A set of numbers will be input at the terminal. The program should compute the sum of the positive numbers and the product of the negative numbers. Use zero as the end-of-data marker.

SAMPLE
OUTPUT

```
ENTER NUMBERS -- USE 0 TO EXIT

?50.2
?-25
?49.8
?-3
?0

THE SUM OF THE POSITIVE NUMBERS IS 100.0

THE PRODUCT OF THE NEGATIVE NUMBERS IS 75
```

1.1. Have the program compute the sum of the squares of the positive input numbers, and also of the negative input numbers. Print each of these sums and the square root of each.

2.0

PROBLEM
STATEMENT

A set of numbers will be input at the terminal. The computer should tell which number in the set was the largest and also print out its value. Use 9999 as the end-of-data marker.

SAMPLE
OUTPUT

```
ENTER NUMBERS -- USE 9999 TO EXIT

?8
?3
?-4
?16.3
?-34
?-9.7
?23
?4
?3
?9999

THE LARGEST NUMBER IS IN POSITION 7

ITS VALUE IS 23
```

2.1. Have the program also print the smallest and its position.

2.2. Have the program print the three largest and the three smallest (and their positions). What should the program do if fewer than six numbers are input?

3.0

PROBLEM
STATEMENT

A set of numbers will be input at the terminal. Printout the median, mean, and standard deviation of the set. Use 9999 as the end-of-data marker.

SAMPLE
OUTPUT

```
ENTER NUMBERS -- USE 9999 TO EXIT

?1
?3
?6
?8
?17
?9999

MEDIAN VALUE: 6

MEAN VALUE: 7

STANDARD DEVIATION: 6.2
```

3.1. Have the program compute the range of the inputs. (Print the smallest input, the largest input, and their difference.)

4.0

PROBLEM
STATEMENT

Write a program to balance a checkbook. The first input should be a starting balance. Deposits should be entered as positive numbers. Checks should be entered as negative numbers. Use 9999 as the end-of-data marker. Include a service charge of 10 cents per check.

SAMPLE
OUTPUT

```
ENTER STARTING BALANCE
?100.25

ENTER CHECKS/DEPOSITS -- USE 9999 TO EXIT
?24.75
?-50.00
?-10.00
?-15.50
?9999

DEPOSITS: 24.75

CHECKS: 75.50   SERVICE CHARGE: .30   TOTAL: 75.80

NEW BALANCE: 46.20
```

4.1. If the new balance is less than zero, print a message, "OVER-DRAWN."

4.2. If at *any point* in the processing, the balance is less than 0, print an overdrawn message. From then on, the program should only accept deposits until the balance becomes positive.

5.0

PROBLEM
STATEMENT

A restaurant pays its employees as follows:

Regular pay = hours worked (up to 40) × regular rate
Overtime pay = hours worked (over 40) × 1.5 × regular rate
Deductions = 0.15 × (regular pay + overtime pay)
Total pay = regular pay + overtime pay − deductions

Write a program that inputs the hours worked and the regular rate for an employee and outputs the total pay.

SAMPLE   ENTER HOURS, PAY RATE
OUTPUT   ?50, 4,00

REGULAR PAY: 160,00

OVERTIME PAY: 60,00

DEDUCTIONS: 33,00

                                  TOTAL PAY: 187,00

5.1.   Alter the program so that it handles up to 30 employees' data. Use 0, 0 as the end-of-data input.

5.2.   Extend the foregoing to print a summary page. The output should include grand totals for the three kinds of pay and the deductions.

6.0

PROBLEM   Write a program that will produce a conversion table of temperatures
STATEMENT   from Fahrenheit to centigrade (Celsius) over a given range. The beginning temperature, the ending temperature, and the increment will be inputs.

SAMPLE   ENTER BEGINNING TEMP, ENDING TEMP, INTERVAL
OUTPUT   ?70,80,2

ITEM	FAHRENHEIT	CENTIGRADE
1	70	21,1
2	72	22,2
3	74	23,3
4	76	24,4
5	78	25,5
6	80	26,7

6.1.   Alter the program so that it will do *either* Fahrenheit to centigrade *or* centigrade to Fahrenheit at the *user's* option.

6.2. Alter the program so that a request that will print more than 20 items will cause the message:

```
SCREEN SIZE EXCEEDED
CONTINUE? (ENTER YES OR NO)
?
```

to appear after each set of 20 lines is printed. The program should continue if the user enters YES and abort otherwise.

7.0

PROBLEM STATEMENT

Print out a table of squares and square roots for any set of positive integers beginning at A and ending at B. A and B are inputs:

SAMPLE OUTPUT

```
TABLE OF SQUARES AND ROOTS

BEGIN AT
?1

END AT
?4

NUMBER          SQUARE              ROOT
1               1                   1
2               4                   1.4
3               9                   1.7
4               16                  2
```

7.1. Test your program to be sure that it deals with possible error conditions. (Fix it if it doesn't.) For inputs use:

TEST	BEGIN AT	END AT
1	5	5
2	4	1
3	-2	-5

7.2. Alter the program so that the power to be used in computing the table is an input.

SAMPLE   `ENTER POWER`
OUTPUT   `?4`

`BEGIN AT`
`?1`

`END AT`
`?4`

NUMBER	POWER	ROOT
1	1	1
2	16	1.18
3	81	1.31
4	256	1.41

8.0

PROBLEM   Write a program to compute the real roots of a quadratic equation. The
STATEMENT   coefficients will be entered as inputs—A, B, C. If there are no real roots,
              the program should print a message to that effect.

SAMPLE   `ENTER COEFFICIENTS: A, B, C`
OUTPUT   `?1,2,-15`

`ROOTS ARE: 3   -5`

`ENTER COEFFICIENTS: A, B, C`
`?10,4,5`

`THE ROOTS ARE NOT REAL`

8.1. Compute the imaginary roots and print them in this form:

`ROOTS ARE: 3+2I     3-2I`

8.2. Test the program thoroughly. In particular, what if any (or all) of
A, B, and C are zero?

8.3. Modify the program so that it also prints out the Cartesian coordinates of the vertex of the parabola defined by the equation.

8.4. Using the form $y = mx + b$, print the values of m and b for the line
tangent to the parabola at its vertex.

9.0

PROBLEM
STATEMENT
Write a program that computes the value of pi. The program should stop
when the newest computed value is within 0.0001 of the last computed
value.

SAMPLE
OUTPUT
Any reasonable output form will do. Print out the computed value for pi
and the number of iterations of the loop that were needed to obtain the
result.

9.1.   Develop a different algorithm for producing the same output. Run
the resulting program. Which of the two programs is the faster?
Why?

10.0

PROBLEM
STATEMENT
Write a program that computes the sums of the following series:

$$1 + 1/2 + 1/3 + 1/4 + \cdots + 1/N$$
$$1 + 1/2 - 1/3 + 1/4 - \cdots + 1/N$$

where N is a positive integer. N is an input to the program.

SAMPLE
OUTPUT
```
ENTER VALUE FOR FINAL DIVISOR, N
?4

SUM: 1+1/2+1/3... IS      2.083
SUM: 1+1/2-1/3... IS      1.416
```

10.1.   Restrict the input to positive, *odd* numbers. Print an error message if the input is not odd.

10.2.   Alter the program so that the running sum is printed as each new
term is computed. Run the program with a very large value of N.
(Try N = 10,000, for example.) What do you notice about the
output? Modify the original program so that the computation
terminates when the new value of the sum is less than 0.0001
larger than the last value.

11.0

PROBLEM
STATEMENT
Two numbers will be entered at the terminal. The computer should find
the smallest value into which both inputs will divide evenly.

SAMPLE   `ENTER TWO NUMBERS`
OUTPUT

`?8,12`

`THE LEAST COMMON DENOMINATOR IS 24`

11.1.   Find a different algorithm for solving the same problem. Code
the program and test it. Which is the better program? Why?

12.0

PROBLEM   Write a program to compute and print out the first 25 prime numbers.
STATEMENT

SAMPLE   `THE FIRST TWENTY-FIVE PRIME NUMBERS ARE:`
OUTPUT   `   1`
`   2`
`   3`
`  .5`
`   7`
`  11`
`   ·`
`   ·`
`   ·`

12.1.   Print the results with five items per line.
Sample output: 1   2   3   5   7
11 13 17 19 23
· · · etc.

12.2.   Alter the program to print the first 50 prime numbers; then the
first 75 primes. How long does each of the three programs take to
run? Does it take three times as long to print 75 as it does to print
25?

13.0

PROBLEM   Write a program that will calculate the exact coins to be returned as
STATEMENT   change for a purchase. Assume the purchase will always be less than one
dollar and that the customer always pays exactly one dollar.

```
SAMPLE OUTPUT:

ENTER AMOUNT OF PURCHASE
?.45

CHANGE RETURNED
1 HALF DOLLAR
1 NICKEL


ENTER AMOUNT OF PURCHASE
?.33

CHANGE RETURNED
1 HALF DOLLAR
1 DIME
1 NICKEL
2 PENNIES
```

Note: Inputs less than 0 or greater than 0.99 should be rejected as invalid.

13.1. Extend the program to handle purchases of up to $100. Try to keep the program as short as possible.

14.0

PROBLEM STATEMENT Write a program that will accept as inputs a dollar amount and a number of years. The output should be a table showing how the dollar amount will grow yearly if invested at these rates: 9%, 10%, 12%, 14%, 16%, 20%. Use compound interest.

SAMPLE OUTPUT

```
ENTER AMOUNT, NUMBER OF YEARS
?100,5

AMOUNT AT END OF YEAR WHEN INVESTED AT
   YEAR   9%   10%   12%   14%   16%   20%
          ---   ---   ---   ---   ---   ---

     1    109   110   112   114   116   120
     2     X     X     X     X     X     X
     3     X     X     X     X     X     X
     4     X     X     X     X     X     X
     5     X     X     X     X     X     X
```

Note: The x's just show where the columns of numbers will be. In the actual program they'll be replaced with the computed values of the amounts.

14.1. Alter the program to allow the user a beginning interest rate, an ending interest rate, and an increment. The table should be computed using that set of rates.

14.2. Allow the user to enter from one to three interest rates in *any order*. Produce the table using those rates, but in ascending order.

15.0

PROBLEM
STATEMENT

The terms of a revolving credit account are as follows:

	Amount	Rate/month
Interest on unpaid balance	$0 – $499.99	1.5
	$500 – $999.99	1.25
	$1000 or more	1.00

	Balance	Payment balance
Minimum payment due	$0 – $9.99	$20
	$10 – $499.99	8% of balance
	$500 or more	

Write a program that inputs the existing balance and a payment and prints out the unpaid balance, interest charged, new balance, and minimum payment due.

SAMPLE
OUTPUT

```
ENTER EXISTING BALANCE, PAYMENT
?500.57, 50.57

UNPAID BALANCE: $450.00

INTEREST CHARGED: $6.75

NEW BALANCE: $456.75    MINIMUM PAYMENT DUE: $20.00
```

15.1. Alter the program to accept a *set* of charges and payments. The output form should remain the same.

15.2. Assume a *credit limit* of $1000. If a balance exceeds the limit, print a message to that effect.

16.0

PROBLEM
STATEMENT
Write a program that will compute the area and circumference of a triangle. The input should be three points specified in (x, y) form.

SAMPLE
OUTPUT

```
ENTER POINTS:
ONE?0,0
TWO?0,3
THREE?4,0

AREA OF TRIANGLE IS 6

CIRCUMFERENCE OF TRIANGLE IS 12
```

16.1.   Alter the program to accept the coordinates of two triangles as input. Print the circumference of the figure formed by their intersection.

16.2.   Have the program input the coordinates of two triangles. Print the area of the figure formed by their intersection.

17.0

PROBLEM
STATEMENT
Find the number of points whose coordinates are integer numbers that lie on or inside the circle defined by the equation:

$$X^2 + Y^2 = C$$

where C is an input.

SAMPLE
OUTPUT

```
ENTER CONSTANT
?4

INTEGER COORDINATES ON OR INSIDE THE CIRCLE
    X          Y

   -2          0
   -1          0
    0          0
    0          1
    0         -1
    0          2
    0         -2
    1          0
    2          0
```

17.1. Alter the program to use the formula:

$$(X - H)^2 + (Y - K)^2 = C$$

where H, K, and C are inputs.

17.2. Alter the program to use the formula for an elipse:

$$(X - H)^2/A + (Y - K)^2/B = C$$

where H, K, A, B, and C are inputs.

18.0

PROBLEM
STATEMENT

Write a program to find sets of numbers A, B, and C such that:

$$A^2 + B^2 = C^2$$

Have the program stop after it computes the first 20 sets.

SAMPLE
OUTPUT

A	B	C
3	4	5
9	16	25

```
         ♦
         ♦
   e t c ♦
```

18.1. Alter the program to compute the first 40 sets. Does it take the same amount of time to compute the second 20 values as it did to compute the first 20? What does this suggest about the distribution of the sets?

18.2. Design an experiment to verify further the conclusion you drew in the foregoing.

19.0

PROBLEM
STATEMENT

Write a program that will print out a depreciation schedule. The inputs should be the cost of the item and the number of years over which it is to be depreciated. The user should be able to select any one of three methods: straight-line, double-declining balance, sum-of-the-digits.

SAMPLE
OUTPUT

```
SELECT DEPRECIATION METHOD:
   ENTER
      1=STRAIGHT-LINE
      2=DOUBLE-DECLINING BALANCE
      3=SUM-OF-THE-DIGITS
      0=EXIT FROM PROGRAM
?1

ENTER AMOUNT, YEARS
?500,5

         YEAR      AMOUNT DEPRECIATED

          1             100.00
          2             100.00
          3             100.00
          4             100.00
          5             100.00


         TOTAL DEPRECIATED: $500.00
```

20.0

PROBLEM
STATEMENT

Write a program that computes the amount of money that must be deposited now at 10% compound interest to have a specified amount of money at some point in the future. This is called a "present value" computation. The desired amount and the range of years to be checked should be inputs.

SAMPLE
OUTPUT

```
ENTER DESIRED AMOUNT
?10000

ENTER FIRST AND LAST OF RANGE OF YEARS TO
     BE INVESTED, AND INCREMENT
?10,12,1

AT 10% INTEREST
IN ORDER TO ACCUMULATE $10000

IN THIS                  YOU MUST INVEST
MANY YEARS               THIS AMOUNT NOW

10                           $3856.53
11                           $3505.08
12                           $3186.74
```

20.1. Alter the program so that the interest rate is a constant.

20.2. Alter the program so that the interest rate is entered as a range—first, last, increment. The output should be a series of tables, each similar to the sample.

20.3. Alter the program to compute the amount that must be deposited at the beginning of each year in order to accumulate the desired amount.

21.0

PROBLEM STATEMENT

Write a program to input, process, and output complex numbers.

r = real part, i = imaginary part:

INPUT	OUTPUT	DESCRIPTION
r, i	r , i	Input r, i from terminal.
r, i	r , i	Output r, i to terminal.
r1, i1	r2 , i2	Output is conjugate of input.
r1, i1, r2, i2	r3 , i3	Output is sum of inputs.
r1, i1, r2, i2	r3 , i3	Output is difference of inputs.
r1, i1, r2,	r3 , i3	Output is product of inputs.

SAMPLE OUTPUT

Any readable output form is acceptable. Run enough tests to verify that the program works for all possible input values.

21.1. FORTRAN provides a special data type for dealing with complex numbers. Read the section on the COMPLEX type in your *FORTRAN Language Reference Manual*. Rewrite the program using the COMPLEX type.

22.0

PROBLEM STATEMENT

Write a program to graph functions of the type: $f(X)=AX^2+C$. A and C should be inputs to the program.

SAMPLE ENTER A,C
OUTPUT ?1,0

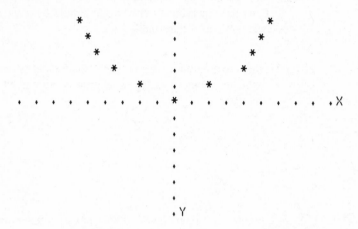

22.1. Modify the program so that the origin of the axes is determined by the integer x, y coordinates closest to the vertex of the curve. Label the original and the axes accordingly.

23.0

PROBLEM   Write a program that simulates the throwing of a pair of dice. Test your
STATEMENT   program by showing that the distribution of 1s, 2s, 3s, etc., is statistically
             correct. (FORTRAN does not have a standard random number generator.
             You will have to write one of your own.)

SAMPLE   HOW MANY THROWS?
OUTPUT   360

	SIMULATED	EXPECTED: 60 EACH
1:	61	
2:	58	
3:	64	
4:	57	
5:	60	
6:	59	

23.1. Load the dice so that threes and fours are 10% more likely to come up than the other numbers.

24.0

PROBLEM STATEMENT The input at the terminal will be a series of numbers. The program should count the number of sets of the same input. A set is a series of three or more occurrences of the same input in a row. For example, in the series:

2, 3, 6, 4, 4, 4, 7, 7, 2, 1, 9, 12, 12, 12, 12, 80, 5, 2

there are two sets—namely, 4, 4, 4 and 12, 12, 12, 12. Use 9999 as the end-of-data-marker.

SAMPLE OUTPUT

```
ENTER THE SERIES OF NUMBERS -- USE 9999 TO EXIT
?5
?3
?3
?3
?6
?6
?9
?23
?23
?23
?23
?5
?0
?2
?2
?9999

THERE ARE   2   SETS IN THIS SERIES
```

24.1. Modify the program to allow the definition of a "set" to be an input. Test the program thoroughly.

25.0

PROBLEM STATEMENT Pick a number between 1 and 100. Have the computer ask you questions about your number and try to guess what it is. The computer should be able to guess it exactly after seven questions.

SAMPLE OUTPUT

```
ANSWER QUESTIONS WITH YES OR NO.

THINK OF A NUMBER BETWEEN 1 AND 100.
```

```
IS THE NUMBER BIGGER THAN 50
?TYES

IS IT LESS THAN 75
?NO

IS THE NUMBER SMALLER THAN 84
?YES

AH, IT'S BETWEEN 75 and 84, IS IT LESS THAN 80
?YES

IS IT BIGGER THAN 77
?YES

IS IT 79
?NO

THEN IT MUST BE 78, NOT BAD, IT TOOK ME 6 QUESTIONS TO
 FIND THE ANSWER,
```

(The output need not be in exactly this form.)

25.1. Modify the program to guess a number between 1 and 1000. What's the maximum number of guesses needed in this case?

26.0

PROBLEM STATEMENT

Write a program to play a game of pickup.

A number of stones are placed in a pile. There are two players, and each may remove one, two, or three stones per turn. The last player to play wins. Just try to get the game to work. Don't try to give the computer a strategy.

The number of stones and whether or not the computer goes first should be inputs.

SAMPLE OUTPUT

```
ENTER NUMBER OF STONES
?8

ENTER (1=COMPUTER GOES FIRST, 0=TERMINAL GOES FIRST)
?1
STONES=8
COMPUTER TAKES: 3
```

```
STONES=5
YOU TAKE
?1

STONES=4
COMPUTER TAKES: 1

STONES=3
YOU TAKE
?3

YOU WIN
```

26.1. Modify the program to give the computer a strategy. It should now play *better* than it did before.

26.2. Modify the program to let the computer play against itself. Use the program to test various strategies.

III
DATA
STRUCTURES

18
LOGIC: DATA STRUCTURES—LISTS

DEFINITIONS

Data Item

A piece of information which is to be stored in the computer's memory.

Data Structure

The general term for the way data is organized for use by the computer.

List

A set of related data items. Logically, a list is a set of data items which are stored in sequence one after another. A list always has a first and a last item.

Index

A number which indicates which one of the items in a list the computer is to deal with at the current moment.

DATA STRUCTURES AND INFORMATION

Most commercial applications of computer programming require data that is *organized* in some way. When we say we *organize* data, we mean that we store it in some special way that makes it easier for us to use. For example, here is some *unorganized* data:

John Smith	804–1166
Sue Jones	Carol Webb
5 Main Street	12 Oak Road
213–8419	223–8017
Al Thomas	8 Ocean Drive
23 Maple Street	616–2043

Unorganized data does not contain much meaning. Another way of saying that is to say that unorganized data does not give us very much information.

If we were to organize the set of data given above into three categories—name, address, and phone number—the result would be *informative*.

NAME	ADDRESS	PHONE NUMBER
John Smith	5 Main Street	804–1166
Sue Jones	23 Maple Street	223–8017
Al Thomas	12 Oak Road	616–2043
Carol Webb	8 Ocean Drive	213–8419

In organizing this data, we have given it a *structure*. We have collected names together, addresses together, and phone numbers together.

It is important to see that in organizing the data we are displaying new information. For example:

What is Carol Webb's phone number?

If you answered 213–8419, it was because the *organized* data associates the phone number 213–8419 and the address 8 Ocean Drive with the name Carol Webb. Notice that it is impossible to get an exact answer to the question from looking at the unorganized data.

You are very used to dealing with organized data; you do it all the time. (In fact, you do it so often that you don't even think about it. In the example, where did we ever say that the list of phone numbers *went* with the list of names? 213–8419 isn't Carol Webb's number; it's Mary Johnson's number. Carol's number isn't even in the list of phone numbers. You should be careful not to jump to conclusions.) Here are some examples of organized, or *structured* data:

- The telephone book for Pittsburgh, Pennsylvania
- A bank statement
- A map of the United States
- *TV Guide* magazine
- Instructions for building a model airplane
- A Zip Code directory for the state of Arizona
- A report card
- The address and phone number of every Exxon station in Cleveland, Ohio

The thing to see here is that if the data stored inside a computer is to be used to provide *information*, it must first be *organized*. It is also important to see that organized data is not different from unorganized data. Organized data is just *arranged* differently. It is the arrangement of the data that provides the information.

Finally, you should never *assume* that just because the data you are looking at appears to be organized, it actually is organized. For example:

NAME	PHONE NUMBER
John Smith	804–1166
Sue Jones	223–8017
Al Thomas	616–2043
Carol Webb	213–8419

This is *a list* of names and *a list* of phone numbers, but there is no reason to assume that the two go together. With one additional piece of data, however, two lists can be connected:

Telephone Directory

NAME	PHONE NUMBER
John Smith	611–8114
Sue Jones	439–6215
Al Thomas	773–6992
Carol Webb	504–3132

Now you know Carol Webb's number for sure (unless someone typed it in wrong or unless she has moved since the directory was compiled.)

The information that comes out of a computer is only as good as the programming that enters and organizes the data. This is why we put so much stress on checking over your algorithms and testing out your programs. A good rule in working with computer output is to keep in the back of your mind the thought that the output might be wrong. Just because a computer printed it doesn't mean it's true.

The next few chapters will deal with the structuring of data and the use of structured data to produce information. As you learn these techniques, however, keep in mind that it's you, and not the computer, that will determine how useful the information is—or, to put it in programmers' terms: GIGO (garbage in; garbage out).

LISTS

In the previous examples, we have shown a number of different *lists*. Here, for example, is a list of phone numbers:

611–8114
439–6215
773–6992
504–3132

A list is a type of data structure. In particular, a *list* is a set of data which are all of the same type and which are related to each other by their positions in the list. To say the data are all of the *same type* means that they are all phone numbers, or all names, or all bank account numbers—all the data items in a list are of the same form.

To say the data items are related to one another by *position* means that if you know how to find any item on the list, you know how to find all of the items on the list. For example, in the list of phone numbers:

611–8114
439–6215
773–6992
504–3132

there are a number of things we can point out about the *list:*

- There is a *first item* on the list (in this case 611–8114).
- There is a *last item* on the list (in this case 504–3132).
- The numbers on the list come in a particular *order*. So if you know how to find the first item, you know that when you get the *next* item it will also be a part of the list. And when you reach the last item, you know you're at the *end* of the list.

Here are some sets of data that are *not* lists:

SET 1	SET 2	
A	JOHN	FRED
2.793		
X		MAX
4.801	SUE	
4.322		BILL
D	JEAN	
F	MIKE	ANN
This set has two different types of data.	This set isn't organized. You can't tell what order the items are in.	

Since a list has a first item and a last item and the items come in a fixed order, we can talk about the list itself as if it were a separate thing. This is important because it lets us talk about entering, printing, and processing lists without worrying about the *exact* values of items on the lists.

If we want to talk about a list this way, the first thing we do is give the list a name. For example, we might call the list of numbers PHONES.

PHONES
611–8114
439–6215
773–6992
504–3132

We also need to be able to talk about the individual data items on the list, so we'll give each of them a number.

PHONES( )
(1)   611–8114
(2)   439–6215
(3)   773–6992
(4)   504–3132

We use PHONES( ) with parentheses to show this is a list and not just a single data item.

Now, if we want to talk about the first item on the list, we can refer to PHONES(1). The word PHONES tells us which *list* to look at, and the (1) tells us which *item* on that list. In the same way, PHONES(3) refers to the third item on the list. The word PHONES is called the *name* of the list. The numbers in parentheses are called *subscripts*.

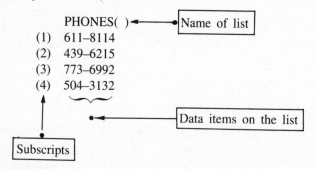

With these conventions we can now talk about the whole list, or any of the items stored on it. For example, we can say:

(1)   PRINT OUT THE LIST OF PHONES( )
With the result: 611–8114
                          439–6215
                          773–6992
                          504–3132

(2)   PRINT OUT THE FIRST ITEM OF PHONES( )
With the result: 611–8114

(3)   PRINT OUT ITEM 3 OF PHONES( )
With the result: 773–6992

(4)   ADD THE ITEM 721–0403 TO THE END OF PHONES( )
With the result: (1)   611–8114
                    (2)   439–6215
                    (3)   773–6992
                    (4)   504–3132
                    (5)   721–0403

All of these *list-processing* operations occur under the control of algorithms. Next we'll look at some of the algorithms used with lists.

ALGORITHMS

The advantage of using *lists* is that entire sets of data items may be processed by referring to a single list name. The following algorithms are basic to using lists. We will use the list of phone numbers as a sample data set.

Enter Data Into a List

    (1)   DEFINE PHONES(10)
    (2)   COUNT = 0
    (3)   LOOP UNTIL end of input data
        (3.1)   Set COUNT up by 1
        (3.2)   INPUT data item into PHONES (COUNT)
    (4)   STOP

Step (1) *defines* the list PHONES( ). Since our computer isn't infinitely large, we need to specify an upper limit on the size of the list. In this case the DEFINE PHONES(10) statement declares PHONES( ) to be a list with room for 10 data items.

We can illustrate the use of the loop at step (2) by doing a trace of the algorithm.

STEP	COUNT	ANSWER AT STEP (3)	DATA VALUE INPUT	DATA STORED AT PHONES (SUBSCRIPT)
(1)	—	—	—	—
(2)	0	—	—	—
(3)	0	NO	—	—
(3.1)	1	—	—	—
(3.2)	1	—	611–8114	PHONES(1)
(3)	1	NO	—	—
(3.1)	2	—	—	—
(3.2)	2	—	439–6215	PHONES(2)
(3)	2	NO	—	—
(3.1)	3	—	—	—
(3.2)	3	—	773–6992	PHONES(3)
(3)	3	NO	—	—
(3.1)	4	—	—	—
(3.2)	4	—	504–3132	PHONES(4)
(3)	4	YES	—	—
(4)	(Stop)			

When step (1) defines the list PHONES (10), the list is *empty*. This means that it contains no data items.

PHONES( )

(1)
(2)
(3)
(4)
(5)
•
•
•
(10)

At step (2), COUNT is set to 1. There *is* input data available, so the answer at step (2.1) is NO, and step (2.2) is executed. At step (2.2), this time the value of COUNT is 1. Since COUNT is being used as the *subscript* for PHONES( ), the data that is input will be stored in PHONES(1). Now the list has a single entry:

PHONES( )

(1) 611–8114
(2)
(3)
(4)
(5)
•
•
•
(10)

Now step (2) is performed and COUNT is increased to 2. There is more data available, so step (2.2) is performed. *This* time at step (2.2), COUNT has the value 2, so the next data input is stored into PHONES(2):

PHONES( )

(1) 611–8114
(2) 439–6215
(3)
(4)
(5)
•
•
•
(10)

This process continues until all four available data inputs have been stored. Notice that when the loop ends, COUNT is set at the count of the data items in the list. We will use COUNT often as a loop control parameter whenever we are processing the data stored in the list.

This first algorithm is essential to getting data into the computer. The remaining algorithms will pick up at step (5). At step (5), the list looks like this:

	PHONES( )	COUNT=4
(1)	611–8114	
(2)	439–6215	
(3)	733–6992	
(4)	504–3132	
(5)		
•		
•		
•		
(10)		

Printing Out a List

(5) LOOP with INDEX going from 1 to COUNT
    (5.1) PRINT PHONES(INDEX)

This is a very simple piece. INDEX counts from one to COUNT and is used as the subscript for PHONES. Each time step (5.1) is performed, the next item in the list is printed. Notice that it is important that we never change COUNT. This is because the value stored in COUNT is what tells us where the end of the list is.

STEP	INDEX	VALUE OF PHONES(INDEX) PRINTED
(5)	1	—
(5.1)	1	611–8114
(5)	2	—
(5.1)	2	439–6215
(5)	3	—
(5.1)	3	773–6992
(5)	4	—
(5.1)	4	504–3132

Finding a Particular Data Item in the List

To locate a particular item on a list, it is necessary to *search* through the list for the desired item and print it if it is found.

Before going on to the search algorithm, we will illustrate another simple, but useful, property of lists. It turns out that if you know the *subscript* of the list location that contains the data item you want to see, you can always print out the item. For example, suppose we wanted to print out the third item on the list. We could do it this way:

(5) Set INDEX to be 3
(6) PRINT PHONES(INDEX)

Step (6) would then print out the data item stored in the list PHONES( ) at location 3.

But by adding a few more instructions we can make the algorithm much more powerful:

    (5)   LOOP FOREVER
          (5.1)   PRINT "PRINT WHICH ITEM?"
          (5.2)   PRINT "ENTER 1 TO", COUNT, "USE 0 TO EXIT"
          (5.3)   INPUT SUBNUM
          (5.4)   IF SUBNUM IS EQUAL TO 0 THEN EXIT LOOP
          (5.5)   IF SUBNUM IS GREATER THAN COUNT OR
                  LESS THAN 1
                  THEN
                  (5.51)   PRINT "SUBSCRIPT ERROR"
                  ELSE
                  (5.52)   PRINT PHONES(SUBNUM)
    (6)

This algorithm will let us select and print out any or all of the items on the list. Step (5) sets up an endless loop. Zero is the end-of-data marker, and step (5.4) provides for leaving the loop when zero is entered. (We choose 0 for end-of-data because there is no 0 subscript in the list.)

Steps (5.1) through (5.3) have the user input the *subscript* of the list location to be printed. Step (5.5) checks to see if the input value is valid—since COUNT is the subscript of the last data item, inputs bigger than COUNT should be rejected. If the input is okay, the contents of that list location are printed at step (5.52).

We will use a similar approach to build the *search* algorithm:

    (5)   LOOP FOREVER
          (5.1)   PRINT "ENTER ITEM VALUE—USE 000–0000
                  TO EXIT"
          (5.2)   INPUT LOOKFOR
          (5.3)   IF LOOKFOR is equal to "000–0000" THEN
                  EXIT LOOP
          (5.4)   Set INDEX to be 0
          (5.5)   LOOP with SUB going from 1 to COUNT
                  (5.51)   IF PHONES(SUB) is equal to LOOKFOR
                           THEN
                           (5.511)   Set INDEX equal to SUB
                           (5.512)   EXIT LOOP
                           ELSE
                           (5.513)   CONTINUE
          (5.6)   IF INDEX is equal to 0
                  THEN
                  (5.61) PRINT "ITEM NOT FOUND"
                  ELSE
                  (5.62)   PRINT "ITEM AT LOCATION", INDEX,
                           PHONES(INDEX)
    (6)

Again, step (5) is an endless loop to allow the user to search for more than one item. Step (5.3) exits from the search routine when the end-of-data marker, 000–0000, is entered. The end-of-data marker was chosen because it is a nonexistent phone number.

LOOKFOR is the input data item. It contains the phone number we are searching for. INDEX is set to zero at step (5.4). If we find an item in the list that matches the item we are searching for, we will set INDEX to the subscript value for that item. If we search the whole list without finding a match, then INDEX will remain at zero. Notice that the IF/THEN/ELSE at step (5.6) prints out the location of the item if the item is found, and a NOT FOUND message if it is not found.

The loop at step (5.5) starts the counter SUB at 1 and counts it up to COUNT in steps of one. So SUB eventually takes on the subscript value of each of the locations which have data items in them. Step (5.51) checks to see if the location for the current value of SUB contains a data item which matches LOOKFOR. If it does, the value of the subscript is stored in INDEX. The item has been found, so the LOOP is exited. If there's no match, step (5.513) continues the loop.

Adding an Item to the End of the List

To add a item to the end of the list, we must do three things:

1. Get the value of the new item.
2. Add 1 to COUNT and check to make sure there is room for the new item.
3. Store the new item in the list.

The algorithm is relatively simple:

```
(5)   PRINT "ENTER NEW ITEM"
(6)   INPUT NEWVAL
(7)   IF COUNT is equal to MAX
      THEN
      (7.1)   PRINT "LIST IS FULL AT SIZE", MAX
      ELSE
      (7.2)   Add 1 to COUNT
      (7.3)   -Store NEWVAL into PHONES(COUNT)
(8)
```

NEWVAL is the input data item which is entered at step (6). Step (7) checks to see if COUNT is equal to MAX. MAX is a parameter that we set at the beginning of the algorithm to be equal to the maximum size of the list. In this case we set the maximum size to be 10 [in the DEFINE PHONES(10) statement], so we would have set MAX to be 10 also.

If COUNT is equal to MAX, then there is no more room in the list and a message is printed at step (7.1). Otherwise COUNT is incremented by 1 and the new value is stored.

Deleting an Item from the List

To delete an item, we first must know the subscript that identifies its location in the list. To use the following algorithm, assume that we've already used the *search* algorithm on page 172 and that INDEX is already set to either 0 or the subscript of the item we want to delete.

> (6) IF INDEX is equal to 0
> THEN
> (6.1) PRINT "DELETION NOT POSSIBLE"
> ELSE
> (6.2) Set PHONES(INDEX) equal to "000–0000"
> (6.3) PRINT "ITEM NUMBER",INDEX,"DELETED"
> (7)

Notice that we "delete" the item by overprinting it with the end-of-data marker. Since the end-of-data marker is not a valid search input, any item with a value of "000–0000" is effectively invisible to the search routine.

PRACTICE

1. We use the data item COUNT to keep track of how many items we have on the list. Instead of this we could have marked the end of the list with a special data item—say 999–9999, for example—and looked for that as a way to control our processing loops. Why is the use of COUNT the better way to do it?

2. The search algorithm finds the *first* occurrence of a particular data item on the list. Rewrite the algorithm so that it prints *all* occurrences of the item.

3. What happens if you perform the search routine with *no* items on the list? Is this what *should* happen?

4. The add routine is correct, but is not the *best* possible approach. The routine asks the user to type in the value to be added first; *then* it checks to see if there is room to add the item. This is inconvenient and may be confusing to the user. Rewrite the add algorithm so that it *first* checks to see if there is room for an addition. If there is room, then it should perform as it does now. If there is *no* room, it should print an error message.

5. The delete routine "deletes" items by erasing their values. Since the add routine can only add new items to new locations at the end of the list, a location that has had its data item deleted is useless from then on. In the worst case the entire list could be filled with "deleted" locations, and no more processing could be done.
    There are two basic ways of handling this problem. Write algorithms to:

    a. Reorganize the list by moving all the "real" data items to the top and "squeezing out" the deleted items.

    b. Rewrite the add routine so that it puts new values into "deleted" locations, if any exist, and only adds a new location if there are no "deleted" ones available.

       Explain the relative advantages and disadvantages of these two solutions to the problem.

6.   Rewrite the delete routine so that when an item is deleted, all of the items below it are moved up to close out the space. This approach will not produce "deleted" locations and fits well with the original add routine. Explain its advantages and disadvantages.

19
SYNTAX: ONE-DIMENSIONAL ARRAYS

DEFINITIONS

Array
A special type of variable that allows more than one piece of data to be stored under the same name.

One-Dimensional Array
The type of array that is used to store *lists*.

Subscript
Also called an *index* or an *address;* a number or variable used to identify the location of a specific piece of data stored in an array.

DIMENSION
The FORTRAN statement that identifies a name as an array variable and reserves space in the computer's memory for the data that will be stored in the array.

ARRAYS

Arrays are special types of FORTRAN variable names. Where normal variables can contain only one value at a time, *array variables* can contain a list of values.

Any legal variable name may be used as an array name. Array names must be defined before the array can be used. This is done with the FORTRAN statement DIMENSION. DIMENSION is shown in the next section.

Just as there are both numeric and character variables, there are both numeric and character arrays. Since the syntax for character arrays is sometimes different for different brands of computers, we will talk only about *numeric* arrays here. To find the syntax rules for character arrays, look in the *FORTRAN Language Reference Manual.* And remember, whatever the *syntax* rules, the *algorithms* for processing numeric arrays work just as well for character arrays.

NUMERIC ARRAYS

```
DIMENSION B(50),I(3)
```

The DIMENSION instruction is used to *define* arrays and must come before the arrays it defines are used in the program. It does not execute, but is used by the computer to reserve space for one or more arrays. In this example, B is an array which has 50 *locations* reserved for use by the program. I is an array with three locations reserved. DIMENSION does not affect the *type* of the variable name. REAL, INTEGER, or CHARACTER are used with array variables in the same way they are used with single variables.

The general form of the DIMENSION instruction is:

```
DIMENSION array name (maximum size)
```

where array name   = any legal FORTRAN variable
  maximum size   = a positive, integer constant that establishes the number of storage locations available in the array.

It is not possible to use a variable name both as an array name and as a single variable name. Notice that the "maximum size" specification must be a *constant*. It cannot be a variable.

In the next set of examples, assume that the instruction:

```
DIMENSION I(3)
```

has been used to define the array I ( ), and that I ( ) is of *type* INTEGER.

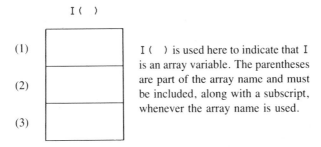

I ( )

(1)

(2)

(3)

I ( ) is used here to indicate that I is an array variable. The parentheses are part of the array name and must be included, along with a subscript, whenever the array name is used.

The three locations can be used to store data by referring to the variable name with a *subscript* inside the parentheses to indicate which of the locations is to be used.

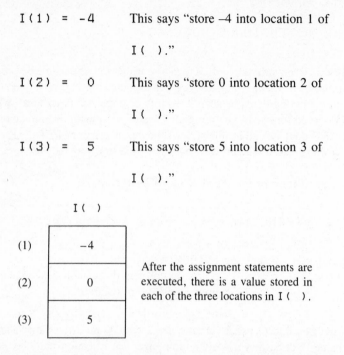

I (1) = −4   This says "store −4 into location 1 of

I ( )."

I (2) = 0   This says "store 0 into location 2 of

I ( )."

I (3) = 5   This says "store 5 into location 3 of

I ( )."

I ( )

(1)	−4
(2)	0
(3)	5

After the assignment statements are executed, there is a value stored in each of the three locations in I ( ) .

The subscript must be an integer and cannot be smaller than 1 or bigger than the value inside the parentheses in the DIMENSION statement. That is, the DIMENSION statement establishes the maximum size of the array.

These are all illegal statements:

I (−2) = 6   Negative subscript.
I (4) = 0   Subscript bigger than 3; see the
DIMENSION statement on page 177.
I (2 , 5) = 9   Subscript not an integer.

Array variables can be used in exactly the same way that regular variables are used:

I (2) = I (3) + I (1)

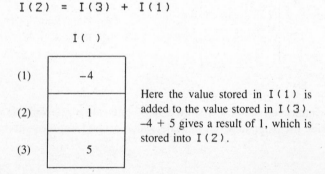

I ( )

(1)	−4
(2)	1
(3)	5

Here the value stored in I (1) is added to the value stored in I (3) . −4 + 5 gives a result of 1, which is stored into I (2) .

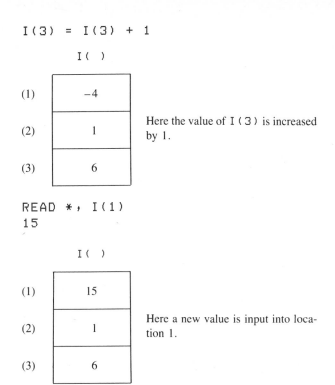

I(3) = I(3) + 1

I( )

(1)	−4
(2)	1
(3)	6

Here the value of I (3) is increased by 1.

READ *, I(1)
15

I( )

(1)	15
(2)	1
(3)	6

Here a new value is input into location 1.

ARRAYS IN LOOPS

The main advantage of using arrays is that variables can be used as subscripts. This program stores the squares of the first five numbers into the first five locations in the array Q( ).

REF.	FORTRAN		Q( )
1	INTEGER Q,K		
2	DIMENSION Q(5)		
3	DO 100 K=1,5	(1)	1
4	Q(K)=K**2		
5	100 CONTINUE	(2)	4
		(3)	9
		(4)	16
For example, when K is 3, Q(3)=3**2 at line 4. So 9 is stored into Q(3).		(5)	25

In this loop the value of the *counter* K goes from 1 to 5. K is also used as a *subscript variable* for the array Q( ). Both Q and K are of type INTEGER, [notice that in the INTEGER statement (line 1) only the *name*, "Q," is used—parentheses are omitted.]

VALUE OF K	VALUE OF K**2	VALUE STORED IN Q(K)
1	1	Q(1) = 1
2	4	Q(2) = 4
3	9	Q(3) = 9
4	16	Q(4) = 16
5	25	Q(5) = 25

Continuing with the *same program*, we will tell the computer to find the sum of the numbers stored in Q( ). S will hold the sum, and J will be the counter. Notice that K is equal to the *count* of the items stored in the array. In this case K is 5.

```
 6       S=0
 7       DO 200 J=1,K
 8       S=S+Q(J)
 9 200 CONTINUE
10       PRINT *, 'THE SUM OF THE FIRST',K, 'SQUARE IS ',S
11       END
```

J is a counter that starts at 1 and goes to K. Remember that K counted the number of values stored in Q( ) so K is equal to 5.

VALUE OF J	VALUE OF Q(J)	VALUE STORED IN S
1	1	1
2	4	5
3	9	14
4	16	30
5	25	55

Output: THE SUM OF THE FIRST 5 SQUARES IS 55

PRACTICE

1. Look at the example program again. Do you understand how it works? Change the program to find the sum of the first N squares where N can be any integer between 1 and 100. For example:

```
RUN
INPUT A NUMBER FROM 1 TO 100
7
THE SUM OF THE FIRST 7 SQUARES IS 140
```

2.   Using the same program as in item 1, change it so that it prints a list of the squares between any two positive integer inputs and also computes and prints the sum. For example:

```
RUN
INPUT A NUMBER FROM 1 TO 100
4
INPUT A NUMBER FROM 4 TO 100
7
NUMBER               SQUARE
   4                   16
   5                   25
   6                   36
   7                   49

SUM IS:   126
```

END-OF-DATA MARKERS

```
        REAL
        DIMENSION P(100)
        DO 10 K=1,100
        READ *, P(K)
100 CONTINUE
```

This loop will read 100 numbers from the terminal and store each one in a different location in the array P ( ) .

VALUE OF K	AT THE TERMINAL	STORED IN P(K)
1	10.3	P(1) = 10.3
2	-9.45	P(2) = -9.45
3	5	P(3) = 5.0
.	.	.
.	.	.
.	.	.
etc.	etc.	etc.

This program insists that 100 numbers be entered at the terminal. Quite often, however, the programmer won't know exactly how many numbers will need to be input at the time the program is to be run. An *end-of-data marker* can be used to control the number of inputs.

```
 1    * ENTERING DATA INTO AN ARRAY
 2    *
 3    * R. W. DILLMAN
 4    * MARCH, 1984
 5    *
 6    * INITIALIZE
 7    *
 8          REAL P, EOD
 9          INTEGER COUNT
10          DIMENSION P(100)
11          EOD=99999
12    *
13    * INPUT ROUTINE
14    *
15          PRINT *, 'ENTER UP TO 100 NUMBERS'
16          PRINT *, '   USE 99999 TO EXIT'
17          COUNT=0
18          DO 100 K=1,100
19             READ*, P(K)
20             IF (P(K) .EQ. EOD) GOTO 101
21             COUNT=COUNT+1
22      100 CONTINUE
23    *
24    * EXIT FROM INPUT LOOP
25    *
26      101 CONTINUE
```

The variable EOD is used to check for the end of the input data. EOD is set equal to 99999 because that number is so large that the programmer doesn't expect it will ever appear as an input value. (Some computers will not accept an integer number as big as 99999. You should find out what the biggest acceptable integer is on your computer.)

The end-of-data marker should be a number that will *never* be a part of the input data. For example, if a program is only supposed to read positive numbers, −1 might be used to mark the end of the data. Obviously, the programmer must know enough about the data the program will be using to choose the end-of-data value correctly.

Looking at the example program again, notice that the input loop ends when *either* the end-of-data marker is found *or* when the value of K exceeds the dimension of the array.

COUNT is then set up by one at line 21. This is done so that the value stored in COUNT is equal to the number of data values stored in the array, not counting the end-of-data marker. The number in COUNT can be used later when the *count of the data* is needed.

Continuing the *same program:*

```
27  *
28  *  PRINT THE CONTENTS OF P( )
29  *
30         DO 200 J=1, COUNT
31          PRINT *, P(J)
32  200 CONTINUE
33     END
```

This output loop will print out the data stored in the array. By using COUNT in the loop control statement, the correct number of data values will be printed no matter how many have been read in.

PRACTICE

3.   This program looks like a shorter way of doing the list input loop. Explain why it doesn't work correctly.

```
        REAL P, EOD
        INTEGER COUNT
        DIMENSION P(100)
        EOD=99999
        PRINT *, 'ENTER UP TO 100 NUMBERS'
        PRINT *, '   USE 99999 TO EXIT'
        DO 100 COUNT=1,100
        READ *, P(COUNT)
        IF (P(COUNT) .EQ. EOD) GOTO 101
    100 CONTINUE
    101 CONTINUE
```

4.   Building on the program given in this chapter, code and test the search, add, and delete algorithms that were developed in Chapter 18.

20
USING THE COMPUTER: A SAMPLE PROBLEM

PROBLEM   Write a program that will read in a set of up to 100 numbers and then print the numbers out sorted from smallest to largest.

PURPOSE   Sort a list of numbers.

SAMPLE
OUTPUT
```
ENTER DATA -- USE 99999 TO EXIT
4
8
0
-3
4
2
99999
SORTED LIST:
-3
 0
 2
 4
 4
 8
```

DATA   NUMBERS( )   A list of up to 100 numbers
        COUNT   The count of the numbers in the list
        EOD   End-of-data marker (99999)
        MAX   Maximum number of items (100)

In reading over the problem we see that we have three main things to do.

1. Read a set of numbers onto a list.
2. Rearrange the numbers in the list so that they are in sorted order from smallest to largest.
3. Print out the list.

There are no special rules involved, other than the rules for sorting the list, which we will discuss shortly.

ALGORITHM

We already know how to do parts 1 and 3 (see Chapters 18 and 19), so we only need to develop an algorithm for part 2. First we initialize our parameters and set up the data input loop.

(1) DEFINE NUMBERS(100)
(2) Set MAX to be 100
(3) Set COUNT to be 0
(4) Set EOD to be 99999
(5) PRINT "ENTER DATA - USE 99999 TO EXIT"
(6) LOOP with K going from 1 to MAX
    (6.1) INPUT NUMBERS(K)
    (6.2) IF NUMBERS(K) is equal to EOD THEN EXIT LOOP
    (6.3) Add 1 to COUNT
(7)

Step (1) defines NUMBERS to be a list with room for 100 items. MAX is the data item that tells us the maximum number of items, so it is set to 100. We choose 99999 for the end-of-data marker because 99999 is bigger than the numbers we expect to be in the input data. If the input was to include numbers as large as 99999, we would have to choose a different value for EOD.

We use K as the loop counter and add 1 to COUNT at step (6.3) only after we know that the input is *not* EOD.

SORTING

To illustrate what the sorting algorithm is supposed to *do*, let's take a set of sample data.

SAMPLE DATA SET: 4,8,0,-3,4,2

If we enter this data onto the list, we get:

```
           NUMBERS( )
      (1)    4
      (2)    8                COUNT = 6
      (3)    0
      (4)   -3
      (5)    4
      (6)    2
      (7)
       •
       •
       •
    (100)
```

Notice that the data items are stored on the list in the order in which they were entered. The object of the sorting algorithm is to rearrange the *locations* of the items on the list so that the smallest value is in location (1), the next smallest in location (2), and so on.

The *result* of the sort will look like this:

```
           NUMBERS( )
      (1)   -3
      (2)    0                COUNT = 6
      (3)    2
      (4)    4
      (5)    4
      (6)    8
      (7)
       •
       •
       •
    (100)
```

These numbers are said to be *sorted* in *ascending* order, from smallest to largest. This is the order that the problem statement asks for. If we wanted to, we could instead sort the numbers into *descending* order, that is, into the order 8, 4, 4, 2, 0, -3—from largest to smallest.

There are *many* different algorithms which solve the sorting problem. The one we are going to develop is a relatively simple one that is *easy* to understand. To put it together, the first thing we need to do is take a look at the list before and after the sort.

BEFORE SORT		AFTER SORT	
NUMBERS( )		NUMBERS( )	
(1)	4	(1)	−3
(2)	8	(2)	0
(3)	0	(3)	2
(4)	−3	(4)	4
(5)	4	(5)	4
(6)	2	(6)	8
(7)		(7)	
•		•	
•		•	
•		•	
(100)		(100)	

In looking, we see that the sorted list has *exactly* the same data items as the input list, but they are stored in different locations. This tells us that our algorithm will need to move items around on the list. Now the question is: How do we decide which items to move, and where?

To answer that, we look at the sorted list once again. What is the item stored in location (1) of the sorted list? That item is −3, the smallest item in the list. So somehow we have to find the smallest item in the input list and move it to location (1). (Remember, although we talk about the "input" list and the "sorted" list, there is really only one list. "Input" refers to the order the list is in just after the data is entered, and "sorted" refers to the order the list is in after the sort has been performed.)

Just to see what happens, then, let's assume we are able to figure out a way to find the smallest item on the list and move it to the top location. What would the results look like?

INPUT LIST		FIND SMALLEST AND MOVE TO TOP	
NUMBERS( )		NUMBERS( )	
(1)	4	(1)	−3
(2)	8	(2)	8
(3)	0	(3)	0
(4)	−3	(4)	4
(5)	4	(5)	4
(6)	2	(6)	2
(7)		(7)	
•		•	
•		•	
•		•	
(100)		(100)	

We found the −3 in location (4). When we moved the −3 to location (1), we had to do something with the 4 that was already there. We couldn't throw it away, so we put it back on the list in the location where −3 used to be. Another way of saying this is to say that we *switched* the items in locations (1) and (4). We can summarize this idea in two steps:

1. Find the smallest item on the list.
2. Switch it with the item in the top location.

Now we're partway to the solution. Let's look at the list again.

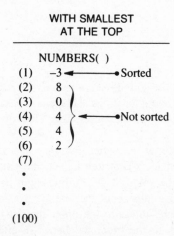

WITH SMALLEST
AT THE TOP

	NUMBERS( )	
(1)	−3	Sorted
(2)	8	
(3)	0	
(4)	4	Not sorted
(5)	4	
(6)	2	
(7)		
•		
•		
•		
(100)		

You can see that what we have done is to sort *one* item. The rest of the items aren't sorted yet, but now we can deal with them. Suppose now that we *ignore* the item in location (1). We can do that because we *know* it's in the right place from the steps we just performed. Now let's look at the *rest* of the data items. Suppose we find the smallest item in *that* set and move it to the top of the set. In this case that means we would find the 0 and switch it with the item in location (2). That would give us this:

AFTER FIRST SORT		AFTER SECOND SORT		
NUMBERS( )		NUMBERS( )		
(1) −3		(1) −3		Sorted
(2) 8		(2) 0		
(3) 0		(3) 8		Not sorted
(4) 4		(4) 4		
(5) 4		(5) 4		
(6) 2		(6) 2		
(7)		(7)		
•		•		
•		•		
•		•		
(100)		(100)		

Now you can see that we have one more sorted item than we did before. If we keep repeating this procedure of finding the smallest item in the set of unsorted numbers and moving it to the top of the set, we will eventually put the entire list into sorted order. We can summarize this idea also:

1. Find the smallest item in the unsorted set.
2. Switch that item with the item at the top of the unsorted set.
3. Repeat steps 2 and 3 until there is only one item left in the unsorted set.

Notice that each time steps 1 and 2 are performed, the unsorted set gets smaller by one. Also notice that we stop repeating step 1 and 2 when there is only one item left unsorted. If there is only one item left unsorted, it *must* be the biggest item in the list. Therefore, we can just leave it where it is—at the bottom.

This is not an algorithm yet, of course. We still have to write the solution in language the computer will be able to deal with. Before we get to that, however, be sure that you understand the *idea* of what we are trying to do.

PRACTICE

1. Take the list as it is after the second sort and show what it would look like after the third sort.

2. In the fourth sort, the unsorted list contains two 4s to be sorted. How should the algorithm deal with this situation?

SORTING

Before we can write down the algorithm, we will have to define some new data items. These are the items that we invented as we were developing the sorting idea.

DATA ITEM	DESCRIPTION
TOP	Location of the top item in the unsorted set
SLOC	Location of the smallest item in the unsorted set
SVAL	Value of the smallest item in the unsorted set
NEXT	Location of the next item in the unsorted list to be checked to see if it is the smallest in the set

Remember we still have NUMBERS( ) and COUNT, which were set in the input loop.

In the algorithm, the value of TOP will be initialized to 1 to indicate location 1 of the list. SLOC will be initialized to 1 and SVAL will be initialized to NUMBER(1). Then NEXT will be set to 2 to indicate location (2) of the list, and NUMBER(NEXT) will be compared with SVAL. If the data item stored in NUMBER(NEXT) is smaller than SVAL, then it is the smallest item found so far, and its location and value will be stored in SLOC and SVAL. When location (2) has been checked, NEXT will be set up to 3 and location (3) will be checked. This will continue until the entire list has been looked at. At this point the smallest value will be in SVAL, and the location of the smallest value will be in SLOC.

The TOP value and the SLOC value will then be switched. This will put the smallest data item in the TOP location. TOP will be set up by one, and the whole process will be repeated until TOP is equal to COUNT.

    (7)   LOOP with TOP going from 1 to COUNT-1
        (7.1)   Set SLOC equal to TOP
        (7.2)   Set SVAL equal to NUMBERS(TOP)
        (7.3)   LOOP with NEXT going from TOP+1 to COUNT
            (7.31)   IF NUMBERS(NEXT) is smaller than SVAL
                    THEN
                    (7.311)   Set SVAL equal to NUMBERS(NEXT)
                    (7.312)   Set SLOC equal to NEXT
                    ELSE
                    (7.313)   CONTINUE
        (7.4)   Set NUMBERS(SLOC) equal to NUMBERS(TOP)
        (7.5)   Set NUMBERS(TOP) equal to SVAL

    (8)

Step (7) starts the TOP location pointer at 1. NUMBERS(TOP) will always be the top location of the *unsorted* part of the list. Steps (7.1) through (7.313) search for the smallest value in the unsorted part of the list. SVAL will always end up containing the smallest value, and SLOC will always end up containing the *location* of the smallest value. Since we always start our search at the top of the unsorted set, the top value is always the smallest value until the search finds a smaller one. Steps (7.1) and (7.2) set SLOC and SVAL accordingly.

In the loop at step (7.3), the NEXT location pointer begins at the location just after TOP and counts down to the bottom of the list. Each time through the loop, the item at location NEXT is compared against SVAL. This happens at step (7.31). If the NUMBERS(NEXT) item is smaller than SVAL, then it is the smallest item found so far, and its value and location are stored into SVAL and SLOC at steps (7.311) and (7.312).

Once the NEXT loop has been completed, steps (7.4) and (7.5) perform the switch. Then the algorithm jumps back to step (7); TOP is set up by one, and the whole process is repeated.

PRACTICE

3. This algorithm may appear to be complicated at first. But if you take the time to work through it slowly, step by step, you will see that it is really a pretty simple idea. To check the algorithm out, use the list of sample input data and fill out the following trace chart. Keep the NUMBERS( ) list on a separate piece of paper and update it each time steps (7.4) and (7.5) are performed.

NUMBERS( )

(1)	4
(2)	8
(3)	0
(4)	−3
(5)	4
(6)	2
(7)	
•	
•	
•	
(100)	

COUNT = 6

STEP	TOP	SLOC	SVAL	NEXT	ANSWER AT STEP (7.31)
(7)					

4. Explain how the algorithm deals with items that are of equal value. This happens at step (7.31).

5. What would happen if step (7.31) read this way?
    (7.31) IF NUMBERS(NEXT) is *greater* than SVAL

PROGRAM

Here is the whole algorithm. This is known as an *exchange* sort.

(1)   DEFINE NUMBERS(100)
(2)   Set MAX to be 100
(3)   Set COUNT to be 0
(4)   Set EOD to be 99999
(5)   PRINT "ENTER DATA - USE 99999 TO EXIT"
(6)   LOOP with K going from 1 to MAX
    (6.1)   INPUT NUMBERS(K)
    (6.2)   IF NUMBERS(K) is equal to EOD THEN EXIT LOOP
    (6.3)   Add 1 to COUNT
(7)   LOOP with TOP going from 1 to COUNT-1
    (7.1)   Set SLOC equal to TOP
    (7.2)   Set SVAL equal to NUMBERS(TOP)
    (7.3)   LOOP with NEXT going from TOP+1 to COUNT
        (7.31)   IF NUMBERS(NEXT) is smaller than SVAL
              THEN
            (7.311)   Set SVAL equal to NUMBERS(NEXT)
            (7.312)   Set SLOC equal to NEXT
            ELSE
            (7.313)   CONTINUE
    (7.4)   Set NUMBERS(SLOC) equal to NUMBERS(TOP)
    (7.5)   Set NUMBERS(TOP) equal to SVAL
(8)   PRINT "SORTED LIST":
(9)   LOOP with K going from 1 to COUNT
    (9.1)   PRINT NUMBERS(K)
(10)   STOP

The translation into FORTRAN is very straightforward. The program will have the following structure:

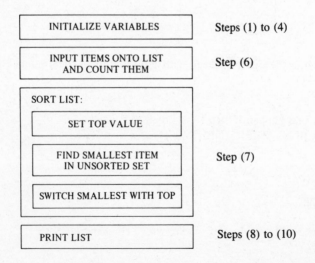

INITIALIZE VARIABLES — Steps (1) to (4)

INPUT ITEMS ONTO LIST AND COUNT THEM — Step (6)

SORT LIST:
  SET TOP VALUE
  FIND SMALLEST ITEM IN UNSORTED SET — Step (7)
  SWITCH SMALLEST WITH TOP

PRINT LIST — Steps (8) to (10)

We will use these variables:

DATA ITEM	VARIABLE NAME
NUMBERS( )	N( )
MAX	MAX
EOD	EOD
COUNT	COUNT
TOP	TOP
NEXT	NEXT
SVAL	SMALL
SLOC	LOC

REFER-ENCE	STEP	FORTRAN CODE
1		```* PROGRAM: SORT```
2		```*```
3		```* SORTS A ONE-DIMENSIONAL ARRAY INTO```
4		```* ASCENDING ORDER```
5		```*```
6		```* R. W. DILLMAN```
7		```* MARCH, 1984```
8		```*```
9		```* GLOBAL VARIABLES:```
10		```* N() -- ARRAY```
11		```* MAX -- MAXIMUM SIZE OF ARRAY (100)```
12		```* EOD -- END OF DATA MARKER (99999)```
13		```* COUNT -- COUNT OF ARRAY ITEMS```
14		```*```
15		```* LOCAL TO SORT ROUTINE:```
16		```* TOP -- POINTER TO TOP OF UNSORTED SET```
17		```* NEXT -- POINTER TO NEXT ITEM TO BE TESTED```
18		```* SMALL -- CURRENT SMALLEST VALUE```
19		```* LOC -- LOCATION OF SMALLEST VALUE```
20		```*```
21		```* INITIALIZE```
22		```*```
23		``` INTEGER N,MAX,COUNT,TOP,NEXT,LOC```
24		``` REAL EOD, SMALL```
25	(1)	``` DIMENSION N(100)```
26	(2), (3), (4)	``` DATA MAX/100/, EOD/99999/, COUNT/0/```
27		```*```
28		```* INPUT ROUTINE```
29		```*```

(continued)

REFER-ENCE	STEP	FORTRAN CODE
30	(5)	* PRINT *,'ENTER UP TO 100 NUMBERS'
31		PRINT*, ' USE 99999 TO EXIT'
32	(6)	DO 100 K=1,MAX
33	(6.1)	READ *, N(K)
34	(6.2)	IF (N(K) .EQ. EOD) GOTO 101
35	(6.3)	COUNT=COUNT+1
36	(6)	100 CONTINUE
37		*
38		* SORT ROUTINE
39		*
40		* [N(TOP) IS TOP VALUE IN UNSORTED SET]
41		101 CONTINUE
42	(7)	DO 200 TOP=1,COUNT-1
43	(7.1)	LOC=TOP
44	(7.2)	SMALL=N(TOP)
45		*
46		* [FIND SMALLEST IN UNSORTED SET]
47	(7.3)	DO 250 NEXT=TOP+1,COUNT
48	(7.31)	IF (N(NEXT) .GE. SMALL) GOTO 250
49	(7.311)	SMALL=N(NEXT)
50	(7.312)	LOC=NEXT
51	(7.3)	250 CONTINUE
52		*
53		* [SWITCH SMALLEST WITH TOP]
54	(7.4)	N(LOC)=N(TOP)
55	(7.5)	N(TOP)=SMALL
56	(7)	200 CONTINUE
57		*
58		* OUTPUT ROUTINE
59		*
60	(8)	PRINT *,' SORTED LIST'
61	(9)	DO 300 K=1,COUNT
62	(9.1)	PRINT*, N(K)
63	(9)	300 CONTINUE
64	(10)	END

PRACTICE

6. Enter, run, and test this program. When you test it, be sure you give it:

a. A list with *no* entries.
b. A list with 100 entries.
c. A list with at least some duplicate entries.

7. In line 26, two of the variables are really constants. Which two are they? Rewrite the line so that the constants are defined as PARAMETERS.

8. Rewrite the algorithm so that the user has the option of choosing either an ascending or a descending sort.

   Sample output:

```
ENTER:   1 FOR ASCENDING SORT
         2 FOR DESCENDING SORT
2
ENTER DATA -- USE 99999 TO EXIT
9
-2
13
99999
SORTED LIST (DESCENDING)
13
 9
-2
```

9. The list-searching algorithm developed in Chapter 18 *must* search the entire list before it can conclude that there is no match for the item for which it is looking. Rewrite the algorithm using a sorted list. Your objective is to make the algorithm run faster in those cases when it is searching for an item that is *not* on the list. *Hint:* Look at these two lists:

LIST( )			LIST( )	
(1)	4		(1)	-3
(2)	-3		(2)	0
(3)	0		(3)	2
(4)	5		(4)	4
(5)	2		(5)	5

   Search for the item value 3. Now ask yourself a question: In each case, *when* do you know that 3 is not on the list?)

10. There are a large number of *different* sorting algorithms in use today. Why do you think there are so many? If you had to choose among five different sorting programs, how would you decide? What criteria would you use to evaluate them?

11. Figure out at least one different method for sorting a set of numbers. Design the algorithm and code and test the program.

21
USING THE COMPUTER: A BAD EXAMPLE

This program contains two simple errors. Without running the program:

1. Explain what the purpose of the program is.
2. Locate and describe how to correct the errors.

REFERENCE	FORTRAN CODE
1	`INTEGER F,X2,L3,Z9`
2	`CHARACTER A*30`
3	`DIMENSION A(201)`
4	`DO 100 K=1,200`
5	`READ *, A(K)`
6	`L3=L3+1`
7	`IF (A(K) .EQ. 'LASTONE') GOTO 101`
8	`100 CONTINUE`
9	`101 CONTINUE`
10	`F=0`
11	`DO 200 X2=1,L3-1`
12	`IF (A(X2+1) .LT. A(X2) GOTO 110`
13	`200 CONTINUE`
14	`IF F=0 THEN 900`
15	`GOTO 101`
16	`110 CONTINUE`
17	`A(201)=A(X2)`
18	`A(X2)=A(X2+1)`
19	`A(X2+1)=A(201)`
20	`F=1`
21	`GOTO 200`
22	`900 DO 901 Z9=1,L3`
23	`PRINT *, A(Z9)`
24	`901 CONTINUE`
25	`END`

This is a very difficult program to decipher. It has no comments. Because of this you don't even know what it's supposed to do in general, let alone what the individual lines of code do. The only way to discover what it does is to do a hand trace. (You could type it in and run it, but it won't work. It has errors.)

The program isn't structured. This makes it hard to trace. If you didn't do a trace, do one now. Notice that the IF instruction at line 12 can send the program down to line 16, and that the GOTO at line 21 sends the program back up to line 13. This is not an error, but it is very confusing. Unstructured jumps like this make programs hard to follow. (Some programmers call this approach "spaghetti code"—because it's so twisted that it looks like a plate of cooked spaghetti.) Line 21 would be better if it said:

```
GOTO 101
```

though that wouldn't fix either of the errors. Also notice that at line 14 the computer might be sent down to line 22, or at line 15 it might be sent up to line 9. These are not loops or IF/THEN/ELSE structures. This is bad programming.

It would be helpful if you could check the code against the algorithm to see if the program was translated correctly. You can't do that, however. There is no algorithm. People who don't design their algorithms first, and then write the code, usually produce bad programs.

If you've completed the trace, you now know what *values* are stored in each variable as the program executes. But do you know what each variable is *used for?* For example, L3 counts the number of items input into the array, F is a switch that is set to 1 whenever lines 17 through 19 are executed, A(201) is a location used as a temporary storage variable in the exchange routine. [The first error is that L3 is incremented before the end-of-data test is performed. L3 will always be off by a count of one. The second error is a typing error in line 19. It should use A(201), not A(200).] If the programmer had included a variable dictionary, then you would have *known* what each variable was for as soon as you began to read. You should also be able to see that comments, especially at lines 10 and 17, would have made the program a lot easier to figure out.

Why is all of this important?

There are relatively few brand-new computer programs written each year. Most of the work that programmers do is altering and repairing programs that *someone else* wrote at some earlier time. A program that cannot be easily read and easily changed may be of little worth, even if it does "work." This is why modern programming puts so much stress on algorithm design and structured coding technique. These are the things that separate the good programmers from the poor ones.

The program is intended to sort a list of strings. Here it is documented and recoded in a structured form.

```
 1   * SORT A STRING ARRAY
 2   *
 3   * R. W. DILLMAN
 4   * MARCH, 1984
 5   *
 6   * VARIABLES:
 7   *   A() -- ARRAY TO BE SORTED
 8   *   COUNT -- COUNT OF ITEMS IN A()
 9   *   TEST -- 1 IF DONE SORTING, 0 IF NOT
10   *   MAX -- MAXIMUM NUMBER OF ITEMS IN A()
11   *   EOD -- END-OF-DATA MARKER ('LASTONE')
12   *   TEMP -- TEMPORARY CHARACTER STRING
13   *
14   * INITIALIZE
15   *
16         CHARACTER A*30,TEMP*30,E*30
17         INTEGER TEST,COUNT,MAX
18         DIMENSION A(200)
19         DATA MAX/200/,COUNT/0/,EOD/'LASTONE'/
20   *
21   * INPUT ROUTINE
22   *
23         PRINT *,'ENTER ITEMS TO BE SORTED'
24         PRINT *,' USE  LASTONE  TO EXIT'
25         DO 100 K=1,MAX
26         READ *, A(K)
27         IF (A(K) .EQ. EOD) GOTO 101
28         COUNT=COUNT+1
29     100 CONTINUE
30   *
31   * SORTING ROUTINE
32   *
33   * [THIS IS A BUBBLE SORT]
34   *
35   * [LOOP REPEATEDLY THROUGH THE ARRAY CHECKING
36   *    PAIRS OF ITEMS,  IF SECOND ITEM IS SMALLER
37   *    THE FIRST, THEN SWITCH THEM.]
38   *
```

```
39    101 CONTINUE
40        DO 200 I=1,MAX
41          TEST=0
42  *
43  * [SET TEST TO ZERO AT START OF LOOP. IF
44  *    SWITCH IS DONE, SET TEST TO 1.  IF TEST IS
45  *    0 AT END OF LOOP, THEN NO SWITCHES WERE
46  *    NEEDED -- WHICH MEANS ITEMS ARE IN SORTED
47  *    ORDER.]
48  *
49          DO 210 K=1, COUNT-1
50            IF (A(K+1) .GE. A(K)) GOTO 210
51  *
52  * [DO THE SWITCH.  TEMP IS TEMPORARY VARIABLE.]
53              TEMP=A(K+1)
54              A(K+1)=A(K)
55              A(K)=TEMP
56              TEST=1
57    210   CONTINUE
58  *
59  * [IF TEST=0 THEN NO SWITCH WAS DONE IN THIS PASS.
60  *    IF SO THEN EXIT.  OTHERWISE DO ANOTHER PASS.]
61  *
62            IF (TEST .EQ. 0) GOTO 201
63    200 CONTINUE
64  *
65  * OUTPUT ROUTINE
66  *
67    201 CONTINUE
68        DO 300 K=1,COUNT
69          PRINT *, A(K)
70    300 CONTINUE
71        END
```

You can see how much easier it is to understand this one than it was to understand the first one.

22
LOGIC: DATA STRUCTURES—TABLES

As we saw in Chapter 18, the *list* is a logical tool that is very useful in dealing with sets of data items that are related to one another. The next data structure we are going to look at is called the *table*. Tables are used to handle *sets* of *lists* that are related to one another.

For example, suppose we have a set of peoples' names, and also suppose that we know each person's phone number:

SUSAN   (219–3841)
CATHY   (818–2293)
BOB   (779–3104)
MIKE   (663–8044)
CAROL   (401–7761)

You can see that we really have *two* lists here—a list of names and a list of phone numbers. (Remember, names and phone numbers cannot be on the *same* list because they are different *types* of data items.)

Let's write the item down as two separate lists:

	NAMES( )		PHONES( )
(1)	SUSAN	(1)	219–3841
(2)	CATHY	(2)	818–2293
(3)	BOB	(3)	779–3104
(4)	MIKE	(4)	663–8044
(5)	CAROL	(5)	401–7761

Now let's sort the list of names into alphabetical order:

	NAMES( )		PHONES( )
(1)	BOB	(1)	219–3841
(2)	CAROL	(2)	818–2293
(3)	CATHY	(3)	779–3104
(4)	MIKE	(4)	663–8044
(5)	SUSAN	(5)	401–7761

Do you see what's happened? At first the two lists were related. Each person's phone number was in the same location in PHONES( ) as the name was in NAMES( ). But when we sorted the NAMES list, we destroyed that relationship. We still know that there is a phone number in the PHONES list for each name in NAMES( ), but we don't know which one goes with which.

We could, of course, look back at the original list and figure out the match-ups:

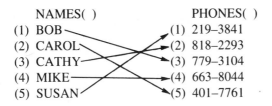

	NAMES( )		PHONES( )
(1)	BOB	(1)	219–3841
(2)	CAROL	(2)	818–2293
(3)	CATHY	(3)	779–3104
(4)	MIKE	(4)	663–8044
(5)	SUSAN	(5)	401–7761

and then we could move the phone numbers around so that the original relationship comes back:

	NAMES( )		PHONES( )
(1)	BOB	(1)	779–3104
(2)	CAROL	(2)	401–7761
(3)	CATHY	(3)	818–2293
(4)	MIKE	(4)	663–8044
(5)	SUSAN	(5)	219–3841

The trouble is that doing this is a lot of work even for small lists of items. You can imagine the work it would take to handle, for example, the phone book (with *three* lists—names, addresses, and phone numbers).

TABLES

To get around this problem we invent a new kind of data structure called a *table*. The general structure of a table looks like this:

TABLE( )

Columns

	(1)	(2)	(3)
Rows (1)			
(2)			
(3)			
(4)			

This table represents three lists put side by side. There are three *columns* in the table. Each column is really a list. So when we speak about *column* 2, we are referring to a set of related items, all of which are the same type of data.

TABLE( )

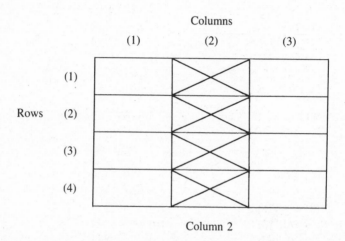

Column 2

Since a table represents a set of *related* lists, there are sets of items, taken one from each column, that are also related. Sets of related items which are of *different* types are called *rows*. The next illustration shows the third row of this table:

TABLE( )

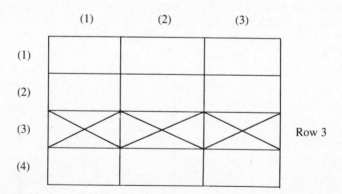

To identify a *particular item* in a table, you must know both the row and the column to which the item belongs. For example, this item:

TABLE( )

	(1)	(2)	(3)
(1)			
(2)			╳	Row 2
(3)			
(4)			

Column 3

is located in the second row of the third column. In a table, we specify the location of a single data item by giving the name of the table, the row location of the item, and the column location of the item—in that order. For example,

TABLE (2,3)

specifies the item at row 2, column 3, of the table named TABLE.

Remember, the form is always

NAME (row,column)

Again, this is the rule: Give the table name, then the row location, then the column location.

TABLE( )

	Col. 1	Col. 2	Col. 3
Row 1	(1,1)	(1,2)	(1,3)
Row 2	(2,1)	(2,2)	(2,3)
Row 3	(3,1)	(3,2)	(3,3)
Row 4	(4,1)	(4,2)	(4,3)

Finally, just as we had to *define* a list by specifying its maximum size, we need to define each table by giving the maximum number of rows and columns. The instruction:

DEFINE TABLE (4,3)

defines a table with four rows and three columns. As always, the first subscript always indicates rows, and the second always indicates columns.

USING TABLES

The main advantage of using tables is that rows of data can be processed very easily. For example, suppose we set up a table and enter some sample data.

DATA ITEM	DESCRIPTION
FRIENDS(100,3)	Phone directory of friends in town
COL 1	Name
COL 2	Street address
COL 3	Phone number

FRIENDS( )

	(1)	(2)	(3)
(1)	BOB	6 MAIN ST	771–4108
(2)	SUE	34 OAK ST	849–4113
(3)	MIKE	216 THIRD AVE	771–2262
• • •			
(100)			

In a table, all of the data in any particular *row* is assumed to be related. If we want Sue's phone number, we do the following:

1. Look down column 1 (NAMES) until we find Sue.
2. In Sue's row (in this case row 2) look up the number in column 3 (PHONE NUMBERS).
3. Return that value as Sue's phone number.

Notice that if we know Sue's row (2), and if we know which column contains phone numbers (3), we can specify exactly the one data item called Sue's phone number. Sue's phone number is in the table called FRIENDS at row 2, column 3—or it's at:

FRIENDS(2,3)

Sue's phone number:

FRIENDS( )

	(1)	(2)	(3)	
(1)				
(2)	SUE		849–4113	Row 2
(3)				
·				
·				
·				
(100)				

Column 3

Now suppose we want to print out Sue's name, address, *and* phone number. Since we know that row 2 is Sue's row, we know where to find each piece of data that we need:

- Sue's name: FRIENDS(2,1)
- Sue's address: FRIENDS(2,2)
- Sue's phone number: FRIENDS(2,3)

So we would write an output instruction like this:

Print FRIENDS(2,1), FRIENDS(2,2), FRIENDS(2,3)

It turns out, in practice, that there are many times when we want to process a whole row, or a whole column of data items. To make it easier to write those kinds of processing algorithms, we introduce a special one-line form of the LOOP instruction.

LOOP (K=1 to 3)   PRINT FRIENDS(2,K)

This means that the counter K will take on the values 1, 2, 3. Each time K takes on a new value, the PRINT will be performed. The first output will be FRIENDS(2,1), the second FRIENDS (2,2), and the last FRIENDS(2,3). This will print the entire row.

ALGORITHMS

We'll continue to use the FRIENDS( ) data set to illustrate four of the basic algorithms used in processing tables. The four are:

1. Enter data into a table.
2. Sort a table.
3. Search for and print out an item.
4. Print the entire table.

These algorithms will be similar to the *list*-processing algorithms that we developed in Chapter 18. You might want to review those before continuing.

INPUT

The input algorithm for tables is identical to the one for lists except that data is entered a row at a time.

```
(1)   DEFINE FRIENDS(100,3)
(2)   Set MAXROW to be 100
(3)   Set MAXCOL to be 3
(4)   Set EOD to be "*END*"
(5)   Set COUNT to be 0
(6)   PRINT "ENTER NAME, ADDRESS, PHONE NO."
(7)   PRINT "USE *END*,X,X TO EXIT"
(8)   LOOP with K going from 1 to MAXROW
      (8.1)LOOP(J=1 TO MAXCOL)INPUT FRIENDS (K,J)
      (8.2)  IF FRIENDS(K,1) is equal to EOD
             THEN
             (8.21)  EXIT LOOP
             ELSE
             (8.22)  Add 1 to COUNT
(9)
```

Step (1) defines FRIENDS( ) to be a table of 100 rows by three columns. Steps (2) through (5) initialize parameters. MAXROW and MAXCOL define the maximum size of the table. *END* is chosen as the end-of-data marker because we have no friends named *END*.

Steps (6) and (7) print the input heading. Note that the user is told to enter *three* data pieces each time. Data is always entered a row at a time. Step (8) is the main input loop. It counts through the rows from 1 to MAXROW. In this case the maximum number of input rows is 100.

Step (8.1) provides the actual input. Within step (8.1), the counter J goes from 1 to MAXCOL. Each time J changes, a new input is accepted. In this case MAXCOL is 3; so each time step (8.1) is performed, three data items will be read into row K of FRIENDS( ). Step (8.2) checks for end of data. When *END* is entered, the input loop finishes. Each time a new row is entered, the COUNT goes up by one. At the end of the loop, COUNT contains a value equal to the number of rows of data entered into the table.

SORTING

The sorting algorithm shown here is identical to the one developed in Chapter 20 except that rows are sorted instead of just single items on a list.

In a table, the decision must be made to sort on a particular column. For example, this table:

FRIENDS( )

	(1)	(2)	(3)
(1)	BOB	6 MAIN ST	771–4108
(2)	SUE	34 OAK ST	849–4113
(3)	MIKE	216 THIRD AVE	771–2262
.			
.			
.			
(100)			

could be sorted on column 1, in which case the names would be in order; column 2, in which case the addresses would be in order; or on column 3, in which case the phone numbers would be in order. Suppose we decide to sort on column 1 by names:

FRIENDS( ) SORTED BY NAME

	(1)	(2)	(3)
(1)	BOB	6 MAIN ST	771–4108
(2)	MIKE	216 THIRD AVE	771–2262
(3)	SUE	34 OAK ST	849–4113
. . .			
(100)			

You can see that this produces a different arrangement of the data then if we had decided to sort on column 3, by phone numbers:

FRIENDS( ) SORTED BY PHONE NUMBER

	(1)	(2)	(3)
(1)	MIKE	216 THIRD AVE	771–2262
(2)	BOB	6 MAIN STREET	771–4108
(3)	SUE	34 OAK ST	849–4113
. . .			
(100)			

It isn't unusual for a table to be sorted a number of different ways depending on the information needed. For example, telephone data is sorted alphabetically for the con-

sumer directory and by phone number for billing purposes. Business numbers are sorted by "type of business" when included in the yellow pages.
The sort uses these data items:

DATA ITEM	DESCRIPTION
FRIENDS( )	Table of data
COUNT	Number of actual rows of data
MAXCOL	Maximum number of columns
SORTCOL	Number of the column which will control the sort
TOP	Location of first item in unsorted set
NEXT	Location of item being tested
SLOC	Row location of smallest item found in unsorted part of column SORTCOL
TEMP	Temporary storage location for use in switch routine

Notice that SVAL is not used here. This is because the smallest *row* must be moved to the top, not just a single value. At the end of each sorting pass, SLOC will contain the number of the row to be switched. Each time we will switch:

FRIENDS(TOP,1) with FRIENDS(SLOC,1)
FRIENDS(TOP,2) with FRIENDS(SLOC,2)
FRIENDS(TOP,3) with FRIENDS(SLOC,3)

The algorithm picks up at step (9) and assumes that the input has already been done.

   (9)   PRINT "SORT ON WHICH COLUMN?"
 (10) INPUT SORTCOL and verify
 (11) LOOP with TOP going from 1 to COUNT-1
      (11.1) Set SLOC equal to TOP
      (11.2) LOOP with NEXT going from TOP+1 to COUNT
           (11.21) IF FRIENDS(NEXT,SORTCOL) is smaller than FRIENDS(SLOC, SORTCOL)
                THEN
                (11.211) SET SLOC EQUAL TO NEXT
                ELSE
                (11.212) CONTINUE
      (11.3) LOOP with K going from 1 to MAXCOL
           (11.31) Set TEMP equal to FRIENDS(TOP,K)
           (11.32) Set FRIENDS(TOP,K) equal to FRIENDS(SLOC,K)
           (11.33) Set FRIENDS(SLOC,K) equal to TEMP
 (12) STOP

Step (10) allows the user to enter the number of the column which is to control the sort. The input number will be checked to insure that it is a valid column number.

Step (11) starts TOP at the first row of the table. Each time through, the smallest unsorted item in column SORTCOL is found. That row of data is then switched with row TOP. TOP is then set up by one, and the process is repeated. This continues until there is only one row of data in the "unsorted" set. At that point the table is in sorted order.

Step (11.1) initializes SLOC to TOP as each new sorting pass begins. At the beginning of the pass, FRIENDS(SLOC,SORTCOL) will be the smallest item found so far. The loop at (11.2) starts NEXT at TOP+1. Each time through this loop the value at FRIENDS(NEXT,SORTCOL) is compared with the value at FRIENDS(SLOC,SORTCOL). If the value at FRIENDS(NEXT,SORTCOL) is the smaller of the two, then *it* is now the smallest one so far and so SLOC is reset to the value of NEXT. When the NEXT loop ends, SLOC will contain the location of the row in the unsorted set which has the smallest value in column SORTCOL. For example, if we are sorting on column 3, the results at the end of the first pass will be:

FRIENDS( )

	(1)	(2)	(3)	
(1)	BOB	6 MAIN ST	771–4108	TOP=1
(2)	SUE	34 OAK ST	849–4113	
(3)	MIKE	216 THIRD AVE	771–2262	SLOC=3
• • •				
(100)				

SORTCOL=3

This indicates that the smallest item in column (3) is at row (3). So the next step would be to switch rows 1 and 3:

FRIENDS( )

	(1)	(2)	(3)	
(1)	MIKE	216 THIRD AVE	771–2262	
(2)	SUE	34 OAK ST	849–4113	Switch rows 1 and 3
(3)	BOB	6 MAIN ST	771–4108	
• • •				
(100)				

SORTCOL=3

Now, with the smallest row in the table moved to the first location, TOP will be set up to 2 and the whole process repeated.

Step, (11.3) performs the switch. The items are switched one column at a time under control of the K loop. The process is:

1. Move the top value into TEMP.
2. Move the SLOC value into the TOP location.
3. Move the TEMP value into the SLOC location.

Three data locations are required to switch two values. Do you see why this is true?

SEARCHING

The following algorithm locates an item and prints out the associated row of data.

DATA ITEMS	DESCRIPTION
FINDVAL	Value of item to be located
FINDCOL	Column which is to be searched
ROWLOC	Row location of located value

      (12)   LOOP FOREVER
           (12.1)   PRINT "SEARCH WHICH COLUMN — 0 TO EXIT"
           (12.2)   INPUT FINDCOL and verify
           (12.3)   IF FINDCOL is equal to 0 THEN EXIT LOOP
           (12.4)   PRINT "SEARCH FOR?"
           (12.5)   INPUT FINDVAL
           (12.6)   Set ROWLOC to be 0
           (12.7)   LOOP with K going from 1 to COUNT
                  (12.71)   IF FRIENDS(K,FINDCOL) is equal to
                            FINDVAL
                            THEN
                            (12.711) Set ROWLOC equal to K
                            (12.712) EXIT LOOP
                            ELSE
                            (12.713) CONTINUE
           (12.8)   IF ROWLOC is equal to 0
                   THEN
                   (12.81)   PRINT "ITEM NOT FOUND"
                   ELSE
                     (12.82)   PRINT "ROW",ROWLOC
                   (12.83)   LOOP(J=1 to MAXCOL) PRINT
                            FRIENDS(ROWLOC,J)
      (13)   STOP

Step (12) sets up an endless loop. Steps (12.1) through (12.3) input the column to be searched and provide a way to end the routine. Steps (12.4) and (12.5) input the value of the item to be located.

The loop at step (12.7) looks at each value in column FINDCOL. If a match to the input value is found, ROWLOC is set equal to the row number and the loop exits to the print routine. If the item is not found, a message is printed. Otherwise the row number and the contents of the row are printed.

To print an entire column, we use a similar statement. For example:

      LOOP (K=1 to COUNT)   PRINT FRIENDS (K,1)

This will print each of the data items in column 1. (COUNT is the count of the rows of data that were read into the table.)

PRINTING THE TABLE

As you would expect, the only difference in printing tables and printing lists is that each line of data to be printed represents a *row* in the table. It is also necessary to label the output by putting a *heading* above each column to be printed.

Sample Output:

```
LISTING OF FRIENDS( )
NAME            ADDRESS              PHONE
BOB          6 MAIN ST           771-4108
SUE          34 OAK ST           849-4113
MIKE         216 THIRD AVE       771-2262
```

Again, we will start at step (9) in the algorithm and assume that the rows of data have already been entered and counted.

    (9)   PRINT "LISTING OF FRIENDS( )"
    (10) PRINT "NAME","ADDRESS","PHONE"
    (11) LOOP with K going from 1 to COUNT
          (11.1)   LOOP(J=1 to MAXCOL) PRINT FRIENDS(K,J)
    (12) STOP

Step (9) prints the *table* heading. Step (10) prints the three *column* headings. Step (11) loops over the rows, and steps (11.1) loops through the columns.

PRACTICE

1. The search routine finds the *first* occurrence of FINDVAL in the table. Redesign the routine so that it prints every occurrence of FINDVAL.

2. Design routines that will add and delete rows of data to and from the table.

23
SYNTAX: TWO-DIMENSIONAL NUMERIC ARRAYS

REVIEW—ONE-DIMENSIONAL ARRAYS

`DIMENSION`
`X(20),Y(10)` — Reserves 20 array locations under the variable name X( ) and 10 locations under the name Y( ).

`X(10) = 26.2` — Stores the value 26.2 into location 10 of array X( ).

`X(M) = Y(J)` — Copies the value currently stored at location J in array Y( ) into location M of array X( ).

TWO-DIMENSIONAL ARRAYS

Each of the one-dimensional arrays illustrated above contains a series of memory locations each of which can be accessed by the use of a single subscript. Singly subscripted arrays are ideal for storing *lists* of data. For example, the list of Social Security numbers for all the employees of a company would be best stored in a one-dimensional array:

```
      INTEGER A
      DIMENSION A(100)
      DO 100 K=1,100
      READ*, A(K)
      IF (A(K) .EQ. 0) GOTO 101
  100 CONTINUE
  101 CONTINUE
```

Sets of data which are arranged as *tables*, however, do not fit as easily into the single-array format. Suppose, for example, that the company wants to store a telephone number and hourly pay rate along with each employee's Social Security number:

SOCIAL SECURITY NUMBER	TELEPHONE	PAY RATE
217640103	2136849	3.60
717619023	8176171	5.21
482771135	4150030	4.82
919968530	2162199	4.80
712449966	3178104	3.97

In this particular table there are five *rows* of data. Each of the five rows contains three *columns*.

	COLUMN 1	COLUMN 2	COLUMN 3
ROW 1	217640103	2136849	3.60
ROW 2	717619023	8176171	5.21
ROW 3	482771135	4150030	4.82
ROW 4	919968530	2162199	4.80
ROW 5	712449966	3178104	3.97

Any data item in the table can be identified by specifying both the row and the column in which it appears. For example, row 3, column 2 specifies the telephone number 4150030. Row 5, column 1 specifies the Social Security number 712449966. This method of identifying a data item by its row and column location can be used, along with a slightly modified type of array variable, to store tables of data.

DEFINING TWO-DIMENSIONAL ARRAYS

```
DIMENSION A(5,3)
```

This DIMENSION statement reserves five rows, of three columns each, under the variable name A ( ). The total number of spaces reserved is 15 ($5 \times 3 = 15$). The DIMENSION statement must come before the array if dimensions is used in the program. Both one- and two-dimensional arrays may be dimensioned in the same DIMENSION statement. A variable name may only be dimensioned as one kind of array.

EXAMPLE   DIMENSION B(10,20), C(8), K(18,5)

This dimensions array B ( ) with 10 rows of 20 columns each, array C ( ) with eight items, and array K ( ) with 18 rows of five columns each. As before, the *types* of B, C, and K are established by means of the CHARACTER, INTEGER or REAL instruction. DIMENSION has no effect on the *type* of a variable.

SUBSCRIPTS

Legal array subscripts include the set of integers from one to the dimensioned size of the array.

Two-dimensional arrays *must always* have two subscripts. The *first* always indicates a *row* position. The *second* always indicates a *column* position.

EXAMPLES   `DIMENSION Q(5,7)`   Here 5 is the row dimension and 7 is the column dimension.

Legal

```
Q(1,3) = 100.21
Q(5,2) = 9
READ *, Q(3,3)
PRINT *, Q(4,1)
Q(5,2) = Q(K,1) + Q(K,3)
```

Illegal

```
Q(7,2) = 4
```
     Row subscript greater than 5 (see `DIMENSION`, above).

```
Q(6) = 3
```
     Column subscript omitted.

```
Q(-3,5) = 201
```
     Negative subscripts not allowed.

INPUTTING DATA INTO ARRAYS

The `DO` instruction provides an efficient tool for entering data into arrays. The following example demonstrates this.

EXAMPLE

```
 1      * READ DATA INTO TABULAR ARRAY AND SORT IT
 2      *
 3      * R. W. DILLMAN
 4      * MARCH, 1984
 5      *
 6      * GLOBAL VARIABLES
 7      *    A() -- TABLE
 8      *    MAXROW -- MAXIMUM NUMBER OF ROWS (100)
 9      *    MAXCOL -- MAXIMUM NUMBER OF COLUMNS (3)
10      *    ROWS -- ACTUAL NUMBER OF ROWS
11      *    EOD -- END-OF-DATA VALUE
12      *
13      * INITIALIZE
14      *
15            REAL A,TEMP,EOD
16            INTEGER MAXROW, MAXCOL,ROWS
```

(continued)

```
17              INTEGER SORTBY,TOP,NEXT,LOC
18              DIMENSION A(100,3)
19              DATA ROWS/0/
20              PARAMETER (MAXROW=100), (MAXCOL=3)
20              PARAMETER (EOD=99999)
21       *
22       * INPUT ROUTINE
23       *
24              DO 100 I=1,MAXROW
25                  READ*, (A(I,J),J=1,MAXCOL)
26                  IF (A(I,1).EQ.EOD) GOTO 101
27                  ROWS=ROWS+1
28          100 CONTINUE
```

Note that ROWS is set (line 27) to count the number of *rows* of actual data stored in the array (the end-of-data marker does not count as a row). The program assumes that three columns of data are supplied for each row. If insufficient data is available at the time the input statement is executed, an error message will be printed.

At line 20 the variables MAXROW and MAXCOL are set equal to the number of rows and columns established in the DIMENSION statement. MAXROW and MAXCOL are *parameters* which will be used later in the program whenever reference to the maximum number of rows or of columns is needed.

The following example *continues* the *previous* program and sorts the data into ascending order. The algorithm for this sort was developed in Chapter 23.

DATA ITEM	VARIABLE NAME
TABLE(100,3)	A(100,3)
COUNT	ROWS
MAXCOL	MAXCOL
MAXROW	MAXROW
SORTCOL	SORTBY
TOP	TOP
NEXT	NEXT
SLOC	LOC
TEMP	TEMP

```
29  *
30  * SORTING ROUTINE
31  *
32  * LOCAL VARIABLES
33  *     SORTBY -- COLUMN TO BE SORTED
34  *     TOP -- INDEX FIRST ROW IN UNSORTED SET
35  *     NEXT -- INDEX OF NEXT ROW TO BE TESTED
36  *     LOC -- INDEX OF ROW WITH SMALLEST VALUE
```

(continued)

```
37    *            IN COLUMN SORTBY
38    *    TEMP -- TEMPORARY VARIABLE USED IN SWITCH
39    *
40    *            [GET SORTBY AND VERIFY]
41    101 CONTINUE
42        PRINT *,'SORT ON WHICH COLUMN?'
43        PRINT*,'   ENTER 1, 2 OR 3'
44        READ *, SORTBY
45        IF (SORTBY .LT. 1) GOTO 101
46        IF (SORTBY .GT. 3) GOTO 101
47    *
48    *            [EXCHANGE SORT]
49        DO 300 TOP=1,ROWS-1
50           LOC=TOP
51    *
52    *    [FIND SMALLEST IN UNSORTED SET]
53        DO 400 NEXT=TOP+1,ROWS
54           IF (A(NEXT,SORTBY) .LT. A(LOC,SORTBY)) THEN
55              LOC=NEXT
56           ENDIF
57    400 CONTINUE
58    *
59    *    [SWITCH SMALLEST WITH TOP -- SWITCH ROWS]
60        DO 500 L=1,ROWS
61           TEMP=A(TOP,L)
62           A(TOP,L)=A(LOC,L)
63           A(LOC,L)=TEMP
64    500 CONTINUE
65    *
66    300 CONTINUE
67    *
68    * OUTPUT ROUTINE
69    *
70      PRINT *,'SORTED TABLE'
71      PRINT *
72      DO 600 I=1,ROWS
73         PRINT *, A(I,1),A(I,2),A(I,3)
74    600 CONTINUE
75        END
```

Lines 45 and 46 check to be sure the sort column input is legal. If it's not, another input is requested. Lines 60 to 64 perform the switch. Notice that although the *decision* as to which is the smallest row is based on the values in just one column, the *entire row* of data must be moved to the top of the unsorted set. After this code is executed, the array will be in this order:

```
A(100,3):
```

ROW	COLUMN 1	COLUMN 2	COLUMN 3
1	217640103	2136849	3.60
2	482771135	4150030	4.82
3	712449966	3178104	3.97
4	717619020	8176171	5.21
5	919968530	2162199	4.80
6	99999	0	0
•			
•			
•			

A printout of the array's contents can be produced by using a similar programming structure. Examples of array outputs are shown in the next section.

The data in the above example was read in one row at a time. This is known as *row order* processing and is the most commonly used approach to array processing. *Column order* processing is similar, the only difference being that data is handled a column at a time instead of a row at a time.

EXAMPLE

```
 1  * COLUMN ORDER INPUT
 2  *
 3  * VARIABLES
 4  *   B() -- ARRAY
 5  *   MAXROW -- MAXIMUM NUMBER OF ROWS (10)
 6  *   MAXCOL -- MAXIMUM NUMBER OF COLUMNS (40)
 7  *   COLS -- ACTUAL NUMBER OF COLUMNS
 8  *
 9      DIMENSION B(10,40)
10      DATA MAXROW/10/,MAXCOL/40/,COLS/0/,EOD/99999/
11  *
12  * INPUT -- OUTER LOOP CONTROLS COLUMNS
13  *          INNER LOOP CONTROLS ROWS
14  *
15      DO 100 I=1,MAXCOL
16        DO 200 J=1,MAXROW
17  *
18  * [NOTE THAT THE READ INSTRUCTION STILL REFERENCES
19  *   B(ROW,COLUMN)]
20  *
21            READ *, B(J,I)
22            IF B((J,I) .EQ. EOD) GOTO 101
23    200 CONTINUE
24        COLS=COLS+1
25    100 CONTINUE
26  *
27  * [EXIT FROM INPUT ROUTINE -- COLS IS COUNT OF COLUMNS]
28    101 CONTINUE
```

In this case the program assumes that 10 data items are available for each column and that zero is the end-of-data marker. Line 24 sets COLS to be the count of the number of columns of data actually read in.

PRACTICE

1. Adding to the program on page 218 write a routine that will print out a list of all employees who earn more than $5.00 per hour.

2. Extend Exercise 1 so that the program asks the user to input a number and then prints a list of employees whose pay rate exceeds that number.

PRINTING TWO-DIMENSIONAL ARRAYS

Two-dimensional arrays usually represent tabular data. The output, then, can usually be thought of as being some number of rows of data with a fixed number of column values in each row.

This output format is generated by using a double loop. The *outer loop* controls the printing of the *rows* and the *inner loop* controls the printing of the individual *column* values.

EXAMPLE   Assume that array B( ) is dimensioned at DIMENSION B(100,4) and that 18 rows of data have been input. Also assume that the following values have been established:

```
MAXCOL = 4      Maximum number of columns
   ROW = 18     Actual number of rows

      * LOOP OVER ROWS
      *
              DO 100 I=1,ROW
      *
      * USE IMPLIED LOOP TO PRINT COLUMNS
      *
              PRINT*, (B(I,J), J=1,MAXCOL)
        100 CONTINUE
```

In this case the program will print 18 lines of data (ROW = 18) with four data items on each line (MAXCOL = 4). It is important to remember that in FORTRAN each execution of a PRINT statement causes a line feed to be printed. So in order to put each row's four items on the same output line, we need to use an *implied* loop. Even though the variable J loops from 1 to 4, and four items are sent as output, the PRINT itself is only executed once per row.

When printing tables of data, it is usually a good idea to print a *heading* above each *column*. In the example above, the spacing of the four values printed in each row is controlled by a comma. To make the headings line up with the columns, commas must also be used.

EXAMPLE

```
* COLUMN HEADINGS
*
        PRINT *, '           SOC-SEC-NO',
     #            '            CITY CODE',
     #            ' TELEPHONE NUMBER',
     #            '            PAY RATE'
*
* DATA ITEMS FROM TABLE
*
        DO 100 I=1,ROW
           PRINT *, (B(I,J), J=1,MAXCOL)
  100 CONTINUE
```

Here the column headings are supplied in a long PRINT statement. Notice that each heading is written as a separate string. This is done to make the headings easier to edit. Each heading contains as many blanks as are needed to center it over the appropriate output column. Output from the program will look like this:

```
SOC-SEC-NO  CITY CODE  TELEPHONE NUMBER  PAY RATE

213887124      12        3017192614        3.72
448112213      28        3018226161        4.20
779332088      42        2036014443        3.62
```

At times it is useful to have the program *number the rows* as it prints them. This is most easily done by printing the row counter at the beginning of each line, just before the first column value.

EXAMPLE

```
* LOOP OVER ROWS
*
        DO 100 I=1,ROW
*
* PRINT ROW NUMBER, ROW OF DATA ITEMS
*
           PRINT *, I, (B(I,J),J=1,MAXCOL)
  100 CONTINUE
```

The output will look like this:

```
1    213887124   12   3017192614   3.72
2    448112213   28   3018226161   4.20
3    779332088   42   2036014443   3.62
4    156021191   31   8149132021   4.11
```

Column headings, of course, can be included as shown before. Since there is now an extra column, no extra heading will be needed.

This method of printing headings is fairly cumbersome. It should be used only when you are not too concerned about the *exact* form of the output. The FORTRAN FORMAT instruction provides a much more powerful way to control output. The FORMAT instruction is discussed in Chapter 33.

PRACTICE

3. Rewrite the above program to include four column headings. The heading for the first column should be NUMBER.

24
LOGIC: DATA FILES

DEFINITIONS

Data Item

A single piece of data.

Data Record

A related set of different types of data items, roughly equivalent to a row in a table.

Data File

A collection of data, usually in the form of similar records, that is permanently stored for use by the computer.

File Definition

The act of locating a file and assigning it for use by a particular program.

File I/O

Input/output operations with files.

THE COMPUTER

As you remember from our first discussions on FORTRAN, a *program* is a set of instructions that causes the computer to manipulate data. Although both programs and data are stored in the computer's memory, they are stored in different places. The program can tell the computer to process the data in its memory, but it can also tell the computer to read data in *from* the outside or print data out *to* the outside.

When your program finishes its processing and "stops," it disappears. In reality it is erased to make room for someone else's program, but the point is that the data also disappears. This is important. Having just entered a set of data, and having gone to all the trouble of getting the data processed the way you want it to be, your program ends and the processed data is gone. What we need to deal with this problem is a way to keep the *data* around after the program is finished.

In terms of the computer system, long-range data storage is accomplished by using hardware devices called *secondary storage* units. Secondary storage is part of the computer itself, and, like the rest of the system, it can be controlled by your programs. Here is the picture of what we would *like* to do:

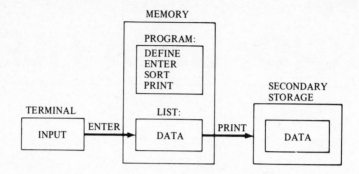

We would like to be able to *copy* our data from the main memory to the secondary storage device and leave it there. That way, when we return to use the system later, we can retrieve it like this:

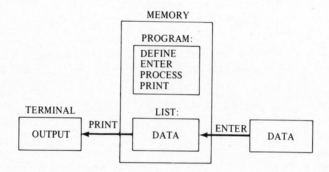

The thing to see here is that we still have only *three* basic computer activities:

INPUT/ENTER   Move data into the main memory.
PROCESS   Manipulate data within the main memory.
OUTPUT/PRINT Move data out of main memory.

In particular, INPUT and OUTPUT are always the same activity. It's just that now we have a new location that can be used as a destination for the output and as a source of input.

In the same way that your program and data take up only a small part of the computer's main memory, your data will take up only a small part of the secondary storage. When you do output the secondary storage, the system reserves part of the device for your data. The reserved area is given a name (so that you can find it later), and is called a data file.

DATA FILES

A collection of data items which is *permanently stored* on the computer media and which can be accessed by your FORTRAN program is called a *data file*.

Data files provide computer users with a way of storing data over long periods of time. Once a file has been established, data items can be added, deleted, or altered by one or many different users' programs. Programs can also read the data items for use in computations or to produce reports.

It is important to distinguish the *physical description* of the file from the *contents* of the file. The physical description of the file includes such information as the size of the file, the types of data it contains, the rules which determine where an individual datum will be stored, and the file's name. The term *contents* always refers to the actual data currently stored in the file.

We emphasize the physical description of data files because we have to establish files before we can use them. Let's take another look at our picture:

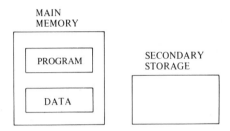

If we want to have our program copy a set of data into a file on the secondary storage device, our first problem is that there is no file there.

Remember that a file is *permanent* storage. Once we set a file up and put data into it, the file will remain in existence until we tell the computer system to destroy it. Since there are many people using the computer, careful track must be kept of how many files exist, what their names are, and who they belong to. So before you use a file for the first time, you must ask the system to *create* it.

When you create the file, you give it a name. The computer reserves space on the secondary storage device under that name. From then on you can use the file anytime you want to by supplying the system with the file name.

It is important to see that the CREATE command that sets up your data file is *not* a part of FORTRAN. Like RUN and LIST, it is a computer system command. The *Computer System User's Manual* for your brand of computer will show you how to create and destroy files. The command will be something like this:

```
CREATE "DFILE", 100
```

which would set up a file named DFILE with room for 100 data items. Once the file has been created, our picture looks like this:

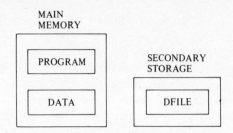

Now the file exists on the secondary storage device.

Our next problem is that although we want our FORTRAN program to have the computer copy data out to the file, the *program* doesn't know that the file exists.

When we use the PRINT instruction, the program assumes that we are sending output to the terminal. What we need is a PRINT-to-FILE instruction that will send the output to a data file. To do that, however, we need to be able to specify to *which* file the output should go.

We do that by inventing an instruction whose purpose is to locate the file by looking up its name on the secondary storage device and then to tell the program how to find it. The instruction looks like this:

OPEN #1, "DFILE"

Later in the program we will do output to the file by saying:

Write #1: ITEM1,ITEM2,ITEM3

Notice that Write is a new output instruction. From now on in our algorithms Print will be used to specify that output is to go to the computer terminal, and Write will be used to send output to data files (or to other output devices). So this:

Print ITEM 1, ITEM 2, ITEM 3

automatically prints three values at the terminal, while:

Write #K: ITEM 1, ITEM 2, ITEM 3

sends output to file number K. K must be an *integer* number, and K *must* have been used in an OPEN statement somewhere earlier in the program. Here, for example, is an algorithm for reading some data from the terminal and storing it in a file. (From now on, we will always assume that the files we use have already been CREATEd.)

(1) OPEN #3, "MYFILE"
(2) Set EOD to be 99999
(3) LOOP with K going from 1 to 100
    (3.1) INPUT ITEM1,ITEM2
    (3.2) IF ITEM1 is equal to EOD THEN EXIT LOOP
    (3.3) WRITE #3: ITEM1,ITEM2
(4) STOP

Step (1) finds the data file MYFILE on the secondary storage device and assigns it as file number 3 for the program. There is no particular reason for choosing 3. On the secondary storage device the file exists by name only. The program can assign any number it wants to, and it can assign different numbers at different times.

Step (3.1) allows the user to enter data at the terminal. Step (3.2) checks for end-of-data. Step (3.3) writes the data out to the file. When step (4) is performed, the program will be erased, but MYFILE will continue to exist. Later, if we want to print this data back out at the terminal, we'll need another program.

(1) OPEN #1, "MYFILE"
(2) LOOP FOREVER
    (2.1) READ #1: ITEM1,ITEM2
    (2.2) IF ENDFILE THEN EXIT LOOP
    (2.3) PRINT ITEM1,ITEM2
(3) STOP

Step (2.2) illustrate a feature of files that we haven't seen before. When you store data into a data file, you expect the computer to maintain that data for you until you ask for it back again. Because of this, it is very important for the computer to know *exactly* where the *end* of your data is. To eliminate any possible errors (for example, by programmers who forget to include an end-of-data marker in their data), the computer attaches its *own* end-of-data marker to every file.

When your program finishes printing data *to* the file, the computer sets the marker (called, for files, the end-of-file marker or EOF). When you do input *from* a file, your program can test for the EOF and exit from the input loop when the end is found. This is what happens in step (2.2).

Notice also that in this program we opened the file MYFILE as file number 1. Again, we can choose whatever number we want to inside the program as long as we identify the file by its proper name.

PROCESSING DATA FILES

You should see by now that a file is a *place* where we store data until we need to use it. Programs which process the data stored in the file usually take on this basic form:

PROGRAM SECTION	DESCRIPTION

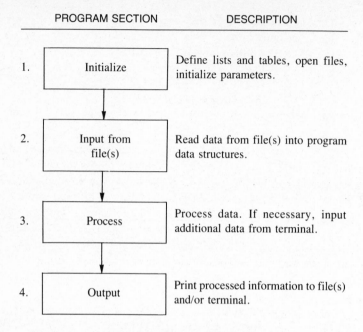

1. **Initialize** — Define lists and tables, open files, initialize parameters.

2. **Input from file(s)** — Read data from file(s) into program data structures.

3. **Process** — Process data. If necessary, input additional data from terminal.

4. **Output** — Print processed information to file(s) and/or terminal.

To make it easier to read from and print to the files, we usually try to keep the data in the same form both in memory and in secondary storage. To do this, we process the data in the form of records.

A *record* is a set of related data items. Records are very similar to *rows* of data in tables, and are used for the same purpose. By storing data in record form, entire sets of data can be accessed by retrieving a single record.

To define a record, the following information is needed:

- The record name
- The names, data types, and sizes of the data items to be in the record
- The order in which the items will appear in the record
- The total size of the record

Suppose, for example, a company wants to store the following data for each of its employees:

1. Employee's identifying number
2. Employee's Social Security number
3. Hourly pay rate
4. Overtime pay rate

During processing, this data will be kept in a table in the computer's main memory.

TABLE( )

	(1)	(2)	(3)	(4)
(1)	16	221370144	10.25	15.75
(2)	27	889663031	9.35	14.00
(3)	29	219304122	9.83	14.20
. . .				

ID   SOCSEC   REG   OVERTIME

Eventually, however, it will be printed out to a file. To make the file I/O easier to handle, the file record definition can be set up to match the table.

FILE NAME: EMPDATA

	DATA ITEM	TYPE	SIZE
1.	ID NUMBER	INTEGER	2
2.	SOCIAL SECURITY NO.	INTEGER	9
3.	REGULAR RATE	DECIMAL	5.2
4.	OVERTIME RATE	DECIMAL	5.2

RECORD SIZE: 21

SAMPLE RECORD:

```
1   3                    12      17        21
1 6 2 2 1 3 7 0 1 4 4 1 0 . 2 5 1 9 . 3 5
```

The file name is the name the file will be given when it is CREATEd on the secondary storage device. It is also the name that will be used when the file is OPENed in a program.

Notice that the four data items are arranged in the same order in the record as they are in each row of the table. This way, when the time comes to print the data to the file, the WRITE statement will simply print each row in order:

LOOP(J=1 to 4) WRITE #3: TABLE(K,J)

where K is any row and J goes from 1 to 4 to output each item in the row. And, of course, since the data is stored in the file in row order, input *from* the file can be done exactly the same way.

The data item *types* and *sizes* are given to help the programmer with the coding. For example, some small computer systems are only accurate to eight digits in their integer numbers. On a system like that, the nine-digit Social Security number could not be processed. Obviously it's important for the programmer to know that.

Three major types of data are used in data processing. *Integer* data is numeric but contains no fractional (or decimal) part. *Decimal* data is numeric and does contain a fractional part. *Character* data is alphanumeric. That means it may contain letters, digits, or symbols. Character data is covered in more detail in Chapter 30. Notice that the size of a decimal data item is specified as A.B, where A is the total size (*including* the decimal point) and B is the number of digits to the *right* of the decimal point.

The *total size* of the record is useful on those systems that require you to specify a *file size* when you CREATE a file. In this example, if the company had 50 employees, the file would need room for 50 × 21 = 1050 data pieces.

The *sample record* is given to help the programmer visualize the actual data. The numbers at the top (1, 3, 12, 17, 21) show where each item begins in the record. These sections of the record are sometimes called *fields*.

ALGORITHMS

Since the actual processing of data occurs in main memory, we will concern ourselves primarily with file input/output operations. There are two general rules which, if followed, will help make file I/O easy to do:

1. Read and write data from and to files a record at a time. This means that each WRITE should write an entire record, and each READ should read an entire record. Moving data in and out of main memory in record-sized chunks makes it less likely that you will accidentally store data items in the wrong place.
2. If at all possible, make the record description and the table or list description match. It is less confusing when the data items are in the same order everywhere.

This algorithm reads a set of data from the terminal, sorts the data, and copies it out to a file. The data record is defined this way:

FILE NAME: EMPDATA

	DATA ITEM	TYPE	SIZE
1.	ID NUMBER	INTEGER	2
2.	SOC SEC NO.	INTEGER	9
3.	REGULAR RATE	DECIMAL	5.2
4.	OVERTIME RATE	DECIMAL	5.2

RECORD SIZE: 21

SAMPLE RECORD:

```
 1    3                      12           17          21
| 2 | 2 | 6 | 1 | 9 | 4 | 4 | 0 | 8 | 1 | 2 |   | 9 | . | 2 | 5 | 1 | 4 | . | 0 | 0 |
```

We'll assume up to 100 possible records in the file. The file will have been created on the secondary storage device as:

```
CREATE "EMPDATA", 2100
```

and will be read into a table called PAYDAT( ) that looks like this:

PAYDAT( )

	(1)	(2)	(3)	(4)
(1)	22	6194410812	9.25	14.00
(2)				
(3)				
.				
.				
.				
(100)				
	ID	SOCSEC	REG	O.T.

Notice that the columns in the table match the order of the fields in the records.
    This is the algorithm:

    (1)   DEFINE PAYDAT(100,4)
    (2)   Set MAXROW to be 100
    (3)   Set MAXCOL to be 4
    (4)   Set EOD to be 0
    (5)   Set COUNT to be 0
    (6)   PRINT "ENTER ID,SOCSEC,REG,O.T."
    (7)   PRINT "   USE 0,0,0,0 TO EXIT"
    (8)   LOOP with K going from 1 to 100
        (8.1)   LOOP (J=1 to 4) INPUT PAYDAT(K,J)
        (8.2)   IF PAYDAT(K,1) is equal to EOD THEN EXIT LOOP
        (8.3)   ADD 1 to COUNT
    (9)   PERFORM SORT on PAYDAT using Column 1
  (10)   OPEN #1, "EMPDATA"
  (11)   LOOP with K going from 1 to COUNT
        (11.1)   LOOP (J=1 to 4) WRITE #1: PAYDAT(K,J)
  (12)   STOP

Step (1) defines the table; steps (2) to (5) initialize parameters. Steps (6) to (8) allow the user to enter data into the table from the terminal. Step (9) performs the sort using a previously developed sorting routine. We specify that PAYDAT( ) is the table to be sorted, and we specify that column 1 is to control the sort. The result of step (9) will be that the rows in the table will be rearranged with the ID numbers in order.

Step (10) opens the file EMPDATA as file 1. Steps (11) and (11.1) copy the table into the file. We copy exactly COUNT rows. We could copy the entire table, including the empty rows, but with a large table that approach wastes a lot of time.

Step (12) stops the algorithm. We assume that when the routine stops, the file will be released by the system. On some computers a file may be OPENed by only one user at a time. Those systems supply a command:

```
CLOSE #1
```

which is used to give the file back to the system when a program is finished with it.

The next algorithm reads the set of data back from the file EMPDATA and prints a report. Again we assume that EMPDATA has been set up and that the sorted table has already been copied into it.

    (1)   DEFINE REPDAT(100,4)
    (2)   Set MAXROW to be 100
    (3)   Set MAXCOL to be 4
    (4)   Set COUNT to be 0
    (5)   OPEN #1, "EMPDATA"

(6) LOOP with K going from 1 to MAXROW
    (6.1)   LOOP (J=1 to MAXCOL) READ #1: REPDAT(K,J)
    (6.2)   IF ENDFILE THEN EXIT LOOP
    (6.3)   Add 1 to COUNT
(8) PRINT "PERSONNEL REPORT"
(9) PRINT "ID","SOC-SEC","REGULAR","OVERTIME"
(10) LOOP with K going from 1 to COUNT
    (10.1) LOOP (J=1 to MAXCOL) PRINT REPDAT(K,J)
(11) STOP

    In step (1) we set up the table to be used in this routine. Notice that the name is different, but the sizes are the same as were used before. The reason the *file description* is so important is that it tells the programmer how the data file is structured. Without this information it is very difficult to *use* the file.

    Step (5) opens the file. Again, we must know the file's *name* to be able to access it. Step (6) inputs data from the file to the table. Notice that if we don't have the dimensions of the table defined correctly, data items will end up in wrong columns. Step (6.2) checks for the system's end-of-file marker and exits the loop when the end is reached. Step (7) releases the file since this routine doesn't need it any more. Steps (8) to (11) print out the data in the table at the terminal.

SUMMARY

A data file is a place on one of the computer system's secondary storage devices where data can be stored for long periods of time. Data is printed out to the file for storage and read back into main memory for processing.

    The majority of the problems that come up in using files happen because of errors in file I/O. It is a good idea to put your data in *record* format and do your I/O in terms of records. It is also a good idea to match the data structures inside your program to the record structure of the file.

PRACTICE

1. Using the *Computer User's Manual* for your system, or by asking your instructor, find out how to create and destroy files on your system.
2. Some systems have a special system program (often called an EDITOR) that allows users to make changes in a data file directly, at the terminal. Check to see if your system allows this.

25
SYNTAX: DATA FILES

DEFINITIONS

Open
: The act of locating a data file by name and connecting it to the computer for use by a program.

OPEN
: The FORTRAN instruction used to open data files

CLOSE
: The FORTRAN instruction used to disconnect an open file. Once closed, a file is no longer available for use.

Unit Number
: An integer number used to identify an open data file. Each open file must have a different number. The unit number is used in READ and WRITE instructions.

READ
: The FORTRAN instruction used to transfer data from a program to a data file.

WRITE
: The FORTRAN instruction used to transfer data from a data file to a program.

IOSTAT= Variable
: A special variable, used by OPEN and CLOSE. The IOSTAT variable is set to zero if no errors occur during the operation.

END= Line Number
: A special line number, used in READ statements. When the end of a data file is reached, the computer jumps to the line number indicated in the END= specification.

CREATING DATA FILES

Before a data file can be used, it must be created on the disk. The system commands used to create files differ greatly from computer to computer. You should check the *Computer User's Manual* for your computer to find out the exact set of commands for your system. We will assume that any files we use in this chapter have already been created.

OPENING DATA FILES

Before data can be read from a file, the file must be connected to your program by means of an OPEN statement. The general form of the open statemnent looks like this.

```
OPEN( unit number, FILE='file name', IOSTAT=integer variable)
```

The word OPEN tells the computer that a file connection is needed. For any particular file, the OPEN statement is executed only once. OPEN must be used before the file is accessed for the first time.

The *unit number* is an integer number which will be used later in the program to identify this file in READ and WRITE statements.

IMPORTANT   Your particular computer system has two *standard* unit numbers that are used to control reading and writing to your terminal. You should *not* use these numbers in OPEN statements. Many systems reserve the numbers 5 and 6 for this purpose; check the *FORTRAN Reference Manual* for your system to be sure.

The FILE= specifier is used to supply the name of the file to be opened. The file name must be enclosed in single quote marks.

The IOSTAT variable is used to check for errors while the system is trying to open the file. If no error occurs, the IOSTAT variable will be given a value of zero. If an error does occur, the variable will be given a nonzero value. The nonzero error codes differ from computer to computer. Check the *FORTRAN Reference Manual* for your system to find the codes for your particular computer.

Here is an example of an OPEN instruction. Assume that the file MYDATA already exists on the disk.

```
OPEN(9, FILE='MYDATA', IOSTAT=K)
```

When this statement is executed, the system will search for the file named MYDATA and try to open it for use by the program. If the system is successful, then K will be set to zero and the file will be available for reading and writing as unit number 9. If the system is not successful, then K will not be zero.

The IOSTAT variable is used to do error checking in cases where an invalid file name is used. For example:

```
1              INTEGER ERR
2              CHARACTER FNAME *8
3        100   CONTINUE
4              PRINT *, 'ENTER FILE NAME'
5              READ *, FNAME
6              OPEN(9, FILE=FNAME, IOSTAT=ERR)
7              IF (ERR .NE. 0) GOTO 100
```

Here the name of the file to be opened will be supplied at the terminal and stored into the character variable, FNAME. At line 6, the system will try to open the file. If the file doesn't exist, or if some other error occurs, then the integer variable ERR will be set to some nonzero value. The IF test at line 7 checks for this and requests another file name if an error did occur.

READING AND WRITING DATA FILES

Once a file has been OPENed, its *unit number* can be used in READ and WRITE statements. For example:

```
1              OPEN(14, FILE='MYDATA')
2              DO 100 I=1,100
3                 READ(14, END=101) NUMB
4                 COUNT=COUNT+1
5        100   CONTINUE
6        101   CONTINUE
7              PRINT *, 'THERE ARE ',COUNT,' NUMBERS IN THE F
```

Notice that the file is opened with a unit number of 14. That unit number is then used in the READ instruction at line 3. Once a file has been opened, its unit number is used to identify it in the READ and WRITE statements that follow. Also notice that the file was OPENed without the use of an IOSTAT variable. If you are not concerned about possible opening errors, then the IOSTAT variable can be omitted.

In the READ statement at line 3, the END= specifier is used to tell the computer what to do when the end of the data file is reached. In this case the computer will jump to line 101 when the end-of-data condition occurs. The general form for the READ instruction is:

READ(unit number, END=line number) variable list

The unit number must have been set previously in an OPEN statement. If the unit number is omitted, the system will supply the standard value that identifies your terminal.

When data is entered into a data file, the computer system supplies its own end-of-data marker. The END= specification tells the computer to look for this marker while it's reading the file. When it sees that the end-of-data marker is the next thing in the file, the computer will not try to read it. Instead it will jump to the line number indicated in the END= specification. This technique is most often used to exit from an input loop that is reading from a data file.

FORMATTED OUTPUT

Many computer systems allow data to be stored in files through the use of a systems program called a *text editor*. You should check the *Computer User's Manual* for your computer system to see if this can be done. If your system does not have this capability, then you must be able to write a program whose job will be to take data from the terminal and store it into a file. This is done by using what is known as the *formatted* WRITE instruction.

The general form of the formatted WRITE instruction is:

WRITE(unit number, format list) variable list

The unit number is the number under which the file to be written to was OPENed. The variable list is a list of variable names, the values of which are to be written out to the file. The format list is a list of special codes that tell the computer the exact form of the data to be written.

In Chapter 24 we showed how *records* are used to define the size and types of data items to be stored in a file. If you don't remember how records are described, go back and review that section. In the WRITE instruction, the variable list and the format list are used to output *records* of data to a data file. Suppose, for example, that we wanted to build a file to contain a list of people—their names, heights and weights. The record for the file would look like this:

FILE NAME: PERDAT

	DATA FIELD	TYPE	SIZE
1.	PERSON'S NAME	CHARACTER	30
2.	HEIGHT IN INCHES	INTEGER	2
3.	WEIGHT IN POUNDS	REAL	5.1

RECORD SIZE: 38

SAMPLE RECORD:

```
1                                          32  34        38
B O N N I E   J O N E S                    6 6 1 2 0 . 3
```

The alogrithm for building the file is very simple. (As always, we assume that the empty file has already been created on the disk.)

(1) OPEN the data file
(2) LOOP FOREVER
    (2.1) Read NAME, HEIGHT, WEIGHT
    (2.2) IF NAME is end-of-data THEN EXIT LOOP
    (2.3) Write NAME, HEIGHT, WEIGHT to data file in record form
(3) CLOSE the file
(4) Stop

We already know how to OPEN the file, and we know how to do the input in step (2.1). We'll use *END* as the end-of-data marker for the terminal input. Notice that the algorithm doesn't write out an end-of-data marker to the file; the computer system will supply its own *end-of-file* mark when the file is closed.

Except for the WRITE statement, we can write the entire program.

```
 1              CHARACTER NAME*30
 2              INTEGER HEIGHT
 3              REAL WEIGHT
 4              OPEN(12, FILE='PERDAT')
 5              PRINT *, 'ENTER NAME, HEIGHT, WEIGHT
 6              PRINT *, ' USE   *END*,0,0   TO EXIT'
 7              DO 100 I=1,2,0
 8                 READ *, NAME, HEIGHT, WEIGHT
 9                 IF (NAME .EQ. '*END*') GOTO 101
10                    WRITE TO FILE (SEE BELOW)
11          100 CONTINUE
12          101 CONTINUE
13              CLOSE(12)
14              END
```

Line 1 defines NAME to be a character variable with a maximum length of 30 characters. Lines 2 and 3 define HEIGHT and WEIGHT. Line 4 opens the data file under unit number 12. We don't exepect any OPENing errors, so we omit the IOSTAT variable. Lines 5 and 6 print the input heading. Line 7 establishes an endless loop. Line 8 reads the data from the terminal into the three variables NAME, HEIGHT, and WEIGHT. Line 9 checks for the end of the input data, and exits from the loop when the end is found.

Line 13 *closes* the data file. CLOSE is the opposite of OPEN. It disconnects the file from the program. On most computer systems, when a program ends, all currently open files are automatically closed. None-the-less it is a good habit to close a file when your program is finished using it.

At this point we have only to write the WRITE statement to finish the program. We need to be able to write the data contained in the variables NAME, HEIGHT, and WEIGHT out to the file. We also must be sure we write the data with all three items on the same line, in the order specified in the *record-description*. To do this, we use a version of the WRITE instruction that specifies file number 12 and then gives the three variable names. We also need to include data to specify the exact form, or *format*, of the output:

```
WRITE(12,'(A30,I2,F5.1)') NAME, HEIGHT, WEIGHT
```

In this case, the 12 identifies the file PERDAT, the information enclosed in single quotes specifies the *format* of the output, and the list of variables specifies the values to be sent to the file. The final program looks like this:

```
1              CHARACTER NAME*30
2              INTEGER HEIGHT
3              REAL WEIGHT
4              OPEN(12, FILE='PERDAT')
5              PRINT *, 'ENTER NAME, HEIGHT, WEIGHT'
6              PRINT *, ' USE  *END*,0,0  TO EXIT'
7              DO 100 I=1,2,0
8                 READ *, NAME, HEIGHT, WEIGHT
9                 IF (NAME .EQ. '*END*') GOTO 101
10                WRITE(12,'(A30,I2,F5,1)') NAME, HEIGHT, WEIGHT
11      100 CONTINUE
12      101 CONTINUE
13             CLOSE(12)
14             END
```

FORMAT CODES

FORTRAN has a very powerful set of special codes that allow the programmer completely to specify the form of a program's input and output. The full set of FORMAT codes is described in Chapter 33. Here we will describe the three basic codes that are needed to do elementary file processing.

The purpose of a format code is to tell the computer two things. First the *type* of the data to be transfered is specified. This is done by means of a letter. I means integer, F means real, and A means character. (If your version of FORTRAN's PRINT * uses the first character in every print line to control the line spacing on the printer, you might expect the WRITE instruction to do the same. In fact it does, but only if the output is to a *printer*. Since file output does not go through a printer, however, the first character is *not* truncated, and so you won't need to supply a blank at the front of each line.)

Second, the exact form of the data is specified. In the case of the A and I formats, this is done by supplying a number that tells the computer the maximum number of characters or digits to expect. In our example, A30 tells the computer to put out the value of NAME as a field of characters of length 30. I2 tells the computer to put out the value stored in HEIGHT as a two digit integer.

In the case of the F format code, both the maximum length of the field and the *precision* (the number of digits to the right of the decimal point) must be specified. The general form of the F code is

Fw.p

where w is an integer that specifies the length of the field (*including* the decimal point), and p specifies the precision. In our example, F5.1 tells the computer to put out the value stored in WEIGHT as a four-digit real number, plus a decimal point, with one digit to the right of the decimal point.

There are two places where errors often arise in using FORMAT codes. Both are easy to avoid if you write your code carefully. First of all, there must be as many codes in the FORMAT list as there are variables in the variable list. The FORMAT codes must also match the types of the variables. For example, both of these are *incorrect:*

```
WRITE(12,'(I2,A30,F5.1)')NAME,HEIGHT,WEIGHT
```

Here the types don't match:

```
WRITE(12,'(I2,F5.1)') NAME, HEIGHT, WEIGHT
```

Here there are only two codes, but there are three variables.

If you make either of these errors, the computer will print an error message and refuse to execute the program.

The second kind of error arises when the value stored in the variable is longer than the length specified in the FORMAT code. As an example, look at this piece of code:

```
INTEGER XYZ
XYZ=12345
WRITE(12,'(I3)') XYZ
```

Here XYZ contains five DIGITS, but the FORMAT code only specifies three. The computer usually will not print an error message in this case. Instead, the output will occur as a field of three asterisks. Like this:

```
***
```

The asterisks indicate that the output value would not fit into the specified field width. This problem can be avoided by making sure that the FORMAT codes you write match the *record description* that you've prepared for the file.

The FORMAT code can be supplied as a character variable. For example, the program we did earlier could have been done like this:

```
CHARACTER FVAR*40
FVAR='(A30,I2,F5.1)'
        .
        .
WRITE(12,FVAR) NAME, HEIGHT, WEIGHT
```

We set the length of FVAR to be 40 just to be sure that it's big enough to hold our FORMAT string. We would get an error message if the variable was too short, and it's alright if it's too long. Notice that the numbers used in the FORMAT codes *must* be integer *constants*. Variables or parameter names are not allowed.

Most people find the A and I codes fairly easy to understand. If you would like to read more about them, look at Chapter 35. Here are some additional examples of the F code.

If this is the variable:

```
REAL FROG
FROG=1234.5678
WRITE(12,FRFORM) FROG
```

then these FORMATS will have the following results:

FORMAT CODE	OUTPUT	COMMENT
FRFORM='(F9,4)'	1234,5678	Fits the data exactly
FRFORM='(F6,1)'	1234,5	One-digit precision
FRFORM='(F5,0)'	1234,	The smallest legal field for this value
FRFORM='(F4,0)'	****	Field width too small
FRFORM='(F9,2)'	1234,56	Extra width filled out with blanks

FORMATs are really fairly simple, and with practice you'll find them very easy to use. For now the main thing to remember is that the *easiest* way to avoid errors is to design the file record structure *first,* and then write all of your FORMAT codes to fit the record design.

FORMATTED INPUT

To read data from a file in an efficient way your program must use FORMAT codes. To write the proper codes then, you must know the format of the data records in the file. This is another good reason for creating and keeping file record documents—they become very helpful whenever file I/O is required.

Let's assume that we now have a data file named PERDAT into which we have stored a number of lines of data by using the "write-to-file" program that we saw earlier. Now we would like to read the data from the file and compute and print out the average weight of the people listed there.

Since we already know how to compute an average, we will just use that same program. We will, of course, have to modify it slightly to get our input from the file instead of from the terminal. The new program looks like this:

```
1           * COMPUTE AVERAGE
2           *
3           * R. W. DILLMAN
4           * MARCH 1984
5           *
6           * VARIABLES
7           *  COUNT, SUM -- COUNT AND SUM OF DATA ITEMS
8           *  AVERAG -- AVERAGE OF DATA ITEMS
9           *  REC -- FORMAT FOR INPUT STATEMENT
10          *
11                INTEGER COUNT, HEIGHT
12                REAL SUM, AVERAGE, WEIGHT
13                CHARACTER FILNAM*10, NAME*30, REC*20
14          *
15          * INITIALIZE VARIABLES AND OPEN DATA FILE
16          *
17                DATA COUNT/0/, SUM/0/, REC/'(A30,I2,F5.1)'/
18          *
19                PRINT *, 'ENTER DATA FILE NAME '
20                READ '(A)', FILNAM
21          *
22                OPEN(8, NAME=FILNAM, IOSTAT=IOERR)
23                IF (IOERR .NE. 0) THEN
24                   PRINT *, 'CANNOT OPEN FILE ', FILNAM
25                   PRINT *, '  ERROR CODE IS ', IOERR
26                   STOP
27                ENDIF
28          *
29                DO 100 I=1,2,0
30                   READ(8,REC, END=101) NAME, HEIGHT, WEIGH
31                   COUNT=COUNT+1
32                   SUM=SUM+WEIGHT
33             100 CONTINUE
34          *
35          * COMPUTE AVERAGE AND PRINT
36          *
37             101 CONTINUE
38                IF (COUNT .EQ. 0) THEN
39                   PRINT *, 'NO DATA IN FILE ', FILNAM
40                   STOP
41                ENDIF
42          *
43                AVERAG=SUM/COUNT
44          *
45                PRINT *,'THE AVERAGE WEIGHT IS ', AVERAG
46                END
```

At lines 11 through 13 we define our variables. We have to include NAME and HEIGHT. Even though we are not going to do anything with them, in order to get WEIGHT, we need to read all three from the file. At line 20 we get the data file name. Here we use an (A) as an input format for the terminal. The * format requires the user to enter the file name with quote marks around it. With the (A) format, the user can eliminate the quote marks. This fits our general approach of trying to make our programs easy to use.

Lines 22 to 27 open the file as unit 8 and check for possible errors. If an error occurs, a message is printed and the program stops. Lines 29 to 33 are an endless loop that reads the data from the file. The END = 101 instruction in the READ will cause the computer to exit to statment number 101 when the end of the data file is reached. Line 30 reads the data from file number 8. REC is a character variable that contains the input FORMAT code. We use the same format that we used when we wrote the file, so there should be no problems here.

The data items are counted and summed as they are read. When the loop terminates, the average is computed and printed out with an appropriate label.

PRACTICE

1. Use the two programs developed in this chapter to create a data file like PERDAT. Test out both programs and make sure that they work correctly.

2. The averaging program does not contain a CLOSE statement. Where is the proper place to insert one?

3. Write a program that reads the file and prints out the average weight of the people in the following catagories:
    Under five feet tall
    Between five and six feet tall
    Over six feet tall

4. Modify the program you developed in Exercise 2 so that the names of the people in each of the three categories are printed. The lists should be in alphabetical order.

26
USING THE COMPUTER: A SAMPLE PROBLEM

FORTRAN does not allow character and numeric data to be stored in the same array. This problem shows how programmers deal with this situation.

PROBLEM   A teacher plans to write a program to compute and print out grades for the students in the class. The teacher plans to give four tests during the semester, and grades will depend on how well the students have done on the tests. The data for each student is to be kept in a data file in this form:

DATA ITEM	TYPE	DESCRIPTION
Student name	Character	Maximum of 30 letters
Student ID number	Integer	Always nine digits
Test scores	Real	Between 0 and 100

SAMPLE   Mike Jefferson, 213144967, 78, 83, 77, 90
RECORD

The data file is kept on the school's computer. Programs already exist for entering students' records into the file and for adding test scores to records as the tests are given.

The teacher's program will be run once, at the end of the semester. The output should look like this:

```
WESTERN MARYLAND COLLEGE
COMPUTER SCIENCE 106
SECTION A6
FALL 1984


    NAME                    SCORES           TOTAL      GRADE


    JOHN SMITH     56     75   68    77       276         C
    CAROL JONES    77     81   75    80       313         B
                                     ·
                                     ·
                                     ·
                                   etc·

                                         CLASS AVERAGE: 281.7
```

The grades will be computed using the following rules:

IF TOTAL SCORE IS	THEN THE GRADE IS
Greater than average + (0.2 × average)	A
Less than an A, but greater than average + (0.15 × average)	B
Less than a B, but greater than average − (0.15 × average)	C
Less than a C, but greater than average − (0.2 × average)	D
Less than a D	F

ANALYSIS

The sample output is given in the problem statement. The program will need to know the name of the file in which the student data is kept. To make the program general, we will ask for the file name as an input when the program executes. The program will expect to find a name, ID number, and four scores for each student. We will have to include error checking, though, just in case some records are not in the correct form.

The grading rules seem clearly defined. If, for example, a student's score is *exactly* equal to average + (0.2 × average), then the student will receive a B. We know that grading schemes change frequently, so we will be especially careful to write that part of the program in a way that makes it easy to modify.

To store the data in the computer's memory, we will need to set up two arrays. One will be a character list that will store the names. The other will be a table that will store the test scores. The ID number is not used in the report, but since that might change in the future, we will also store the ID number in the table. The problem doesn't say how many students to expect. We'll set the program up to handle 50 students, but we'll also make it so that the maximum number of students is easily changed. So we need the following data items:

DATA ITEM	TYPE	DESCRIPTION
NAMES(50)	CHARACTER	Student names
TAB(50,5)	REAL	*Columns* 1. ID number 2. Test 1 3. Test 2 4. Test 3 5. Test 4
FILENAM	CHARACTER	Name of data file
SUM	REAL	Total score
COUNT	INTEGER	Number of students
AVERAGE	REAL	Average of scores
GRADE	CHARACTER	Student's letter grade
LETTER(5)	CHARACTER	Possible letter grades (A, B, C, D, F)
LEVEL(4)	REAL	Grade level cutoff values 1. 1.20 2. 1.15 3. 0.85 4. 0.80
NUMLEV	INTEGER	Number of levels (four)

LEVEL( ) contains the values needed to compute the grades. To make the computation simpler, the rules have been converted to a single number. If a score is greater than $1.20 \times$ average, it's an A. If it's $1.20 \times$ average or less, but greater than $1.15 \times$ average, it's a B, and so on.

The overall structure of the algorithm will look like this:

1. Initialize variables. Get file name. Open file.
2. Read data from file into arrays. Count the records.
3. Compute each student's total score.
4. Compute the class average.
5. Compute the grades and print the report.

In looking at this we notice that we have not yet created a variable to hold each student's total score. Since we have to print out the total for each student, we now decide to add another column to the table and put the total in there. Since we might some day want to modify the program to work with more that four tests, we'll put the total score into column 2. We also need the maximum row and column parameters. After these revisions, we have this:

DATA ITEM

TAB(50,6)   1. ID number   2. Total score   3–6. Test scores

MAXCOL=6
MAXROW=50

ALGORITHM
Part 1. Initialize variables; open data file

We'll set the global parameters here. We'll also input the data file name and open the file.

(1) DEFINE NAMES(50), TAB(50,6), LEVEL(4), LETTERS(5)
(2) Set MAXCOL to be 6
(3) Set MAXROW to be 50
(4) Set LETTERS(1)='A', LETTERS(2)='B', LETTERS(3)='C',
     LETTERS(4)='D', LETTERS(5)='F'
(5) Set NUMLEV=4
(6) Set LEVEL(1)=1.20, LEVEL(2)=1.15, LEVEL(3)=0.85,
     LEVEL(4)=0.80
(7) READ FILNAM
(8) OPEN #1, FILNAM—IF error print a message and STOP

Part 2. Read data from file and count the number of students

We also have to remember to check for input errors while reading.

(9)   Set COUNT to be 0
(10) LOOP with I going from 1 to MAXROW
      (10.1) IF end of file THEN EXIT LOOP
      (10.2) LOOP(J=1 to 6) INPUT #1: NAMES(I), TAB(I,J)
              (8.21) IF input error print a message and STOP
      (10.3) COUNT=COUNT+1

At this point we see that we have a problem. Column 2 of the table is to contain the student's total score. The data file, however, does not contain a value to be stored there. To make the INPUT instruction match the file record, we decide to put the ID number in column 2 of the table and the total score in column 1. So our data definition now looks like this,

DATA ITEM

TAB(50,6)   1. Total Score   2. ID number   3–6. Test scores and we can rewrite the algorithm so that the first column of TAB( ) is left empty.

> (9)　Set COUNT to be 0
> (10)　LOOP with I going from 1 to MAXROW
> 　　　(10.1)　IF end of file THEN EXIT LOOP
> 　　　(10.2)　LOOP(J=2 to 6) INPUT #1: NAMES(I), TAB(I,J)
> 　　　　　　(8.21)　IF input error print a message and STOP
> 　　　(10.3)　COUNT=COUNT+1

Now no data is read into TAB(I,1). When we begin to compute the total scores, we will have to initialize each of those locations to zero.

Part 3. Compute each student's total score

Here we loop through the table, add up the scores in each row, and put the total into column 1.

> (11)　LOOP with I going from 1 to COUNT.
> 　　　(11.1)　Set TAB(I,1) to be 0
> 　　　(11.2)　LOOP with K going from 3 to MAXCOL
> 　　　　　　(11.21)　TAB(I,1)=TAB(I,1)+TAB(I,K)

Part 4. Compute the class average

Once again we loop through the table. First we compute the total of the students' total scores; then we compute the average. SUM is a variable that holds the class total.

> (12)　Set SUM to be 0
> (13)　LOOP with I going from 1 to COUNT
> 　　　(14.1)　SUM=SUM+TAB(I,1)
> (14)　AVERAGE=SUM/COUNT

Here we recognize that if COUNT is 0, the division in step 12 will be illegal. We will have to be sure to check for this error condition at the end of Part 2.

Part 5. Compute the grades and print the report

First we will print the report headings. To do the grades, we will loop through the table and compare each student's total score with the average. Based on the values stored in LEVEL( ), we will compute a grade and store it in GRADE. Finally, we will print an output line for that student.

(15) Print headings
(16) LOOP with I going from 1 to COUNT
    (16.1) Set GRADE to be LETTER(1)
    (16.2) LOOP with K going from 1 to NUMLEV
        (16.21) IF TAB(I,1) is less than or equal to
                LEVEL(K)*AVERAGE then
                GRADE=LETTER(K+1)
    (16.3) Print NAMES(I),
                LOOP(L=3 to MAXCOL) TAB(I,L),
                TAB(I,1),
                GRADE
(17) Print 'CLASS AVERAGE ', AVERAGE
(18) Stop

The array LETTER contains the actual symbols to be printed as "grades." We set these up as parameters because they might change. (For example, in the future the school might decide to start giving plus and minus grades.) NUMLEV specifies the maximum number of checks to be made in order to compute a grade. Notice that if the score is less than LEVEL(NUMLEV)*AVERAGE, the student receives the letter grade stored in LETTER(NUMLEV+1). There are other ways to arrange this, but this way works correctly and is easy to understand.

PROGRAM

```
 1   *  PRINT STUDENT GRADES
 2   *
 3   *  R. W. DILLMAN
 4   *  MARCH, 1984
 5   *
 6   *  GLOBAL VARIABLES
 7   *   NAMES() -- CONTAINS STUDENT NAMES
 8   *   TAB() -- TABLE OF NUMERIC DATA
 9   *      COLUMNS
10   *         1: TOTAL SCORE
11   *         2: ID NUMBER
12   *         3-6: TEST SCORES
13   *   MAXROW -- MAXIMUM NUMBER OF STUDENTS
14   *   MAXCOL -- NUMBER OF COLUMNS IN TAB()
15   *   COUNT -- ACTUAL NUMBER OF STUDENTS
16   *   AVERAG -- AVERAGE OF STUDENTS SCORES
17   *
18   *  LOCAL VARIABLES
19   *   FILNAM -- NAME OF DATA FILE
```

(continued)

```
20   *   SUM -- TOTAL OF ALL STUDENTS SCORES
21   *   LETTER() -- SYMBOLS PRINTED AS GRADES (A,B,C,D,F)
22   *   LEVEL() -- PERCENTAGE OF AVERAGE USED TO DETERMINE GRADES
23   *   NUMLEV -- MAXIMUM NUMBER OF LEVELS
24   *   GRADE -- CONTAINS A PARTICULAR STUDENT'S GRADE
25   *
26   * INITIALIZE
27
28   *       CHARACTER NAMES*30, LETTER*1, GRADE*1, FILNAM*10, REC*40
29           INTEGER COUNT, MAXROW, MAXCOL, NUMLEV
30           REAL TAB, SUM, AVERAG
31   *
32           DIMENSION TAB(50,6), NAMES(50), LETTER(5), LEVEL(4)
33   *
34           DATA MAXROW/50/, MAXCOL/6/, NUMLEV/4/,REC/'(A30,I9,4I3)'/
35           DATA LETTER/'A','B','C','D','F'/
36           DATA LEVEL/1.2,1.15,.85,.80/
37   *
38   * OPEN DATA FILE
39   *
40           PRINT *, 'ENTER DATA FILE NAME'
41           READ (A), FILNAM
42           OPEN(9, NAME=FILNAM, IOSTAT=IOERR)
43           IF (IOERR .NE. 0) THEN
44              PRINT *, 'CANNOT OPEN FILE', FILNAM
45              PRINT *, '  ERROR CONDITION IS ', IOERR
46              STOP
47           ENDIF
48   *
49   * READ DATA FROM FILE
50   *
51           COUNT=0
52           DO 100 I=1,MAXROW
53              READ(9,REC, END=101, ERR=102), NAMES(I), (TAB(I,J),J=2,6)
54              COUNT=COUNT+1
55       100 CONTINUE
56   *
57   *            [INPUT ERROR ROUTINE]
58       102 CONTINUE
59           PRINT *,' ERROR IN READING FILE'
60           PRINT *,' LAST ITEM SUCCESSFULLY READ WAS:'
61           PRINT *,'    ITEM NUMBER: ',COUNT
62           PRINT *,'    NAME: ', NAME(COUNT)
63           STOP
64   *
65   * COMPUTE STUDENTS' TOTAL SCORES
```

(continued)

```
66   *
67      101 CONTINUE
68   *
69   *          [CHECK FOR EMPTY FILE]
70         IF (COUNT .EQ. 0) THEN
71            PRINT *,' NO DATA IN FILE', FILNAM
72            STOP
73         ENDIF
74   *
75         DO 200 I=1,COUNT
76            TAB(I,1)=0
77               DO 210 K=3,MAXCOL
78                  TAB(I,1)=TAB(I,1)+TAB(I,K)
79      210      CONTINUE
80      200 CONTINUE
81   *
82   * COMPUTE CLASS AVERAGE
83   *
84         SUM=0
85         DO 300 I=1,COUNT
86            SUM=SUM+TAB(I,1)
87      300 CONTINUE
88         AVERAG=SUM/COUNT
89   *
90   * COMPUTE GRADES AND PRINT REPORT
91   *
92   *          [HEADINGS]
93         PRINT *,'WESTERN MARYLAND COLLEGE'
94         PRINT *,'COMPUTER SCIENCE 106'
95         PRINT *,'SECTION A6'
96         PRINT *,'FALL 1984'
97         PRINT *
98         PRINT *, '                NAME            ',
99       #          '              SCORES         ',
100      #          '  TOTAL  ',
101      #          '  GRADE  ',
102  *
103  *          [NAMES AND GRADES]
104        DO 400 I=1,COUNT
105           GRADE=LETTER(1)
106           DO 410 K=1,NUMLEV
107              IF (TAB(I,1) .LE. LEVEL(K)*AVERAG) GRADE=LETTER(K+1)
108     410   CONTINUE
109           PRINT *, NAMES(I), (TAB(I,L),L=3,MAXCOL), TAB(I,1), GRADE
110     400 CONTINUE
111        PRINT *,'                    CLASS AVERAGE: ', AVERAG
112        END
```

In line 28 the character variables are defined. FILNAM is established as a ten-character string. If your system uses longer file names, you may have to adjust the length of FILNAM. Lines 35 and 36 determine the characteristics of the grading scheme. The grade-level cutoff percentages may be changed by editing line 36. Additional grades (e.g., B+, C–) can be added by editing both lines. Note that there must be one more grade symbol in LETTER than there are percentages in LEVEL.

In line 53 the READ statement gets data from the file. (The file was opened as unit number 9 at line 42.) When the end of the file is reached, the END instruction will cause the computer to jump to statement number 101. If any other kind of input error occurs, the ERR instruction will send the computer to statement number 102. Although the IOSTAT instruction can be used in READ and WRITE statements, its effectiveness requires that the programmer know the error-numbering scheme particular to the computer on which the program is to be executed. END and ERR do not give as much *specific* information as IOSTAT, but since they work the same way on all computers, their use is preferable. Notice that the error routine tries to identify the *place* in the data file where the error occurred. This is to help the user locate and fix the problem.

Lines 70 to 73 make sure the file is not empty. This is necessary to prevent a division by zero error at line 88. The PRINT statement from lines 98 to 101 is structured the way it is in order to line up the headings over the appropriate columns. This type of output control is better done with FORMAT statements, as is shown in Chapter 33.

PRACTICE

1. Enter this program into your computer. Set up a test data file and run the program. (If your computer system does not have a text editor for files, you may need to write a program that will let you build the data file.)

2. Alter the program so that it handles six tests instead of four.

3. The teacher would like to run the program at various times during the semester to see how the class is doing. Alter the program to make this possible. Among other things, this means that there will need to be some sort of end-of-line marker for each line in the data file. It will also be very important to check that each student has taken the same number of tests. This is not a trivial problem. Be sure to make your changes in the algorithm and test them out before you start to code.

4. The teacher would like to see the grade report in order of ID numbers. Add a sorting routine to the program. Where is the best place to insert such a routine in the code?

5. The heading information is specific to a single course. To make the program more general, modify the system so that the heading data is stored at the beginning of the data file. The program will read the heading data as input and print it as part of the output routine.

SUMMARY
FOR PART III

The main purpose of computer programs is to manipulate data. The way the data is *organized* when it is stored into the computer is important because the organization, or structure, of the data often determines the kinds of algorithms the programmer must develop to get the data processed. We looked at three kinds of data structures.

Lists are sets of data, all of the same type, that follow one another in sequence. By using lists a programmer can use a small set of instructions to tell the computer to manipulate large sets of similar data. This allows programs to be very powerful while remaining relatively small in size. There are many ways of coding list structures in computer languages. We looked at one of the easiest ones to use, the one-dimensional array.

Tables are sets of lists. Much commercial programming is concerned with processing tabular data. We looked at one way of doing this, namely, the two-dimensional array.

Files are sets of data, usually organized in the form of records, and usually stored *outside* of the computer's main memory. We looked at the *elementary* algorithms and input/output techniques that are used when processing files. In commercial environments data files are often extremely large. This means that programmers have to be very concerned with the amount of *time* it takes a program to locate a particular data item prior to processing it. There are books and courses whose only concern is how to do file processing efficiently.

PROGRAMMING PROBLEMS

The problems in this set are considerably more difficult than the ones at the end of Part II. You should read the problems very carefully before you begin to design your algorithms. You should spend time at the beginning thinking through the kinds of data structures that you will need. You should be prepared to throw away your algorithm and start over if it turns out that the structure you've chosen won't work. Don't be depressed if this happens—good programmers are willing to start over as many times as it takes to get the best algorithm. Time spent getting the right algorithm will save you hours of debugging and testing.

1.0

PROBLEM STATEMENT

Write a program to:

1. Input Roman numerals and output their integer equivalents,
2. Input integer numbers and output their Roman equivalents.

The user should be given a choice as to which routine is to be used. Roman numerals should be limited to 10 characters.

SAMPLE OUTPUT

```
ENTER NUMBER TO CHOOSE OPTION:
   1=ROMAN TO INTEGER
   2=INTEGER TO ROMAN
   0=EXIT


1
ENTER ROMAN NUMERAL (LIMIT OF TEN DIGITS) -- USE E TO EXIT
?XVII


RESULT: 17


ENTER ROMAN NUMERAL (LIMIT OF TEN DIGITS) -- USE E TO EXIT
E


ENTER NUMBER TO CHOOSE OPTION
   1=ROMAN TO INTEGER
   2=INTEGER TO ROMAN
   0=EXIT


2
ENTER INTEGER -- USE 0 TO EXIT


34


RESULT: XXXIV
```

1.1. Write a program to add Roman numerals. Also include subtraction.

1.2. Extend the above to include multiplication and division.

2.0

PROBLEM STATEMENT

Write a program which, given a date, will print out a calendar showing the week before and the week after the date given.

The date should be in the form: mm,dd,yy. Example, December 5, 1983, is given as 12,05,83.

The program should deal with dates in the range 1900 to 2050 (or thereabouts).

SAMPLE   ENTER TARGET DATE
OUTPUT   10,20,82

```
                    ** OCTOBER **
MONDAY   TUESDAY  WEDNESDAY  THURSDAY  FRIDAY  SATURDAY  SUNDAY
                     13         14       15       16       17
  18       19        20         21       22       23       24
  25       26        27
```

2.1. Print out any month on request. Include in the printout the last two days of the previous month and the first two days of the following month.

2.2. Compute and display the number of days between any two dates.

3.0
PROBLEM   Write a general-purpose graphing routine. Inputs should come from data
STATEMENT files. The program should be given the names of two data files. It should
           open both files, read the data contained in them, and plot a graph of one
           against the other.

SAMPLE   File #1: 3, −2, −6, 4, 4, 9
DATA   File #2: 45, 34, 30, 76, 98

SAMPLE   GRAPH OF DAT1 VERSUS DAT2
OUTPUT

```
             10,

              ,

              8,

              ,

              6,

              ,

              4,                              *        *

              ,                        *

              2,

     DAT1     ,

              0,   ,   ,   ,   ,   ,   ,   ,   ,   ,
              ,   10  20  30  40  50  60  70  80  90  100
             -2,                    *

              ,

             -4,

              ,

             -6,            *

              ,

             -8,

              ,

            -10,
                                DAT2
```

NOTE: EXTRA DATA IN DAT2

3.1. Calculate and display the correlation coefficient for the two sets.

4.0

PROBLEM STATEMENT

Write a program that will accept as input the daily price data on two stocks. The output should be a chart showing the relative performance of the stocks over the time period used.

SAMPLE DATA

Time period: 10/12/82 to 10/19/82 (closing price)
Stock #1: 112   112.4   112.2   112.6   113.1   113.2   113.5
Stock #2: 43.2   43.5   43.9   44.1   44.4   44.3   43.9

SAMPLE OUTPUT

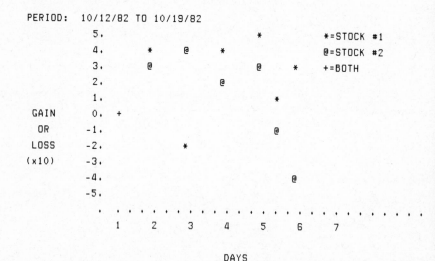

Note: Input data should be kept in a data file if possible, and preferably one stock per file.

The type of graph shown here is not necessarily the best way to do it. Use a better method if you find one.

4.1. Modify the program to graph three stocks.

4.2. Based on the data, project the trends of the stocks. Graph these points as day "T" on the chart (following day 7).

5.0

PROBLEM STATEMENT

A restaurant keeps track of the number of breakfasts, lunches, and dinners sold on any given day. Breakfasts are identified as meal type 1, lunches are identified as type 2, and dinners as type 3. The restaurant also keeps track of the total amount collected for each type of meal and the overall total amount collected. Write a program to automate this bookkeeping. Use zero as the end-of-data marker.

SAMPLE
OUTPUT

```
ENTER TYPE, AMOUNT -- USE 0,0 TO EXIT
1,5,23
1,4,09
2,6,50
1,3,22
2,5,89
2,7,25
3,11,36
0,0
```

TYPE	NUMBER SOLD	AMOUNT COLLECTED
----	------	---------
BREAKFAST	3	12,54
LUNCH	3	19,64
DINNER	1	11,36

```
TOTAL: 43,54
```

5.1. The restaurant must pay 5% sales tax on each meal sold. After-tax print are estimated as follows:

> Breakfast: 6%
> Lunch: 10%
> Dinner: 5%

Modify the program to print the sales tax and estimated profit for each type of meal.

6.0

PROBLEM
STATEMENT

Create two data files. In each file put a set of integer numbers, one per line, arranged in ascending order. Each file should contain a different set, and the sets should be of different lengths.

Write a program that will read the two files and produce a third file that contains the data from the first two merged together. This means that the third file should end up with all of the numbers, arranged in ascending order. (Note: The program should *not* use a sorting algorithm.)

SAMPLE
OUTPUT

```
FIRST FILE DATA: 1,3,5,5,7,8
SECOND FILE DATA: 2,3,3,5,9,10,16,23
RESULTING FILE: 1,2,3,3,3,5,5,5,7,8,9,10,16,23
```

6.1. Modify the program to merge three or more files. The names of the input files and the output file should be input by the user. What is the maximum number of files that can be merged by this program running on your computer?

7.0

PROBLEM STATEMENT   A data file contains information on people arranged as follows:

name, height, weight, sex, hair color, eye color, age

Set up a data file with at least 25 lines of data. Write a program to print out the names of everybody who has matches one or two particular characteristics.

SAMPLE OUTPUT

```
ENTER CHARACTERISTIC(S) FOR SEARCH -- USE * IF NULL
CHOOSE FROM:
          HEIGHT, WEIGHT, SEX, HAIR, EYES, AGE

SEX,EYES

SEX TYPE (M OR F)? M
EYE COLOR (BROWN, BLUE, GREEN, GREY)? GREEN

JAMES SMITH
MIKE JONES
TOMAS JOHNSON

ENTER CHARACTERISTICS FOR SEARCH -- USE * IF NULL
CHOOSE FROM:
          HEIGHT, WEIGHT, SEX, HAIR, EYES, AGE
AGE
ENTER AGE 23
MIKE JONES
SUSAN THOMAS
BEVERLY SMITH
BILL CONNERLY
```

7.1.   Modify the program to let the user ask for a match on from one to six input characteristics.

7.2.   Write a separate program that will allow you to modify the data in the file. You should be able to alter existing records, and to add and delete records.

8.0

PROBLEM STATEMENT   The Census Bureau is evaluating data obtained in the last census. One set of data includes the number of people living in a household, the total income of the household, its Zip Code, and a six-digit identifying number.

Write a program to analyze the data as follows:

A. Calculate the average household income grouped by the number of people in the household.
B. List the Zip Codes of the households whose incomes are above average for their respective groups.
C. Print a list of households that fall below the poverty line. The poverty level is based on the number of people in the household (n):

$$p = \$7500 + \$1000 * (n - 1.75)$$

Create a data file using data similar to this:

IN	ZIP	PEOPLE	INCOME
362357	20443	3	21365
378091	45701	5	16207
398801	22018	2	31804
		.	
		.	
		.	
		etc.	

SAMPLE OUTPUT

```
NUMBER IN
HOUSEHOLD        AVERAGE INCOME     ID NUMBERS
    1                21150            565443
                                      330567
                                      404556
    2                28440            202556
                                      403220
                                      332032
    3                24621            303324
                                      452401

POVERTY LINE             ID NUMBER
   14600                  450023
   16509                  479112
```

9.0

PROBLEM STATEMENT A college bookstore uses the following parameters to estimate sales of textbooks:

TYPE OF BOOK	PERCENTAGE OF STUDENTS ENROLLED WHO WILL BUY ONE
Required, new	95
Required, used before	70
Recommended, new	45
Recommended, used before	20

The following information is kept in each book: ID number, cost, number on hand, recommended/required, whether it was used last term (new/old).

Write a program that will input a set of book ID numbers and class sizes and print the number of books that must be ordered and the cost of the order.

SAMPLE
OUTPUT
```
ENTER BOOK NUMBER, CLASS SIZE -- 0,0 TO EXIT
2259, 30
8182, 135
      ,
      ,
      ,
    etc
0,0
BOOK: 2259 -- REQUIRED -- NEW -- $15.32
ON HAND: 8                     NEEDED: 22
COST: $306.40
                    ,
                    ,
                    ,
                  etc
TOTAL COST OF ORDER: $45204.45
```

9.1.   A second file contains records in the following form:

Book number, title, author, edition, publisher, publisher's address

Write a program that will take as input the book number and number needed (as generated by the first program) and will create a set of purchase orders. There should be one purchase order for each publisher.

SAMPLE
OUTPUT
```
Holt, Rinehart and Winston
401 Broadway
New York, N.Y. 10116
```

Title	Author	Edition	Number	Price	Total
Problem Solving with FORTRAN	Dillman	1	30	15.00	450.00
Geology	Smithfield	2	20	30.00	600.00
Modern Art	Brown	1	100	20.00	2000.00
			,		
			,		
			,		

```
Total $213317.26
```

10.0

PROBLEM
STATEMENT

Information on library books is stored in a data file as follows:

Title of book

Author

Catalog number

Checked out to (student ID number, 0 if not out)

Date due to be returned

Create a file with at least 25 entries. Write a program to:

A. Print a list of the titles of all books that are checked out. This should include the date they are due.

B. Given a date, print a list of all books due after (but not on) that date and the ID numbers of the students who have checked them out.

C. Given a student ID number, print a list of books checked out to that student.

SAMPLE
OUTPUT

Any easily readible form of output will do.

10.1. Given a catalog number, print out all the data about the book. Add this option to the program.

10.2. Write a separate program that allows books to be added to and deleted from the file.

10.3. Write a separate program that updates the "checked out to" and "date due" fields. Catalog number, student ID number, and date due should be input sequentially from another file.

11.0

PROBLEM
STATEMENT

Write a program to help a person choose a menu that fits within a set of dietary restrictions. The person should enter the name of the meal (breakfast, lunch, dinner), the maximum number of calories allowed, and any other restrictions (low sodium, low fat, high calcium, etc.). The program should present a series of selections and allow the user to choose. Dietary data should be kept in a file or series of files.

```
SAMPLE      SELECT MEAL
OUTPUT       ENTER
              1=BREAKFAST
              2=LUNCH
              3=DINNER
             3
             ENTER MAXIMUM NUMBER OF CALORIES FOR THIS MEAL
             1000
             SELECT DIETARY RESTRICTIONS
              ENTER
               1=LOW SODIUM
               2=LOW FAT
               3=HIGH PROTEIN
               4=HIGH CALORIE
              YOU MAY ENTER MORE THAN ONE -- USE 0 TO TERMINATE ENTRY
             1
             0
             MAIN DISH -- SELECT ONE -- CALORIES SO FAR: 0
              ENTER
               1=BROILED FLOUNDER (200)
               2=BAKED CHICKEN (300)
             1
             APPETIZER -- SELECT ONE -- CALORIES SO FAR: 200
              ENTER
               1=GREEN SALAD, LOW SALT DRESSING (75)
               2=BROILED MUSHROOMS, CRABMEAT STUFFING (110)
               3=BREADSTICKS (95)
```

And so on. At the end, the menu should be printed along with the calorie
total and any other necessary information.

11.1 Given a meal type as input, print a list of all low-sodium foods for
      that meal. Include calories for each food.

11.2 Extend the above to handle all of the available diet restrictions.

12.0

PROBLEM   Write a program to score true/false exams. Input data should come from a
STATEMENT   data file and should be in the following form:

      Student number,1,1,0,0,1,0,1,0,1,1,1,0,1,0,1,1,1

The student number is a four-digit integer. There should be one line of data for each student taking the test.

The first line of data in the file should provide the correct answers as follows:

1,1,0,0,1,1,0,1,1,1,0,1,0,1,1,1,1,9

where the 9 indicates end of data and is used to get the count of the number of answers.

The output should include for each student the student number, number of questions correct, and a list of questions answered incorrectly. The number of students taking the test should also be printed.

Assume a maximum of 40 students and a maximum of 50 questions per test.

SAMPLE OUTPUT	STUDENT	CORRECT	INCORRECT
	2135	15	3 17
	2204	17	
	3106	10	2 3 4 6 8 9 11
	2228	14	12
	4018	13	4 6 12 16

NUMBER OF STUDENTS TAKING THE TEST: 5

12.1. Compute the range, average, and standard deviation of the correct scores by student.

12.2. Based on the normal curve, with C as the average grade, print a letter grade for each student.

13.0

PROBLEM STATEMENT A weaver uses a number of different color threads in weaving cloth. The colors available are numbered as follows:

1.	White	8.	Pink
2.	Black	9.	Sky blue
3.	Gray	10.	Purple
4.	Yellow	11.	Orange
5.	Red	12.	Beige
6.	Blue	13.	Brown
7.	Green	14.	Light green

The weaver's loom is computer controlled and uses an input pattern of the following form:

:2:12:12:8:1:2:14:7:7:7:10:4:0:

where :n: indicates the next color thread to be chosen, and :0: indicates the end of a weaving sequence.
Write a program to:

1. Scan input strings such as the one above and verify that the data is in the correct form (i.e., never two colons together and no numbers bigger than 14).
2. Allow the weaver to enter "not allowed" sets of colors which may not appear together. For example, if [14,7] were a "not allowed" set, then the pattern :14:7: could not appear in the input string above. The program should scan the string and make a note of all occurrences of "not allowed" sets.

SAMPLE
OUTPUT

```
ENTER DATA FILE NAME
TESTDAT

ENTER 'NOT ALLOWED' SETS -- USE 0,0 TO EXIT
14,7
10,4
0,0

STRING NUMBER 1

ERROR SCAN COMPLETE: NO ERRORS

NOT ALLOWED        POSITION
:14:7:                7
:10:4:               11

RUN COMPLETE
```

Note: There will be a series of weaving input strings in the file, each terminated by :0:. The program should check each of them.

14.0

PROBLEM
STATEMENT

Write a subroutine or set of subroutines that simulates a standard deck of 52 cards. The program should be able to:

1. Shuffle the deck.
2. Deal out N hands of C cards each (up to a limit of 52), where N and C are inputs.
3. Deal out one card at a time on request.

The cards may be represented internally as numbers, but printouts should be in symbolic form.

SAMPLE
OUTPUT

```
ENTER NUMBER OF HANDS, CARDS PER HAND
5, 3
            HAND      CARDS
             1        10C   QH   3D
             2              JS   4C   7S
             3              KH   AD   2C
             4              QC   3H   5D
             5              6S   JD   8H
```

Note: This program is best done by using functions and subroutines to do each of the shuffling and dealing tasks. The hands should be displayed in sorted order (C, D, H, S).

14.1. Test the program to verify that (a) no card will ever show up twice in the same deal, and (b) each card is equally likely to be dealt.

14.2. Use the routine(s) to deal hands and have the computer play any of the following games:

Hearts   Gin rummy
Bridge   Poker

15.0

PROBLEM
STATEMENT

A peg game is played on the board pictured below. Each X represents a peg placed in a hole; the 0 represents an empty hole:

```
            X X X
            X X X
        X X X X X X X
        X X X O X X X
        X X X X X X X
            X X X
            X X X
```

```
      A B C
      D E F
  G H I  J K L M
  N O P Q R S  T
  U V W X Y Z 9
      8 7 6
      5 4 3
```

This pattern is used as a reference to let the player input his or her move.

A move is made by jumping a peg over an immediate neighbor into a hole adjacent to the neighbor. The jumped peg is then removed from the board. The object of the game is to remove all of the pegs except one.

SAMPLE
OUTPUT

```
MOVE: 1                    S ; Q    PEGS REMOVED: 1
              X X X
              X X X
      X X X X X X X
      X X X X O O X
      X X X X X X X
              X X X
              X X X
```

Note: The results of a first move are shown. S;Q means "peg in hole S moved to hole Q," using the lettering scheme shown above. A "move" may consist of a series of "jumps," as in checkers.

15.1. Run the game with differing starting configurations. Demonstrate that your algorithm will find a solution if one is possible.

15.2. Modify the algorithm so that it tries to leave the last peg in the center position.

16.0

PROBLEM
STATEMENT

A familiar puzzle/game is played by sliding eight numbered tiles back and forth in a three-by-three square as shown below:

```
  6 3 2
  5 4
  1 7 8
```

The tiles can slide into the empty space, but cannot be moved otherwise.

The object is to find a sequence of moves that produced the following configuration:

```
  1 2 3
  8   4
  7 6 5
```

SAMPLE
OUTPUT

```
MOVE: 1                           TILE: 8
          6      3      2
          5      4      8
          1      7

MOVE: 2                           TILE: 7
          6      3      2
          5      4      8
          1             7

             etc.
```

16.1. Demonstrate that your algorithm will find the solution in a minimum number of moves.

17.0

PROBLEM
STATEMENT

The rules for the game of Life were published in *Scientific American* in October 1970 (pages 120–123). Write a computer program that plays Life.

SAMPLE
OUTPUT

```
ENTER INITIAL CONFIGURATION -- USE Z TO EXIT
      1 2 3 4 5
      6 7 8 9 A
      B C D E F
      G H I J K
      L M N O P
C
D
E
Z
INITIAL CONFIGURATION IS:

         * * *

CONFIRM
YES
GAME BEGINS:

1     * * *

2       *
        *
        *

3     * * *

         etc.
```

17.1. Some patterns will need more room than is available on the screen. Modify your program so that the current and two prior patterns are stored in ARRAYS. Allow the user to center the display on any section of a pattern.

17.2. Modify the program so that the sequence of patterns is stored in a data file. Allow the user to print the data file (after the run is complete, of course) as hard copy or display selected patterns on the screen.

18.0

PROBLEM
STATEMENT

Write a program that finds a path through a maze. Represent the maze as a two-dimensional array with each array location being either clear (part of a path) or blocked (part of a wall). Input the maze from a data file. Print the maze as below. Output the path as a series of (x, y) coordinates.

SAMPLE
MAZE

```
X O X O X X X X X X
X O X O O O O X O X
X O X X X X O X O X
X O O O O X O X O X
X X X O X X O X O X
X O O O X X O O O X
X O X O O X X O X X
X O X X O X X O X X
X X X O X X X O O X
X O O O O X O O X X
X X X X X X O X X X
```

SAMPLE
OUTPUT

```
ENTER
(11,4)
(10,4)
(10,5)
(10,6)
(10,7)
(9,7)
(8,7)
   .
   .
   .
(2,8)
(2,7)
(1,7)
EXIT
```

18.1.   Alter the program so that the path through the maze is displayed graphically as a series of "+" characters.

18.2.   Time the computer as it solves the sample maze. Rewrite the program so that it finds the solution faster. Run a series of tests to verify that the second one is, in fact, the faster algorithm.

IV
SUBPROGRAMS, STRINGS, AND FORMATTED OUTPUT

27
LOGIC: MODULAR PROBLEM SOLVING

DEFINITIONS

Module	A small algorithm or computer language routine which performs one specific activity.
Interface	The passing of data values into and out of a module.
Global Data	Data items which are accessible by all modules in a program.
Local Data	Data items which cannot be used outside of the module in which they are defined.
Stepwise Refinement	A way of doing program design by starting with a broad description of the solution and then gradually adding details until the final solution is evolved.
Top-down Design	The general name given to the use of a collection of program design, coding, and testing techniques, including stepwise, modular design and structured programming.

STEPWISE REFINEMENT

As the problems a programmer is asked to solve grow more difficult, the solutions tend to grow larger and more complex. At some point the algorithm becomes too much to keep in mind all at once. Stepwise refinement is a design tool which deals with this situation.

We have been using stepwise refinement for some time now, though we have not described it by name. In developing algorithms for the longer problems, we've first sketched out a "summary" solution. For example, in Chapter 26, we summarized the solution to the grading problem as:

Part 1. Initialize variables and open the data file.
Part 2. Read data from the file.
Part 3. Compute student totals.
Part 4. Compute class average.
Part 5. Compute grades and print report.

If you examine each of these "parts," you will see that each one can exist independently of the others. We can, for example, read data from the file without worrying about what the data will be used for later. To write the part of the program that computes the class average, all we need to know is what the table looks like. We don't need to know what the specific values of the data are.

In dividing the problem into pieces like this, we are doing what is called *modular design*. Each "part" is a module. A module is a small (usually one page or less) algorithm that performs one specific activity. The set of modules used together solve the problem.

Stepwise refinement is a design technique which is applied to modules. In using stepwise refinement, a programmer first writes a general description for a module. This is called the first *level* of the module's design. The first level for module 2 in our example is:

Module 2
Level 1

Read data from file and count the number of students.

Notice that this is *not* an algorithm. It will become one eventually, but at the beginning the idea is to give a *general* description and leave out the details. In level 2 we will expand the description somewhat.

Level 2

Read data from file and count students.

      (1)   Initialize COUNT to 0
      (2)   LOOP until end of file or input error
          (2.1)   READ data record into table
          (2.2)   Add 1 to COUNT

You can see that what we've done is add more detail to the description given in level 1.

Here is why stepwise refinement is useful. At the beginning, when we were thinking about the *whole problem*, the most important thing was that we managed to identify all the *tasks* we needed to perform in order to solve the problem. At that point we didn't care *how* we would accomplish the tasks, but we did need to know *what* we had to accomplish. The first level of the design is simply a list of "things to be done."

There may be things on the list that we already know how to do. In our example, module 1 is to open the file. Since we have opened files before, we don't expect to have to do much work on that module. (Just knowing this is useful; by considering at each of the modules in the list we can get a rough estimate of how much time it is going to take us to solve the problem.) In fact, it will usually happen that some modules are easier to design than others. Professional programmers often work in teams, with the easiest modules being given to the less experienced members of the team.

Once we have organized the first level, we can begin to think about *how* to accomplish the tasks that are outlined in the individual modules. If a particular task looks difficult, we can continue by breaking the module up into a set of subtasks. This is what we did to get level 2 of the example.

You can see that level 2 is still not a complete algorithm. What it is is a more detailed breakdown of level 1. Where level 1 gives a general description of the task, level 2 gives a general description of the steps we'll have to go through to perform the task. From this we can develop level 3:

Level 3

Read data from file and count students.

    (1)   Set COUNT to be 0
    (2)   LOOP with I going from 1 to MAXROW
        (2.1)   IF end of file THEN EXIT LOOP
        (2.2)   INPUT #1: NAMES(I), LOOP(J=2 to 6) TAB(I,J)
            (2.21)   IF input error print a message and STOP
        (2.3)   COUNT=COUNT+1

Now we have an actual algorithm. But we also have something else—because *this* algorithm was developed from a level 1 description, and because that level 1 description was part of the set of descriptions that we know we need to solve the problem, we are *sure* that this algorithm will fit into our final overall solution.

For small problems, this knowledge isn't too important. If we can think the entire problem through in a couple of hours, the odds are that we'll be able to make everything work with no trouble. Commercial programming problems, however, are seldom that small. A typical problem may take five programmers six months to complete. In that kind of situation, *top-down modular* design (which is what this whole process is called) provides the framework that holds everything together.

INTERFACES

There is one part of the top-down modular design process that we haven't talked about yet. If you look at the module 2 example, you notice that it sits all by itself. It isn't connected to any other algorithms the way it was in Chapter 26.

This is an advantage in that the algorithm can be developed independently of the algorithms in the other modules, but it carries a disadvantage in that the person who is developing it doesn't know anything about the data names being used in the other modules.

With *local* data items this doesn't matter. Since those variables won't be accessed by any other part of the final program, the programmer can set them up however he or she wants to. In this example the local items are I and J, both of which are loop counters. The *global* data items are:

NAMES( ) List of student names
TAB( )   Table of numeric data
COUNT   Count of the students

These items are used in many different places in the design. Since their values must be passed into this particular module from somewhere else, and then passed on after this module finishes its processing, the programmer must make sure that the names and values match up correctly. This connection between any one module and the rest of the design is called an *interface*. The interface specifies what data must be *input to* and/or *output from* a module for it to function correctly. If the interface is not *exactly* correct, that is, if the right values are not stored into the right data names, the module will produce incorrect results.

For example, here are the interfaces for the problem we did in Chapter 26:

MODULE	GLOBAL DATA USED	NEW GLOBAL DATA PRODUCED
1. Initialize Open file	None	NAME(50) defined TAB(50,6) defined LEVEL(4) LETTERS(5) MAXROW MAXCOL NUMLEV FILNAM file is opened
2. Read data Count inputs	MAXROW	NAME( ) TAB( ) COUNT
3. Compute total score	COUNT MAXCOL TAB( )	TAB( ) column 1
4. Compute class average	COUNT TAB( )	AVERAGE
5. Compute grades Print report	COUNT TAB( ) NAME( ) AVERAGE LETTER( ) LEVEL( ) NUMLEV MAXCOL	None

Module 1 is the first to be executed. It defines the arrays, inputs the data file name, and opens the file. Although it *produces* no actual data, it sets everything up for the rest of the program. Module 2 is an *input* module. It moves data *into* the data structures that were defined in module 1. Modules 3 and 4 are *processing* modules. They manipulate data stored in global variables. Module 5 is a processing and *output* module. It manipulates global data, but it also moves data *out of* the computer so that it can be displayed for the user to see.

Since different modules are often designed by different programmers (who use different names for the data items), and since keeping close track of the module interfaces is so important, the information is usually kept in a special chart. The chart lists the global items that are used in each module and also specifies the variable names to be used in the final program. This chart allows each programmer to make up his or her own data item names while ensuring that the correct variable names will be used to replace the item names when the program is coded. The chart for our example might have looked like this:

| | MODULE NUMBER | | | |
DESCRIPTION	1	2	5	VARIABLE
Name list	NAMES( )	NAMDAT( )	NAMES( )	NAME(50)
Data table	TAB( )	TABLE( )	TABLE( )	T(50,6)
Maximum rows	MAXR	ROWLIMIT	RMAX	MAXROW
Maximum columns	MAXC	COLIMIT	CMAX	MAXCOL
Number of students	NUMBS	SNUMB	SNUMB	COUNT
•	•	•	•	•
•	•	•	•	•
•	•	•	•	•

and so on, until all the global variables are listed. Notice that the names used in the various modules can be the same or different. It depends on the programmer's choice. If only one or two people are designing the program, then it's usually a good idea to use the same names throughout all the modules.

Along with the module interface chart goes a data structure chart. This chart tells what each list, or column in a table, is used for.

Variable Name: T

Description: Main data table

Size: 50 rows, 6 columns

Columns:

1. Total score
2. ID number
3. Test score no. 1
4. Test score no. 2
5. Test score no. 3
6. Test score no. 4

By using this chart, each programmer can set the proper subscript values at the beginning of a module. This can be done *after* the logic for the module has been developed. If you look back at the algorithms we developed in Chapter 26, you'll see that we used constant numbers for the column variables. These can now be replaced with parameters. Here, for example, is what modules 2 and 3 would look like:

Module 2

Read data from data file and count students.

Level 3

```
(0)  GLOBAL MAXCOL, MAXROW, COUNT
(0)  GLOBAL NAMES(MAXROW), TAB(MAXROW,MAXCOL)
(0)  FIRST=2, LAST=MAXCOL
(1)  Set COUNT to be 0
(2)  LOOP with I going from 1 to MAXROW
     (2.1)  IF end of file THEN EXIT LOOP
     (2.2)  INPUT #1: NAMES(I), LOOP(J=FIRST to LAST)
            TAB(I,J)
            (2.21) IF input error print a message and STOP
     (2.3)  COUNT=COUNT+1
(3)  RETURN
```

Module 3

Compute each student's total score.

Level 3

```
(0)  GLOBAL MAXCOL, MAXROW, COUNT
(0)  GLOBAL NAMES(MAXROW), TAB(MAXROW,MAXCOL)
(0)  TOTCOL=1, TEST1=3, TESTEND=MAXCOL
(1)  LOOP with I going from 1 to COUNT
     (1.1)  Set TAB(I,TOTCOL) to be 0
     (1.2)  LOOP with K going from TEST1 to TESTEND
            (1.21)  TAB(I,TOTCOL)=TAB(I,TOTCOL)+TAB(I,K)
(2)  RETURN
```

Here, the steps numbered (0) are not really part of the algorithm. Instead they describe the interface. They provide information that explains where the module is to access the global data that it needs. We add the RETURN at the end of each module to indicate where it ends. We will see how modules like these are connected together and run in the next chapter, but an example of the code for module 3 might look like this:

```
1                      SUBROUTINE TOTALS(MAXCOL,MAXROW,COUNT,NAMES,TAB)
2          *
3                      INTEGER MAXCOL,MAXROW,COUNT,TOTCOL,TEST1,LAST
4                      CHARACTER NAMES*30
5                      REAL TAB
6          *
7                      PARAMETER (TOTCOL=1, TEST1=3, LAST=MAXCOL)
8          *
9                      DIMENSION NAMES(MAXROW), TAB(MAXROW,MAXCOL)
10         *
11                     DO 100 I=1,COUNT
12                        TAB(I,TOTCOL)=0
13                        DO 200 K=TEST1,LAST
14                           TAB(I,TOTCOL)=TAB(I,TOTCOL)+TAB(I,K)
15         200        CONTINUE
16         100 CONTINUE
17                     RETURN
18                     END
```

This is an example of a *subroutine*. Line 1 defines the interface to the routine. Line 18 marks the physical end of the routine; line 17 indicates the logical exit. In line 9 we dimension the arrays by using data names. This is allowed in subroutines, but *only* if the data names are part of the interface. The next chapter will explain the syntax of subroutines and the other kind of FORTRAN module, the function.

PRACTICE

1. Rewrite all of the algorithms in Chapter 26 as modules. Be sure to specify the interfaces.

2. Module 2 is the only module that uses the file, but the file is opened in module 1 (It is never closed.). Rewrite modules 1 and 2 so that the file name is input in module 1, but the file is opened, read, and closed entirely in module 2.

3. Design a new module which will sort the data in NAMES() and TAB() into ascending order based on the student ID numbers.

28
SYNTAX: FUNCTIONS AND SUBROUTINES

DEFINITIONS

Main program	A set of FORTRAN code, terminated by an END statement. The main program is always executed first when the main program is executed.
Subprogram	A set of FORTRAN code which is isolated from the main program. A subprogram must include at least one RETURN statement and must terminate with END.
Function	A type of subprogram that returns a value in its name.
Subroutine	A type of subprogram that is called by a CALL instruction.
FUNCTION	The FORTRAN instruction used to define functions.
SUBROUTINE	The FORTRAN instruction used to define subroutines.

SUBPROGRAMS

Subprograms are independent sets of code that a programmer places after a main program and then calls into use during the execution of the main program. There are two types of subprograms: subroutines and functions. This picture shows the setup of a typical program using subprograms:

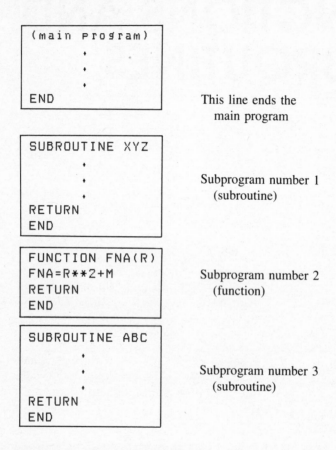

This line ends the
main program

Subprogram number 1
(subroutine)

Subprogram number 2
(function)

Subprogram number 3
(subroutine)

There is no limit to the number of subprograms a program can have. Notice that the very *last* instruction in the main program and in *each* subprogram is END.

SUBROUTINES

A *subroutine* is a set of FORTRAN statements which is separated from the main program and which is called into use whenever it is needed. The CALL instruction is used to invoke a subroutine. The RETURN statement is used to leave a subroutine.

EXAMPLE

MAIN PROGRAM

```
* MAIN PROGRAM
*
*
      X=0
      CALL ABC
        ↓
        ↓
        ↓
      END
```

SUBROUTINE

```
* SUBROUTINE ABC STARTS HERE
*
      SUBROUTINE ABC
      REAL VAR, Q
      READ *, Q
      VAR=VAR*Q
      PRINT *, VAR
        ↓
        ↓
        ↓
      RETURN
      END
*
* SUBROUTINE ABC ENDS HERE
```

A subroutine is a set of FORTRAN instructions. Its purpose is to give the programmer flexibility in designing and coding programs. By using subroutines, a program may be written and tested in small "chunks," which will be merged together to produce the final version. This approach is called *modular programming*. Most professionals agree that programmers who use modular programming techniques finish their programs sooner and make fewer errors than programmers who do not.

Subroutines are called into use by the execution of a CALL instruction. The CALL sends the computer to the *first line* of the subroutine. Inside the subroutine, the execution of a RETURN instruction sends the computer back to the *next line after the CALL*.

In the example above, the CALL statement sends the computer down to the line where the subroutine begins. Notice that subroutines are called by name, in this case ABC. Once the computer reaches the subroutine, it continues to execute until it comes to a RETURN statement. The RETURN instructs it to go back to the line of the original CALL and continue on from there.

The syntax for the CALL is very simple:

CALL subroutine name

A subroutine *must* have at least one RETURN statement. It may have more than one. Subroutines may contain CALLs which call other subroutines, but care should be taken to ensure that a subroutine does not call itself.

EXAMPLE   Incorrect use of CALL

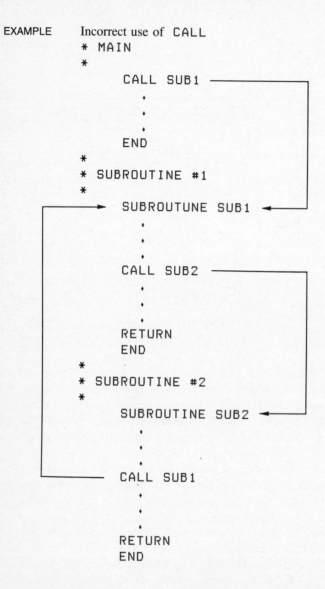

```
* MAIN
*
         CALL SUB1
            .
            .
            .
         END
*
* SUBROUTINE #1
*
         SUBROUTUNE SUB1
            .
            .
            .
         CALL SUB2
            .
            .
            .
         RETURN
         END
*
* SUBROUTINE #2
*
         SUBROUTINE SUB2
            .
            .
            .
         CALL SUB1
            .
            .
            .
         RETURN
         END
```

In this case the main program calls subroutine SUB1. SUB1 then calls SUB2. This is perfectly legal, but before a RETURN is reached in SUB2, SUB1 is called again. This sets up an endless loop of subroutine calls that quickly exhausts the computer's ability to remember the sequence of returns necessary to get back to the main program. At that point an error message prints out and the program stops.

EXAMPLE   Correct use of CALL

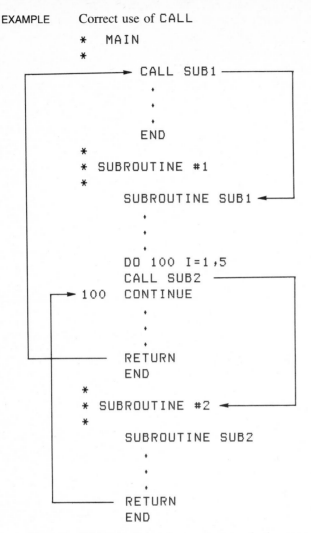

```
*    MAIN
*
         CALL SUB1
           ·
           ·
           ·
         END
*
* SUBROUTINE #1
*
         SUBROUTINE SUB1
           ·
           ·
           ·
         DO 100 I=1,5
         CALL SUB2
100      CONTINUE
           ·
           ·
           ·
         RETURN
         END
*
* SUBROUTINE #2
*
         SUBROUTINE SUB2
           ·
           ·
           ·
         RETURN
         END
```

Here the CALL in the main program sends the computer to SUB1. SUB1 then calls SUB2. SUB2 completes its processing and returns to SUB1. Since the call statement in SUB1 is inside of a loop, SUB2 will be called again. In fact, SUB2 will be called five times in succession before the RETURN in SUB1 is reached and the computer returns to the main program.

We can now describe a general structure for *all* FORTRAN programs. The first module in any FORTRAN program *must* be the main program. The main program may be defined by a PROGRAM statement such as this:

```
PROGRAM TESTIT
    ·
    ·
    ·
END
```

The `PROGRAM` statement is not required, however, and is usually omitted. The last line of the main program *must* be an `END` statement. In fact, the last line of *every* FORTRAN program or subprogram must be an `END` statement.

Subprograms must begin with either a `SUBROUTINE` statement or a `FUNC-TION` statement (we'll look at FUNCTIONS later on). Subprograms *must* end with `END` statements. Subprograms must be listed after the main program. There is no limit to the number of subprograms you can have, but they may not contain each other. This, for example, is illegal:

```
SUBROUTINE QRST
       ¹
       ¹
       ¹
SUBROUTINE INSIDE
       ¹
       ¹
       ¹
RETURN
END
```

Once a subprogram has been started, no additional subprograms may be started until the first one ends.

USING SUBROUTINES

Subroutines are used to divide the work a program has to do into small sets of instructions called *modules*. Modules are not a part of FORTRAN itself, but are logical constructs which are used by the programmer to make programs easier to design, code, and test.

For example, suppose you are designing a program to read in a set of numbers and print out the sum of all the numbers in the set that are above the average. In analyzing this problem, you identify four tasks the computer will have to do:

1. Read in the set of numbers and count them.
2. Compute the average of the set.
3. Compute the sum of the numbers greater than the average.
4. Print the result.

Each of these tasks can be programmed independently. This means, for example, that you can write a FORTRAN routine to compute the average of a set of numbers *without* knowing exactly what the specific numbers will be. A task that can be set up this way is called a *module*. As an example we will show the program for the second of these four tasks.

In this example, to compute the average, you only need to know the name of the array in which the values are stored, and the count of the values in the array.

Inputs to Module

Array name: A (   )
Number of values to be averaged: COUNT

Output from Module

Average: AVG

FORTRAN Code

```
 1    *  COMPUTE AVERAGE
 2    *
 3    *  GLOBAL VARIABLES
 4    *     A() -- LIST TO BE AVERAGED
 5    *     COUNT -- NUMBER OF ITEMS ON THE LIST
 6    *     AVG -- AVERAGE OF LIST
 7    *
 8    *  LOCAL VARIABLES
 9    *     SUM -- SUM OF ITEMS ON LIST
10    *
11          SUBROUTINE AVERG(A,COUNT,AVG)
12          REAL A, SUM, AVG
13          INTEGER COUNT
14    *
15    *  INITIALIZE
16    *
17          DIMENSION A(COUNT)
18          SUM=0
19    *
20    *  COMPUTE SUM AND AVERAGE
21    *
22          DO 100 I=1,COUNT
23              SUM=SUM+A(I)
24      100 CONTINUE
25    *
26          AVG=SUM/COUNT
27    *
28          RETURN
29          END
```

This routine is designed to be called in by some other routine, probably the main program. Line 11 defines the subroutine. Notice that the *interface* to this routine is contained within the parentheses after the subroutine name. In this case the array A and the COUNT are *inputs* to the subroutine, while the variable AVG is an *output*.

Lines 12 and 13 define the variables. Remember that the *names* used to identify the variable locations in the subroutine do not have to be the same names that were used in the routine that called the subroutine. For example, the CALL statement for this subroutine might look like this:

```
CALL AVERG(DATLIS,NUMB,AVRAG)
```

Any names may be used in the subroutine. There are only two restrictions:

1. There must be *exactly* the same number of variable names in the SUBROUTINE interface list as there are in the CALL statement for that subroutine.
2. When the CALL variables and the SUBROUTINE variables are lined up on a one-to-one basis, the corresponding variables must be of the same type. For example:

```
CALL AVERG(DATLIS,  NUMB,  AVRAG)
SUBROUTINE AVERG(A,   COUNT,   AVG)
```

Types: DATLIS and A—REAL
NUMB and COUNT—INTEGER
AVRAG and AVG—REAL

If the types do not match, an error message will be printed and the program will stop.

At line 17 we dimension the array. We use the interface variable COUNT to supply the size of the dimension. Variables may be used to dimension arrays within subprograms, but *only* if they are integers and *only* if they are interface variables. (PARAMETER names may be used also, of course, but remember that PARAMETER names are not variables.)

A special case arises when character variables are passed through a subprogram interface. The CHARACTER statement insists that the *length* of the variable be declared as an integer constant. If this rule were strictly enforced, the programmer would have to know the exact length of each character string in the interface ahead of time. This is often very difficult to do, so to avoid the problem, FORTRAN allows a special use of CHARACTER which applies *in subprograms only*.

```
        SUBROUTINE ABC(INCHAR)
*
        CHARACTER INCHAR*(*)
*
            .
            .
            .
        RETURN
        END
```

Here (*) is used as the length declaration. Its effect is to set the length of INCHAR to be exactly the same as the length of the variable used in the CALL to this routine. Generally *all* character variables in subprograms should be defined this way.

Lines 18 to 26 compute the average of the numbers in A ( ). The average is stored in the variable AVG. Since AVG is an interface variable, its value will be *passed back* to the calling routine when the RETURN statement is executed.

Thus the entire averaging program can be written as a series of modules each of which is coded in FORTRAN as a subroutine.

Good programmers tend to write *all* of their programs as a series of subprograms. Each subprogram does a specific job, and each is called in when it is needed. The next chapter contains an example—the program we developed in Chapter 26 is shown rewritten in modular form.

FUNCTIONS

A function is a special type of subprogram. Rather than starting with the word SUB-ROUTINE, functions start with the word FUNCTION. There are two ways in which FORTRAN functions differ from FORTRAN subroutines. Other than that they are *exactly* identical.

The first difference is that the *name* of a function actually identifies a variable location in the computer's memory. This is not true of subroutine names. Here is an example of a function that finds the larger of two numbers:

```
1     *  MAIN
2     *
3            REAL X,Y
4     *
5            PRINT *, 'ENTER TWO NUMBERS'
6            READ *, X,Y
7     *
8            PRINT *, 'THE BIGGEST IS ', BIGONE(X,Y)
9            END
10    *
11    *  SUBPROGRAM
12    *
13            REAL FUNCTION BIGONE(X,Y)
14    *
15            REAL X,Y
16            IF (X .GT. Y) THEN BIGONE=X ELSE BIGONE=Y
17            RETURN
18            END
```

Look at the function first. The name of the function is BIGONE. In line 16 the variable X and Y are compared, and the larger of the two values is stored into BIGONE. Notice that the *name* of the function acts like a variable.

IMPORTANT In a FORTRAN function, the name of the function *must* assigned a value before the RETURN is executed. The name of a subroutine *cannot* be assigned a value.

If no value is assigned, an error will occur.

Function names follow the same rules that regular variable names do. Because this function name begins with the letter B, it is automatically real. In line 13 we could omit the REAL specifier. We put it in because we always try specifically to define the types of our major variables.

Now look at the main program. Two numbers are input at line 6. These are passed to the function in the interface list when the function is *invoked* in the middle of the PRINT statement in line 8.

IMPORTANT   A FORTRAN function *must* have at least one variable name in its interface list. This is not true of subroutines.

The function stores the larger value in BIGONE and returns. When the function is called, the computer has just finished printing THE BIGGEST IS in line 8. When the RETURN at line 17 is executed, the computer continues on in line 8 and prints out the contents of BIGONE.

INTRINSIC FUNCTIONS

A number of "built-in" or *intrinsic* functions are supplied as part of the FORTRAN language. These functions have already been defined, and may be used at any time. A partial list is given below. Refer to the *FORTRAN Language Reference Manual* for additional information.

Types of inputs and outputs are specified as R = real, I = integer, C = character. Some functions return a value of the same type as the input where the input can be either real or integer. These are identified as I/R.

| | | TYPE OF | | |
FUNCTION	NAME	INPUT	OUTPUT	FUNCTION RETURNS
INT(X)	Truncate	R	I	Integer part of X.
MOD(X,Y)	Remainder	I/R	I/R	Remainder of X/Y.
MAX(X1,X2,...)	Maximum	I/R	I/R	Largest of the set of inputs.
MIN(X1,X2,...)	Minimum	I/R	I/R	Smallest of the set of inputs.
LEN(X)	Length	C	I	Number of characters in X.
INDEX(X,Y)	Substring	C	I	Location of beginning of substring Y in string X. Zero if Y is not contained in X.
EXP(X)	Exponential	R	R	e^X
LOG(X)	Log e	R	R	Natural LOG of X.
LOG10(X)	Log 10	R	R	LOG base-10 of X.
SIN(X)	Sine	R	R	Sine of X, X in radians.
COS(X)	Cosine	R	R	Cosine of X, X in radians.
TAN(X)	Tangent	R	R	Tangent of X, X in radians.
CHAR(X)	Collate	I	C	Character equivalant of I in the computer's collating sequence. See *Computer User's Guide*.
ICHAR(X)	Collate	C	I	Position of C in the computer's collating sequence.

PRACTICE

1. Write a subroutine that inputs an array and returns the array in sorted order. Why is it better to use a subroutine than a function for this task?

2. Write a function that inputs an integer number that is larger than 0 and returns:

   1—if the number is odd.
   2—if the number is even.
   0—if the number is an error.

3. Write a function that inputs a character string of digits and returns the integer number equivalent. Be sure to check the input string to make sure that it contains only digits. What value will the function return if there *is* an input error? Be sure to handle both positive and negative integers.

4. Modify the function in Problem 3 so that it handles real numbers.

29
USING THE COMPUTER: A SAMPLE PROBLEM

Here is the program we developed in Chapter 26 rewritten using subprograms.

PROGRAM

```
1    * COMPUTE STUDENT GRADES
2    *
3    * R. W. DILLMAN
4    * MARCH, 1983
5    *
6    * GLOBAL VARIABLES
7    *   NAMES() -- CONTAINS STUDENT NAMES
8    *   TAB() -- TABLE OF NUMERIC DATA
9    *     COLUMNS
10   *        1: TOTAL SCORE
11   *        2: ID NUMBER
12   *        3-6: TEST SCORES
13   *   MAXROW -- MAXIMUM NUMBER OF STUDENTS
14   *   MAXCOL -- NUMBER OF COLUMNS IN TAB()
15   *   COUNT -- ACTUAL NUMBER OF STUDENTS
16   *   AVERAG -- AVERAGE OF STUDENTS SCORES
17   *
18   * SUBPROGRAMS
19   *   GETDAT -- READ DATA FROM FILE -- (SUB)
20   *   TOTALS -- COMPUTE STUDENTS' TOTAL SCORES -- (SUB)
21   *   AVG    -- COMPUTE CLASS AVERAGE -- (SUB)
22   *   GRADES -- PRINT GRADE REPORT -- (SUB)
23   *   SYMBOL -- COMPUTE GRADE FOR A GIVEN SCORE -- (FUN)
24   ****************************************************************
```

(continued)

```
25      * MAIN PROGRAM
26      * INITIALIZE GLOBALS
27      *
28              CHARACTER NAMES*30
29              INTEGER COUNT, MAXROW, MAXCOL
30              REAL TAB, AVERAG
31      *
32              DIMENSION TAB(50,6), NAMES(50)
33      *
34              DATA MAXROW/50/, MAXCOL/6/
35      *
36      * [OPEN FILE AND READ DATA]
37      *
38              CALL GETDAT(NAME,TAB,COUNT,MAXROW,MAXCOL)
39      *
40              IF (COUNT .EQ. 0) THEN
41                  PRINT *,' IN MAIN, RETURN FROM GETDAT'
42                  PRINT *,' NO DATA IN FILE '
43                  STOP
44              ENDIF
45      *
46      * [COMPUTE EACH STUDENT'S TOTAL SCORE]
47      *
48              CALL TOTALS(TAB,COUNT,MAXCOL)
49      *
50      * [COMPUTE AVERAGE]
51      *
52              CALL AVG(TAB,COUNT,MAXCOL,AVERAG)
53      * [COMPUTE GRADES AND PRINT REPORT]
54      *
55              CALL GRADES(NAME,TAB,COUNT,MAXCOL,AVERAG)
56      *
57              STOP
58              END
59      *
60      ******************************************************************
61      *
62      * OPEN DATA FILE
63      *
64              SUBROUTINE GETDAT(NAME,TAB,COUNT,MAXROW,MAXCOL)
65      *
66      * LOCAL VARIABLES
67      * FIR, LAS -- FIRST AND LAST INPUT COLUMNS IN TAB()
68      * FILNAM -- DATA FILE NAME
69      * REC -- FORMAT CODES FOR FILE INPUT
70      *
```

(continued)

```
71          REAL TAB
72          INTEGER COUNT,MAXROW,MAXCOL,FIR,LAS
73          CHARACTER NAME*(*), FILNAM*10, REC*40
74          DATA REC/'(A30,I9,4I3)'/
75          PARAMETER (FIR=2, LAS=6)
76    *
77          DIMENSION NAME(MAXROW), TAB(MAXROW,MAXCOL)
78    *
79    *
80    * OPEN FILE
81    *
82          PRINT *, 'ENTER DATA FILE NAME'
83          READ '(A)', FILNAM
84          OPEN(9, NAME=FILNAM, IOSTAT=IOERR)
85          IF (IOERR .NE. 0) THEN
86             PRINT *, 'IN ROUTINE GETDAT'
87             PRINT *, 'CANNOT OPEN FILE', FILNAM
88             PRINT *, '  ERROR CONDITION IS ', IOERR
89             STOP
90          ENDIF
91    *
92    * READ DATA FROM FILE
93    *
94          COUNT=0
95          DO 100 I=1,MAXROW
96           READ(9,REC, END=101, ERR=102), NAMES(I), (TAB(I,J),J=FIR,LAS
97           COUNT=COUNT+1
98     100 CONTINUE
99    *
100   *      [NORMAL EXIT -- END OF FILE REACHED]
101    101 CONTINUE
102        RETURN
103   *
104   *         [ERROR IN FILE INPUT]
105    102 CONTINUE
106        PRINT *, 'IN ROUTINE GETDAT'
107        PRINT *,' ERROR IN READING FILE', FILNAM
108        PRINT *,' LAST ITEM SUCCESSFULLY READ WAS:'
109        PRINT *,'    ITEM NUMBER: ',COUNT
110        PRINT *,'    NAME: ', NAME(COUNT)
111        STOP
112        END
113   *
114   ***********************************************************
115   *
```

(continued)

```
116  * COMPUTE STUDENTS' TOTAL SCORES
117  *
118         SUBROUTINE TOTALS(TAB,COUNT,MAXCOL)
119  *
120  * LOCAL VARIABLES
121  *  TOTCOL -- COLUMN WHERE TOTALS ARE STORED
122  *  FIRST -- COLUMN WHERE FIRST TEST SCORE IS STORED
123  *
124         INTEGER COUNT,MAXCOL,TOTCOL,FIRST
125         REAL TAB
126  *
127         PARAMETER (TOTCOL=1, FIRST=3)
128  *
129         DIMENSION TAB(COUNT,MAXCOL)
130  *
131  * COMPUTE TOTALS
132  *
133         DO 200 I=1,COUNT
134            TAB(I,TOTCOL)=0
135               DO 210 K=FIRST,MAXCOL
136                  TAB(I,TOTCOL)=TAB(I,TOTCOL)+TAB(I,K)
137     210         CONTINUE
138     200 CONTINUE
139         RETURN
140         END
141  *
142  ****************************************************************
143  *
144  * COMPUTE CLASS AVERAGE
145  *
146         SUBROUTINE AVG(TAB,COUNT,MAXCOL,AVERAG)
147  *
148  * LOCAL VARIABLES
149  *  SUM -- SUM OF SCORES
150  *  TOTCOL -- COUMN IN WHICH TOTALS ARE STORED
151  *
152         REAL TAB, AVERAG, SUM
153         INTEGER COUNT,MAXCOL,TOTCOL
154  *
155         PARAMETER (TOTCOL=1)
156  *
157         DIMENSION TAB(COUNT,MAXCOL)
158  *
159  * COMPUTE AVERAGE
160  *
```

(continued)

```
161          SUM=0
162          DO 300 I=1,COUNT
163              SUM=SUM+TAB(I,TOTCOL)
164      300 CONTINUE
165          AVERAG=SUM/COUNT
166          RETURN
167          END
168  ******************************************************************
169  *
170  * COMPUTE GRADES AND PRINT REPORT
171  *
172  * FUNCTION INPUTS SCORE AND AVERAGE, OUTPUTS LETTER GRADE
173  *
174          CHARACTER*(*) FUNCTON SYMBOL(SCORE, AVERAG)
175  *
176  * LOCAL VARIABLES
177  *   SCORE -- TEST SCORE (RANGE=0 TO 100)
178  *   TOP -- HIGHEST LETTER GRADE
179  *   LETTER() -- ARRAY OF REMAINING LETTER GRADES
180  *   LEVEL() -- PERCENTAGES OF AVERAGE THAT DETERMINE GRADES
181  *   NUMLEV -- NUMBER OF ITEMS IN LEVEL()
182  *
183  * INITIALIZE
184  *
185          CHARACTER LETTER*1,TOP*1
186          INTEGER NUMLEV
187          REAL SCORE, LEVEL,AVERAG
188  *
189          DATA LETTER/'B','C','D','F'/,TOP/'A'
190          DATA LEVEL/1.2,1.15,.85,.80/
191          DATA NUMLEV/4/
192  *
193  * COMPUTE LETTER GRADE
194  *
195  * [INITIAL GRADE IS TOP. IF SCORE IS BELOW FIRST ITEM IN LEVEL
196  *  MULTIPLIED BY THE AVERAGE, THEN GRADE IS SET TO FIRST ITEM IN
197  *  LETTER. THIS PROCESS REPEATS NUMLEV TIMES.]
198  *
199          SYMBOL=TOP
200          DO 100 K=1,NUMLEV
201              IF (SCORE .LE. LEVEL(K)*AVERAG) SYMBOL=LETTER(K)
202      100 CONTINUE
203          RETURN
204          END
```

(continued)

```
205  *
206  ****************************************************************
207  *
208  * PRINT GRADE REPORT
209  *
210        SUBROUTINE GRADES(NAME,TAB,COUNT,MAXCOL,AVERAG)
211  *
212  * LOCAL VARIABLES
213  *  TOTCOL -- COLUMN IN TAB() THAT WAS TOTAL SCORES
214  *  FIRST -- COLUMN IN TAB() WHERE TEST SCORES BEGIN
215  *  SYMBOL -- CHARACTER FUNCTION -- COMPUTES LETTER GRADE
216  *
217        CHARACTER NAME*(*), SYMBOL*1
218        INTEGER COUNT, MAXCOL, TOTCOL, FIRST
219        REAL TAB,AVERAG
220  *
221        PARAMETER (TOTCOL=1, FIRST=3)
222  *
223  * DO REPORT
224  *
225  *             [HEADINGS]
226        PRINT *,'WESTERN MARYLAND COLLEGE'
227        PRINT *,'COMPUTER SCIENCE 101'
228        PRINT *,'SECTION A6'
229        PRINT *,'FALL 1984'
230        PRINT *
231        PRINT *, '                    NAME                ',
232       #        '              SCORES            ',
233       #        '  TOTAL ',
234       #        '  GRADE '
235  *
236             [NAMES AND GRADES]
237        DO 100 I=1,COUNT
238          PRINT *, NAMES(I), (TAB(I,L),L=FIRST,MAXCOL),
239       #          TAB(I,TOTCOL), SYMBOL(TAB(I,TOTCOL),AVERAG)
240    100 CONTINUE
241        PRINT *
242        PRINT *,'                              CLASS AVERAGE: ', AVERAG
243        RETURN
244        END
245  *
246  ****************** END OF PROGRAM **************************
247  ****************************************************************
```

DISCUSSION

In lines 6 to 16 we describe the global variables. Local variables are described at the beginning of the routine in which they are used. Notice also that we use comment lines to identify the beginning of each subprogram. We also add comments (lines 36, 46, 50, 53) to indicate the purpose of each CALL statement.

We use the same names for all of the global variables in all of the subprograms. FORTRAN does *not* require this. We could, for example, call the NAMES() array NAMES in the main program and something else, say PERSON, in the GETDAT subroutine. If we did that, the CALL/SUBROUTINE sequence would look like this:

In the main routine

```
CALL GETDAT(NAMES,TAB,COUNT,MAXROW,MAXCOL)
```

In the subroutine

```
SUBROUTINE GETDAT(PERSON,TAB,COUNT,MAXROW,MAXCOL)
CHARACTER PERSON*(*)
DIMENSION PERSON(MAXROW)
            ·
            ·
            ·
READ(9,*,END=101,ERR=101),PERSON(I),(TAB(I,J),J=FIR,LAS
            ·
            ·
            ·
```

Because NAMES is the first thing in the CALL GETDAT interface list and the first thing in the SUBROUTINE GETDAT interface list, the computer treats them as the same array. This means that a name read into PERSON() in the GETDAT subroutine will be available to the computer in NAMES() in the main routine. The calls to the subroutines are at lines 38, 48, 52, and 55. The corresponding subroutines are at lines 64, 118, 146, and 210. You can see that in each case the interface list of the CALL matches up with the interface list of the SUBROUTINE. It is essential that this be true, otherwise the data in the interface will not be communicated correctly between the routines. We will discuss interfacing at greater length in Chapter 30.

The main program begins at line 28 and ends at line 58. The first job of the main routine is to initialize the global variables. It then calls the subprograms in the proper order. Notice that in line 40 we check the result of the call to GETDAT. If no data is found (in which case the COUNT will be 0), an error message is printed and the program stops. This is necessary to avoid a possible "division by zero" error in line 165. Good programs explicitly check for predictible errors whenever possible.

The GETDAT subroutine (64–112) asks the user to input the data file name, opens the file, and reads the data into NAMES() and TAB(). We assume that the data file has been created in the form specified in the format variable REC. (If this isn't true, the error routine at statement number 102 will be executed.) GETDAT contains all of the information needed to do its job. If we later decide to change the makeup of the data file, all of the changes (with the exception of redefining the global variables TAB ( ), NAME ( ), MAXROW, and MAXCOL in the main routine) would be done in GETDAT. Remember that one of the major reasons for using modular programming is to make it easy to modify programs later on.

The TOTALS routine (118–140) and the AVG routine (146–167) are straightforward. Each performs computations on the data. Notice, by the way, that *only* the variables actually needed by the subprogram are passed in the interface list.

The GRADES subroutine (210–244) uses a function called SYMBOL (174–204). The function inputs a score and the average. It compares the score against the average (using the data in LEVEL), and outputs the student's letter grade.

SYMBOL is defined in line 174. The CHARACTER*(*) instruction means that the function variable SYMBOL is of type CHARACTER and that its size is determined by the calling routine—in this case GRADES. Notice that in line 217 of GRADES, the name SYMBOL is defined to be of type CHARACTER*1. When the function SYMBOL is called from the subroutine GRADES, the variable location symbol will be defined as CHARACTER*1. (If this seems complicated, it's because it *is* complicated. Take the time to think about how it works. Be sure you understand it. If you need to, reread the section on functions in Chapter 28.)

The "what-letter-does-this-score-deserve" part of the computation is done in a function to make the program easy to modify if the grading scheme changes later on. At some time in the future, for example, the teacher might decide to have the program read the grade cutoff levels from a data file. (In fact,the cutoff levels might be stored in the same data files as the students' test scores. This way each class could be graded on its own set of percentages.) If this does happen, the only part of the program that will have to be changed will be the SYMBOL function.

It is also important to see that the GRADES subroutine does no computation. It only prints, (SYMBOL is called in from the middle of a PRINT statement at line 239. This is an especially useful way to apply functions.) Because GRADES only does printout, if in the future the *form* of the output is to change, GRADES will be the only routine that has to be modified. We keep stressing this point only because it is so important. In modern programming, progams are often modified, and "good" programs are ones that are easy to change.

PRACTICE

1. Modify this program so that the level cutoff percentages can be stored in the file with the students' grades. The output heading data should be stored in the same file and read into the program at run time. This is *not* a trivial problem; be sure you take time to design your changes before you begin to code them.

2. Modify the grading scheme for this program as follows:

PERCENTAGE OF AVERAGE	GRADE
Over 1.28	A+
Over 1.25	A
Over 1.22	A–
Over 1.20	B+
Over 1.18	B
Over 1.15	B–
Over 1.10	C+
Over 1.00	C
Over 0.85	C–
Over 0.75	D
0.75 and below	F

3. Combine Problems 1 and 2 so that the new grading scheme can also be read from the data file. The *same* program should be able to process files with either type of grading scheme.

30
PROCESSING CHARACTER STRINGS

DEFINITIONS

Character	The code sent to the computer when a key on the keyboard is pressed, in particular the letters A to Z, the digits 0 to 9, the punctuation marks, and the operators.
String	A set of zero or more characters. A string which has no characters in it is called an "empty" or "null" string.
Length	The number of characters in a string.
Character Variable	A special type of variable into which strings can be stored.
Character Operators	Special operators which allow the programmer to have the computer manipulate strings and string variables.

CHARACTER STRINGS

A string is a set of characters. So that the computer can tell the difference between strings and comments or variables (which are also sets of characters), strings are enclosed in single quotation marks.

> 'ABCDEF'   This is a string
> ABCDEF   This is not a string.

Strings can include any of the characters that can be typed on the keyboard. For example, these are legal strings:

```
'A$B,XY?'
'+-/*'
'B3Q97L'
'123,45'
```

Notice that the last example string looks like a number. It is not, however; it is a string of character digits. Strings cannot be used in arithmetic operations. For example:

```
X='123,4'+9,3
```

is illegal and will cause an error message to be printed.

Strings can be assigned to special types of variables called string variables. String variables must be defined before they are used. String definition is done with the CHARACTER instruction. There are two basic forms of this instruction. This one:

```
CHARACTER BOX*2, FROG*5, ALPH*50, XYZ*25
```

defines each variable name to be a string. The asterisk and integer number attached to each name determine the maximum length the string may take on. If all of the strings in a CHARACTER statement are to be of the *same* maximum length, the instruction can be abbreviated like this:

```
CHARACTER*30 FIRST, SECOND, THIRD, LAST
```

In this case each of the four strings will have a maximum length of 30 characters.

COMPARING STRINGS

Strings may only be compared with or assigned to other strings. If, for example, the variable ALPH is defined to be of type CHARACTER and the variable NUMB to be of type INTEGER, then these are all illegal statements:

`IF(ALPH ,EQ, 37) X=X+1`	Strings and numbers cannot be compared.
`IF(APLH ,GE, NUMB) GOTO 101`	Strings and numbers cannot be compared.
`ALPH=34,9`	A number cannot be assigned to a string.
`NUMB='THE LAST NUMBER IS'`	A string cannot be assigned to a number.
`NUMB=ALPH*34+(2*NUMB)`	Strings cannot be used in arithmetic.

The following, however, are legal:

```
ALPH='FLOWERPOT'
IF(ALPH .EQ. 'DONE') GOTO 209
IF(ALPH .GT. 'H') PRINT *, ALPH
```

Notice that the last example checks to see if the string contained in ALPH is "greater than" the character "H". Strings used in logical tests are compared on a character-by-character basis from left to right. As soon as two differing characters are encountered, the string with the higher valued character is determined to be the "greater" string. If the strings differ in length, the shorter one will be left-justified and filled out with blanks.

EXAMPLE   Is A=B?

A	B	RESULT OF COMPARISON
ABCDE	ABCDE	Strings are equal.
ABCXE	ABCDE	A is greater than B because X is "greater" than D.
ABCDE	ABC	A is greater than B because D is "greater" than blank.
AB246	ABCDE	B is greater than A because C is "greater" than 2.

On most computers the comparison is based on a collating sequence in which:

$$\text{'A'} < \text{'B'} < \text{'C'} < \ldots < \text{'X'} < \text{'Y'}, \text{'Z'}$$

Here we will use the ASCII collating sequence. The *FORTRAN Language Reference Manual* for your computer system will tell you what the collating sequence is for your particular computer. You should look this up before you begin to program with strings—it might be different than the one used here.

The *length* of a string is the count of the number of characters in the string. For example:

'ABCDE'	Length is 5
'M'	Length is 1
'B3Q79'	Length is 5
' '	Length is 1 (the character is a blank)
''	Length is 0

The last example is a string which contains no characters. The string is written by placing the two quotation marks right next to each other, like this: ''. This string is called the *null* string. Its length is always zero.

It is often useful to be able to find out the length of a string while a program is running. To do this, FORTRAN provides a *character function* called LEN( ), LEN( ) takes a string as an argument and returns a number which is equal to the length of the string. For example:

```
CHARACTER A*40
A='ABCDE'
N=LEN(A)
PRINT *, 'THE LENGTH OF A IS ',N
END
```

Notice that while A is a string, LEN(A) is a number. So N=LEN(A) is a legal FORTRAN statement. In this case the number stored into N would be 5. Here are some more examples:

```
A=' '
PRINT *, LEN(A)        Prints out 0. ' ' is the null string.
A='GOAT'
PRINT *, LEN(A)        Prints out 4.
A='BBQ8##9$3, 2'
PRINT *, LEN(A)        Prints out 12. Blank counts as a character.
```

Notice that each time a new string is assigned to A, the length of A changes. On most computers, strings have an initial value of null until a later value is assigned. And on most computers there is an overall maximum length that a string can be defined to have. You should check the *FORTRAN Language Reference Manual* for your computer system to see what limitations apply.

STRING OPERATIONS

Strings are made up of characters. Since the characters in a given string are there in a particular sequence (that is, since they come one after another, *in order*), each character has a unique *position* in the string.

For example, if we have the string variable ALPH:

```
CHARACTER ALPH*20
ALPH='ABCDEFG'
```

we can think of ALPH as looking like this:

```
1 2 3 4 5 6 7 8
A B C D E F G ☒
```

The ⊠ marks the end of the string. In this case the length of the string is 7. The ⊠ is known as the "end-of-string" mark, and it does not count as part of the string itself.

In this example, character 1 of the string is the character "A." Character 5 is "E." The *position* of a character is its location, by number, in the string. The leftmost character is always in position 1; we always count from left to right.

A character or string of characters located within a larger string is called a *substring*. In this example, 'A' is a substring of 'ABCDEFG'. 'B', 'E', and 'F' are also substrings. 'Q', 'Z', and 'M' are not.

Other substrings *contained in* ALPH are:

```
'AB'
'ABC'
'BCDEF'
'DEFG'
'EF'
```

There are, of course, many others. It is important to see that while 'ABCD' and 'DEFG' *are* substrings, 'ABFG' and 'BDEF' are *not*. To be a substring, a set of characters must already exist as a smaller string *inside* the larger one.

In FORTRAN we can identify substrings explicitly by position. For example, the substring "EFQ" is in positions 5, 6, and 7 of ALPH. We can write this as:

```
ALPH(5:7)
```

More generally,

```
STRING(F:L)
```

identifies the substring of STRING beginning a position F and ending with position L. The characters at F and L are each part of the substring. Either F or L may be omitted. This:

```
STRING(F:)
```

identifies the substring beginning at position F and running through to the end of STRING. This:

```
STRING(:L)
```

identifies a substring beginning with the character 1 of STRING and ending with the character at position L. This

```
STRING(M:M)
```

identifies exactly *one* character, namely the one at position M.

So in our example, if ALPH='ABCDEFG', then

THIS INSTRUCTION	PRODUCES THIS OUTPUT
PRINT *, ALPH(3:6)	CDEF
PRINT *, ALPH(:4)	ABCD
PRINT *, ALPH(5:)	EFG
PRINT *, ALPH(5:7)	EFG
PRINT *, ALPH(2:2)	B
PRINT *, ALPH(8:8)	Error; subscript too large.

The substring operator is very useful. Here, for example, is a program that prints a string out one letter per line:

```
CHARACTER ALPH*10
ALPH='ABCDEFG'

DO 100 I=1, LEN(ALPH)
    PRINT *, ALPH(I:I)
100 CONTINUE
END
```

Although this particular program doesn't do much itself, the *idea* of using a loop counter to index a string is exceptionally useful in programs that need to search for and process smaller parts of larger strings. An example of this kind of processing is given in the next chapter.

A special string function, called INDEX, is available to help with substring operations. INDEX is called with two string arguments. If the second argument is a substring of the first, then INDEX returns the position at which the substring begins. If the second argument is not a substring of the first, then INDEX returns zero. For example:

```
CHARACTER ALPH*10
ALPH='ABCDEFG'
PRINT *, INDEX(ALPH, 'CDE')        Prints out 3.
PRINT *, INDEX(ALPH, 'BCDEF')      Prints out 2.
PRINT *, INDEX(ALPH, 'FROG')       Prints out 0.
```

INDEX is an integer function and may be used any time you need to know the position of one string inside of another.

PRACTICE

1. Write a program that will print out all the possible substrings of an input string, for example:

```
INPUT:    ABC
OUTPUT:   ABC AB BC A B C
```

CONCATENATION

Two strings may be combined, or concatenated by using / / as a string operator.

```
M = 'ABC'//'XYZ
PRINT *, M
           Output:   ABCXYZ
```

The two strings are made into one string. They are put together in the order in which they are written in the FORTRAN statement.

This piece of code, for example, is often used in "friendly" computer programs:

```
CHARACTER ALPH*3, NAME*30
ALPH='HI '

PRINT *, 'WHAT''S YOUR NAME?'
READ '(A)', NAME
PRINT *
PRINT *, ALPH//NAME

          Output:
          WHAT'S YOUR NAME?

          SUE
          HI SUE
```

Notice that in the first PRINT statement, we use two ''s to indicate an apostrophe. This is the way FORTRAN gets around the fact that the ' character is used to specify strings. Also notice that we include a blank on the end of ALPH so that HI SUE will be spaced properly. We also could have done it like this:

```
ALPH='HI'
    .
    .
    .
PRINT *, ALPH// ' ' //NAME
```

As usual, there are many ways to write the same program. This produces results that are identical to the first one.

STRING ARRAYS

String arrays are similar to numeric arrays (see Chapter 18) except that they contain character data instead of numbers. String arrays must be dimensioned before they are used. The dimension statement, DIMENSION, tells the computer how much room to set aside to use for the array.

```
CHARACTER*5 A
DIMENSION A(20)
```

This reserves room for a string array named A. The array will have 20 strings. Each string will have a maxmum length of five characters. Each string in the array can be processed by using the string operators, in the same way that single strings are processed.

EXAMPLE
```
CHARACTER ALPH*30
INTEGER COUNT
DIMENSION ALPH(20)

COUNT=0
DO 100 I=1,20
READ '(A)', ALPH(I)
IF (LEN(ALPH(I)) .EQ. 0) GOTO 101
COUNT=COUNT+1
100 CONTINUE
101 CONTINUE
```

This reads data into the string array ALPH. ALPH can hold up to 20 strings. Each string can be a maximum of 30 characters long. Here the null string is used as the end-of-data marker. The null string is entered from the terminal by typing a carriage return. The following program inputs a list of names and sorts them into alphabetic order.

```
1       * SORT A LIST OF NAMES
2       *
3       * R. W. DILLMAN
4       * APRIL, 1983
5       *
6       * VARIABLES:
7       *   LIST -- THE LIST OF NAMES
8       *   MAX -- THE MAXIMUM NUMBER OF NAMES
9       *   COUNT -- ACTUAL NUMBER OF NAMES ENTERED.
10      *
```

(continued)

```
11          *  INITIALIZE
12          *
13                  CHARACTER LIST*30, TEMP*30
14                  INTEGER COUNT, MAX
15          *
16                  PARAMETER (MAX=100)
17          *
18                  DIMENSION LIST(MAX)
19          *
20          *  INPUT NAMES
21          *
22                  PRINT *,' ENTER UP TO ',MAX,' NAMES'
23                  PRINT *, '    FORM IS: LAST NAME, FIRST NAME'
24                  PRINT *, '    USE CARRIAGE RETURN TO EXIT'
25          *
26                  COUNT=0
27                  DO 100 I=1,MAX
28                      READ '(A)', LIST(I)
29                      IF (LEN(LIST(I)) .EQ. 0) GOTO 101
30                      COUNT=COUNT+1
31            100   CONTINUE
32          *
33          *  EXCHANGE SORT
34          *
35            101 CONTINUE
36                  DO 200 I=1,COUNT-1
37                      DO 250 K=I+1,COUNT
38                          IF (LIST(K) .LT. LIST(I)) THEN
39                              TEMP=LIST(K)
40                              LIST(K)=LIST(I)
41                              LIST(I)=TEMP
42                          ENDIF
43            250     CONTINUE
44            200 CONTINUE
45          *
46          *  PRINT SORTED LIST
47          *
48                  PRINT *, 'SORTED LIST'
49                  PRINT *
50                  DO 300 I=1,COUNT
51                      PRINT *, LIST(I)
52            300 CONTINUE
53                  END
```

Input:

```
JONES, CAROL
ADAMS, TOM
THOMAS, MIKE
BAKER, SUE
```

Output:

```
ADAMS, TOM
BAKER, SUE
JONES, CAROL
THOMAS, MIKE
```

In line 18 we dimension the array L I S T. Since MAX has been set to 100 (line 16), the array will handle up to 100 strings. Since L I S T is of type CHARACTER ∗ 30 (line 13), each of the 100 possible strings can be up to 30 characters long.

Lines 22 to 31 input the list of names from the terminal into the array. A single carriage return as input is interpreted as the null string. Since the length of the null string is 0, the LEN function can be used to check for it as the end-of-data marker (line 29).

The exchange sort is the same one we have seen in earlier chapters. TEMP is a local variable used in the switching routine at lines 39 to 41. Lines 48 to 52 print out the sorted list.

PRACTICE

2. Code and test the alphabetizing program.

3. Modify the program so that the input comes from a data file. The data file name should be entered at run time.

4. Modify the printout part of the program so that the names are printed in the form FIRST LAST. The input form should not change.

31
USING THE COMPUTER: A SAMPLE PROBLEM

In most of the larger programs that we've written, it has been necessary to check for various kinds of errors and print out a message when one occurs. In this chapter we are going to create a general "error message" subroutine. It will input the name of the routine in which the error occurred and a message, and it will output its inputs. We will use it, as a time-saver, whenever we need to print an error message. We will also gain the advantage of having all of our error messages appear in the same format.

SAMPLE
OUTPUT

We would like to be able to call the error routine like this:

```
CALL ERROUT('GETDAT','FILE ERROR; NO DATA IN FILE '//FILNAM)
```

and have the following output appear:

```
ERROR IN ROUTINE: GETDAT

FILE ERROR
NO DATA IN FILE STUDAT
```

In this case F I L N A M is a character variable that contains the name of a data file. The contents of FILNAM are concatenated to the string 'FILE ERROR; NO DATA IN FILE ' in the calling statement's interface list. The semicolon is a special character that the subroutine must recognize as meaning "print a carriage return here." This isn't strictly necessary, but it does give us the ability to print a message that appears on more than one line.

ALGORITHM

The top level of our design looks something like this:

(1)   Get name of routine and message.
(2)   Print out the routine name
(3)   Scan the message string one character at a time
     (3.1) If the character is not a semicolon,
          then print the character;
          otherwise print a carriage return
(4)   Return

This seems to be pretty easy until we remember that *each* time a FORTRAN PRINT instruction is executed, it causes a line feed to be printed. That means that if we do step (3) the way we've outlined it above, the message will print out down the edge of the page, one character per line. Steps (1), (2), and (4) seem alright, so we'll concentrate on step (3).

In thinking about it, we find that another approach to the problem is to print only parts of the message at the points where we actually find the semicolons. For example, with the message string:

```
 1  2  3  4  5 6 7 8 9 10  11   12  .  .  .  .                                    33
┌──┬──┬──┬──┬──┬──┬──┬──┬──┬──┬──┬──┬──┬──┬──┬──┬──┬──┬──┬──┬──┬──┬──┐
│F │I │L │E │  │E │R │R │O │R │; │N │O │  │D │A │T │A │  │I │N │  │F │I │L │E │  │S │T │U │D │A │T │
└──┴──┴──┴──┴──┴──┴──┴──┴──┴──┴──┴──┴──┴──┴──┴──┴──┴──┴──┴──┴──┴──┴──┘
```

we would find a semicolon in position 11. At that point we would print out the substring from 1 to 10, followed by a carriage return. Then we would search forward from position 12 in the string looking for the next semicolon. In this case the next thing we would find would be the end of the string, so at that point we would print out the substring from 12 to 33 and return.

To operate this way, we will need two variables. One will point to the first character in the next substring to be printed. We'll call this variable FIRST, and its initial value will be 1. The second variable will be called LAST. It will contain the location of the character currently being scanned. The initial value of LAST will also be 1.

We'll also create a variable name for the error message. The new version of step (3) then, looks like this:

(3)   Set FIRST to be 1
(4)   LOOP with LAST going from 1 to length of MESSAGE
     (4.1)   IF the character at position LAST is a semicolon
           THEN
           (4.11) Print MESSAGE(FIRST:LAST−1)
           (4.12) Set FIRST to be LAST+1
           ELSE
           (4.13) IF LAST=length of MESSAGE
                THEN
                (4.131)   Print MESSAGE(FIRST:LAST)

In the example given above, the length of the string is 33. The first semicolon will be found when LAST is equal to 11. At that point the test at step (4.1) will be true and steps (4.11) and (4.12) will be performed. Since the value of FIRST is 1, MESSAGE(1:10) will print out; then FIRST will be set to 11+1, or 12.

Next the loop will continue. There are no more semicolons, but eventually LAST will be set equal to 33. At that point the IF test at step (4.13) will become true. Step (4.131) will be performed, and MESSAGE(12:33) will be printed. The loop will try to continue, but since LAST has reached the end, the loop will terminate. This algorithm seems to check out alright.

PROGRAM

The only thing we will add is two extra PRINT statements to add spacing before and after the message.

```
 1      * ERROR MESSAGE ROUTINE
 2      *
 3             SUBROUTINE ERROUT(FROM,MESAGE)
 4      *
 5      * INTERFACE VARIABLES
 6      *  FROM -- THE NAME OF THE CALLING ROUTINE,
 7      *  MESSAGE -- THE MESSAGE TO BE PRINTED,  IN THE
 8      *              MESSAGE, THE CHARACTER ';'  WILL BE USED
 9      *              TO INDICATE THE END OF A LINE,
10      *
11      * LOCAL VARIABLES
12      *  NEWLIN -- SEPERATOR FOR PRINT LINES (;)
13      *  FIRST -- INDEX OF FIRST CHARACTER ON A LINE
14      *  LAST -- INDEX OF LAST CHARACTER ON A LINE
15      *  LENGTH -- NUMBER OF CHARACTERS IN MESAGE
16      *
17             INTEGER FIRST, LAST
18             CHARACTER FROM*(*), MESAGE*(*), NEWLIN*1
19      *
20             NEWLIN=';'
21      *
22      * PRINT MESSAGE
23      *
24             PRINT *
25             PRINT *, 'ERROR IN ROUTINE ',FROM
26             PRINT *
27      *
28             LENGTH=LEN(MESAGE)
29             FIRST=1
30             DO 100 LAST=1,LENGTH
```

(continued)

```
31              IF (MESAGE(LAST:LAST) .EQ. NEWLIN) THEN
32                  PRINT *, MESAGE(FIRST:LAST-1)
33                  FIRST=LAST+1
34              ELSE IF (LAST=LENGTH) THEN
35                  PRINT *, MESAGE(FIRST:LAST)
36              ENDIF
37      100 CONTINUE
38          PRINT *
39          RETURN
40          END
```

This is a good example of a *programming tool*. It is general enough to be used with any program you expect to write. As an example, we'll show how this routine would be called if it were used in the data input module of the program we developed in Chapter 26. First, this is the module as originally written:

```
59      *
60      *****************************************************************
61      *
62      * OPEN DATA FILE
63      *
64          SUBROUTINE GETDAT(NAME,TAB,COUNT,MAXROW,MAXCOL)
65      *
66      * LOCAL VARIABLES
67      *  FIR, LAS -- FIRST AND LAST INPUT COLUMNS IN TAB()
68      *  FILNAM -- DATA FILE NAME
69      *  REC -- FORMAT CODES FOR FILE INPUT
70      *
71          REAL TAB
72          INTEGER COUNT,MAXROW,MAXCOL,FIR,LAS
73          CHARACTER NAME*(*), FILNAM*10, REC*40
74          DATA REC/'(A30,I9,4I3)'/
75          PARAMETER (FIR=2, LAS=6)
76      *
77          DIMENSION NAME(MAXROW), TAB(MAXROW,MAXCOL)
78      *
79      *
80      * OPEN FILE
81      *
82          PRINT *, 'ENTER DATA FILE NAME'
83          READ (A), FILNAM
84          OPEN(9, NAME=FILNAM, IOSTAT=IOERR)
85          IF (IOERR .NE. 0) THEN
86              PRINT *, 'IN ROUTINE GETDAT'
87              PRINT *, 'CANNOT OPEN FILE', FILNAM
```

(continued)

```
 88               PRINT *, ' ERROR CONDITION IS ', IOERR
 89            STOP
 90         ENDIF
 91   *
 92   * READ DATA FROM FILE
 93   *
 94         COUNT=0
 95         DO 100 I=1,MAXROW
 96         READ(9,REC, END=101, ERR=102), NAMES(I), (TAB(I,J),J=FIR,LAS)
 97         COUNT=COUNT+1
 98     100 CONTINUE
 99   *
100   *      [NORMAL EXIT -- END OF FILE REACHED]
101     101 CONTINUE
102         RETURN
103   *
104   *         [ERROR IN FILE INPUT]
105     102 CONTINUE
106         PRINT *, 'IN ROUTINE GETDAT'
107         PRINT *,' ERROR IN READING FILE', FILNAM
108         PRINT *,' LAST ITEM SUCCESSFULLY READ WAS:'
109         PRINT *,'    ITEM NUMBER: ',COUNT
110         PRINT *,'    NAME: ', NAME(COUNT)
111         STOP
112         END
```

Here is the replacement for lines 106 to 110.

```
103   *
104   *         [ERROR IN FILE INPUT]
105     102 CONTINUE
106         CALL ERROUT('GETDAT','CANNOT READ FILE '//FILNAM//';LAST
107       # ITEM SUCCESSFULLY READ WAS:;   NAME: '//NAME(COUNT))
108         PRINT *, '    ITEM NUMBER: ',COUNT
109         STOP
110         END
111   *
112   *****************************************************************
113   *
```

Admittedly this doesn't look very pretty, but the comment is sufficient for other programmers to figure out what the CALL is for, and the ERROUT routine will sort out the message. The reason for using ERROUT is to make error messages easier to write, and to make them print out in a standard form. The subroutine accomplishes both of these objectives.

PRACTICE

1. Test the error message routine. What if the last character in MESAGE is a ";"? What if MESAGE is null?

2. You can see that ERROUT requires the error message to be in the form of a character string. Because of this we cannout use ERROUT to print the value of COUNT in the example shown above. If we had a function (call it STR) that could convert numbers to strings, we would be able to pass the converted values on. For example, like this:

   ```
   CALL ERROUT('TESTER','THE VALUE IN COUNT IS '//STR(COUNT))
   ```

   Write such a function. It should input an integer number and output the corresponding character string.

3. Write another function like the one in Problem 1. It, however, should input real numbers and output their string equivalents.

4. Write an error message routine of your own design. What would you add to or delete from the one developed here?

5. Write a function that inputs three strings. The function should search the first looking for all occurrences of the second. When it finds an occurrence of the second string, it should replace it with a copy of the third string. In string processing this is known as a "search and replace" routine.

32
LOGIC:
DESIGNING OUTPUT

HEADINGS AND LABELS

Good programmers *always* label both their input and their output. There are good reasons for this. Here is an example of a program with unlabeled input.

```
RUN PROG
<. . . long pause . . .>
```

Clearly the user is expected to enter something, but what? Here is a better, but still bad, example:

```
RUN PROG
ENTER THREE NUMBERS
```

Which three numbers? 10, −6.314, and 8? What are the three numbers for? How does the user decide what to type? One more bad example:

```
RUN
ENTER A AND QSUM
```

This probably means something to the programmer. A and QSUM are probably variable names, but the person *using* the program doesn't know what the variables are for. Programs that do input like this can only be used well by the person who programmed them.

IMPORTANT   Programs which can only be used by one person are effectively worthless.

Not only will no one else ever be able to figure out how they work, but after awhile the person who wrote them will forget what A and QSUM were, or what the three numbers were for, and *no one* will be able to use the programs.

315

Here is an example of well-labeled input:

```
RUN
ENTER NAME, AGE
   (ENTER *END*,0 TO EXIT)
```

This explains that the user is to enter sets of people's names and ages. Each name and age should be separated by a comma. The end-of-data marker is *END*,0.

In a similar way, all output should be labeled. Suppose, for example, that in running the program above, the user typed in 35 names and ages, and the printout looked like this:

```
26.5


JOHN THOMPSON
SUSAN SMITH


BILL JONES
CAROL ADAMS
MICHELE BROWN
```

What does this output mean? What is 26.5? Are there two lists of names, or did the computer accidentally skip a line?

IMPORTANT   *Every* distinct set of information that is printed by the computer should be labeled.

Good programmers never assume that the results of their programs will be obvious. They always have their programs print enough extra information to explain the output. For example, *good* output for the situation above would be:

```
AVERAGE AGE:   26.5

PERSONS UNDER 18 YEARS OLD:
   JOHN THOMPSON
   SUSAN SMITH

PERSONS OVER 65 YEARS OLD:
   BILL JONES
   CAROL ADAMS
   MICHELE BROWN
```

Now the output's meaning is easy to see.

OUTPUT FORMAT

The *format* of the output refers to the way in which the data items and their associated labels are arranged on the page after printing. In FORTRAN, format control is handled through the use of specialized *FORMAT* codes. These codes are sent to the output device along with the data to be printed. The codes provide the device with the information it needs to arrange the output properly. The syntax of FORMAT codes is discussed in Chapter 33. This chapter will deal with the *logical* design of output specifications.

JUSTIFICATION

Left justification means that the output items in a column are lined up to be even at the left edge of the column. *Right-justified* items are lined up to be even at the right edge of the column.

EXAMPLE   Left-justified output:

```
21.32          894            -2.6
12.4           6              -0.122
3.619          2100           83.6
-2.93          74             41
562            .803           7.22
```

EXAMPLE   Right-justified output:

```
21.32          894            -2.6
  12.4           6           -0.122
3.619          2100           38.6
-2.93           74             41
  562          .803           7.22
```

LABELS AND HEADINGS

A *label* is a character string which is output for the purpose of describing a particular data item which is to be printed. A label is associated with the data item and is often output as part of the same PRINT or WRITE instruction. Here is an example of a label.

```
PRINT *, 'THE CORRECT ANSWER IS ', CORANW
```

Output: THE CORRECT ANSWER IS 295.6

A *heading* is a character string which is output for the purpose of describing a *group* of data items that are to be printed. Headings are most often used to describe lists or tables. Here is an example of a heading.

```
        PRINT *, '    WEEKLY AVERAGE'
        PRINT *, 'TEMPERATURES FOR JULY'
        DO 100 I=1,TCOUNT
            PRINT *, '      ', TEMP(I)
   100  CONTINUE
```

```
Output:         WEEKLY AVERAGE
            TEMPERATURES FOR JULY
                89.4
                90.3
                90.5
                87.4
```

Labels and headings are often used together. In all cases, the objective is to make the output as easy to read as possible. For example:

```
      PRINT *, 'WEEKLY AVERAGE TEMPERATURE FOR ',MONTH
      PRINT *
      PRINT *, '    WEEK             TEMPERATURE'
      DO 100 I=1,TCOUNT
          PRINT *, '     ',I,'      ', TEMP
  100 CONTINUE
```

```
Output:  WEEKLY AVERAGE TEMPERATURES FOR JULY

              WEEK                  TEMPERATU
               1                       89.4
               2                       90.3
               3                       90.5
               4                       87.4
```

The importance of providing readable output cannot be overemphasized. Whenever possible, a programmer should have a *sample output* available at the beginning of the problem analysis. Certainly the final output form should be specified as part of the program design.

OUTPUT SPECIFICATION

It is important that as part of the original problem statement the programmer obtains a sample of the expected output. There are two major reasons for this:

1. The output requirements play a large role in the design of the input and data processing algorithms. Therefore, the programmer must know exactly what the program is supposed to produce before he or she can even begin to design the code.
2. The sample output provides the standard against which the final output will be judged. In part, the programmer's job is to produce a program whose output format matches the sample. No coding should begin until all concerned with the problem are agreed that the output formats are acceptable.

Usually, once agreement has been reached on the format of the sample output, the sample is translated into more formal *output specifications*. These list the data types and formats for all of the output fields, and they often contain information as to when and for whom the output is to be produced.

EXAMPLE   A program is to be written to analyze the age characteristics of students at a community college. The sample output looks like this:

```
LOCAL COMMUNITY COLLEGE
STUDENT AGE REPORT
OCTOBER 4, 1987

TOTAL NUMBER OF STUDENTS:   14,238
AVERAGE AGE:   24,3

CATEGORY            NUMBER            AVERAGE_AGE
FRESHMEN            6,030               18,9
SOPHOMORES          5,108               19,7
SPECIAL             3,100               30,3

SPECIAL STUDENTS         NUMBER         AVERAGE AGE
SENIOR CITIZENS            54              67,2
HIGH SCHOOL HONORS         12              18,3
WORK CO-OP                 41              27,1
OTHER                   1,095             32,9
NO AGE LISTED:    8
```

There are a large number of different techniques that can be used to record the output specifications for any program. For this example we will use an approach called a *template*.

PROJECT: 317
PROGRAMMER: R.W. DILLMAN
TEMPLATE 1#1, STUDENT AGE REPORT
PAGE 1 OF 2

COLUMN	5 10 15 20 25 30 35 40 ...
Row 1	LOCAL COMMUNITY COLLEGE
2	STUDENT AGE REPORT
3	<. . . date . . .>
4	
5	TOTAL NUMBER OF STUDENTS: <n>
6	AVERAGE AGE: <a>
7	
8	CATEGORY NUMBER AVERAGE AGE
9	FRESHMEN < h1 > < a1 >
10	SOPHOMORES < h2 > < a2 >
11	SPECIAL < h3 > < a3 >
12	
13	SPECIAL STUDENTS NUMBER AVERAGE AGE
14	SENIOR CITIZENS < n4 > < a4 >
15	HIGH SCHOOL HONORS < n5 > < a5 >
16	WORK CO-OP < n6 > < a6 >
17	OTHER < n7 > < a7 >
18	
19	
20	NO AGE LISTED <h8>
21	
22	
23	
24	

The template shows the *constant* heading and labeling information. It also shows exactly which row and column positions will be occupied by this information.

Variable output, data that will change from report to report, is also specified. The < > brackets show what row and column positions will be filled when the program is run. The symbols inside the brackets tell which data items are to be printed. The second page of the template lists the data items, describes their formats, and gives an example of each.

PROJECT: 317
PROGRAMMER: R.W. DILLMAN
TEMPLATE 1, STUDENT AGE REPORT
PAGE 2 OF 2

SYMBOL	DESCRIPTION	FORMAT
Date	Current date	MONTH, DAY, YEAR (OCTOBER 4, 1987)
n	Total of students	xxx,xxx (3,217)
n1	Total freshmen	•
n2	Total sophomores	•
n3	Total special	•
n4	Total senior citizens	•
n5	Total high school honors	Same as
n6	Total work co-op	for n
n7	Total other	•
n8	Total no age	•
a	Average age, all students	xx.x (18.3)
a1 through a7	Average age for total of h1 through h7 students	Same as for a

Notice that page 1 of the template shows *where* each output item goes on the output page. Page 2 of the template shows *what form* each of the variable data items will have. The total of students, for example, is represented by xxx,xxx. This means the totals will always be printed as integer numbers, with commas if necessary, and with a maximum size of 999,999. Similarly, the average age will be a decimal, accurate to one decimal place, and with a maximum of 99.9.

As we pointed out before, there are *many* different ways of doing this step in the program design process. It's not important that you do it any *particular* way, but it is important that you do it.

33
SYNTAX: FORMATTED OUTPUT

FORTRAN format codes are used to specify the form in which output data is to be displayed by the output device. There are a number of different ways that *formatted* output can be performed in FORTRAN. We will show one of these ways. You may want to look up "formatted output" in the *FORTRAN Language Reference Manual* for your computer system to see what the other ones look like.

We choose to use the WRITE instruction to do formatted output. This gives us three basic output options:

PRINT* for unformatted output to the terminal.
WRITE (*, format) for formatted output to the terminal.
WRITE (unit number, format) for formatted output to data files.

We introduced the WRITE instruction in Chapter 25. There a unit number was required to tell the computer which data file was to receive the output. Here the WRITE instruction will be directing its output to the terminal. When that is the case, the unit number can be replaced by an asterisk. So the general form of the WRITE instruction for terminal output is:

WRITE (*, format) list of variables

where format is the statement number of the associated FORMAT instruction.

FORMATTED OUTPUT

In doing formatted output, the instruction that transmits the data to be printed also must transmit information that describes the form the printed output is to take. Here is an example of formatted output:

```
      CHARACTER ALPH*5
      INTEGER INUMB
      REAL RNUMB
      ALPH='ABCDE'
      INUMB=789
      RNUMB=123.45
      WRITE(*, 9000) ALPH, INUMB, RNUMB
 9000 FORMAT(A5,I3,F6.2)
```

Notice that *each* variable in the variable list has a corresponding *format* code in the FORMAT list. Also notice that the *types* of the format codes match up to the types of the variables.

```
   ALPH          INUMB          RNUMB

    A5             I3            F6.2
```

This particular format list *specifies* an output *line* that has three *fields*. The first field is five characters long and will be filled with a string. The A code is for strings. The second field is three characters long and will be filled with an integer number. The I code is for integer numbers. The third field is six characters long and will be filled with a real number. The real number will have two digits of precision. The F code is for real numbes. The line, then, is to look like this:

string	integer	real	:type
5	3	6	:length

At the time the output is performed, the values of the variables will be inserted into their respective fields. (Since the length of the F field is 6, there will be room for five digits plus the decimal point.) The printed result will look like this:

```
      BCDE789123.45
```

Notice that the A is missing, and the fields run together.

The A is missing because of a rather strange rule of FORTRAN output:

IN FORTRAN FORMATTED OUTPUT, THE *FIRST*
CHARACTER OF *EVERY* OUTPUT *LINE* IS USED BY
THE PRINTER AS A CODE THAT TELLS IT HOW
MANY LINE FEEDS TO PERFORM.

This rule is called the "carriage control" rule. Carriage control can get to be very complicated, so we will adopt a simple-minded, but very effective, method for dealing with it.

> IF THE FIRST CHARACTER IN A LINE IS A BLANK,
> THE PRINTER WILL INTERPRET IT TO MEAN "SINGLE
> SPACING." THEREFORE WE WILL HEAD *EVERY*
> OUTPUT *LINE* WITH A BLANK.

There are two ways we can do this. The first is to insert a ' ' in the format list. Like this:

```
9000 FORMAT(' ',A5,I3,F6.2)
```

The second way is to use a new format code, the X code, to specify a blank. The general form of the X code is

```
nX
```

where n is the number of blanks to be printed. We'll use the X code, which means that our FORMAT instruction now looks like this:

```
9000 FORMAT(1X,A5,I3,F6.2)
```

Notice that unlike the other format codes, the number part of the X code comes in *front* of the code. The output from our program now looks like this:

```
ABCDE789123.45
```

We still need spacing between the output fields. To provide that we use the X code again. Suppose we decide to put four blanks between each of the fields:

```
9000 FORMAT(1X,A5,4X,I3,4X,F6.2)
```

Now our output looks like this:

```
ABCDE    789    123.45
```

Next we need to *label* the output. We do that by supplying character strings at the appropriate places within the format list. A character string appearing in a format list will be printed out just as it appears.

```
9000 FORMAT(1X,'APLHA: ',A5,4X,'INTEGER: ',I3,4X,'REAL: ',F6.2)
```

The output is now:

```
ALPHA: ABCDE    INTEGER: 789    REAL: 123.45
```

Notice that we supplied a blank at the end of each of the label strings. Finally, suppose we'd like each of the fields to start on a *new* line in the output. To make this happen, we use the / (slash) format code. The / code tells the computer to print a carriage return followed by a line feed. This has the effect of starting a new line—remember, each line needs a carriage control code. Here is the FORMAT instruction:

```
9000 FORMAT(1X,'ALPHA: ',A5,/,1X,'INTEGER: ',I3,/,1X,'REAL: ',F6.2)
```

and here is the output:

```
ALPH: ABCDE
INTEGER: 789
REAL: 123.45
```

FORMAT CODES

This section will describe the major FORTRAN format codes. There are more codes than we will discuss here, and the codes we do discuss have more to them than we will show. FORTRAN formatting can become very involved. We will show what you need to handle most of the output you'll ever need to do, but after you've finished this section you should look over your *FORTRAN Language Reference Manual* just to see what other formatting capabilities your computer system has.

Character [A]

GENERAL FORM
Aw where w is the width of the output field. The variable associated with an A format code must be of type CHARACTER. On output the value of the variable will be printed, left-justified, in a field of width w. If w is omitted, the size of the print field will equal the length of the string.

EXAMPLE
```
CHARACTER ALPH
ALPH='MIXTURE'
WRITE(*,5) ALPH
5 FORMAT(1X,A10)
```

OUTPUT
```
MIXTURE
```

ERROR
If the string stored in the variable location is longer than the specified width, the extra characters on the right-hand end of the string will not be printed.

Integer [I]

GENERAL
FORM

I w   where w is the width of the output field. The variable associated with the I format code must be of type INTEGER. On output the value will be printed, right-justified, in a field of width w. If the value to be printed contains fewer than w digits, the left-hand side of the field will be filled out with blanks.

EXAMPLE

```
INTEGER TEST
TEST=12345
WRITE(*,56) TEST
56 FORMAT(1X,I10)
```

OUTPUT

```
      12345
```

ERROR

If the number to be printed contains more digits than the field width will hold, the field will be filled with asterisks.

Real [F]

GENERAL
FORM

F w . p   where w is the field width and p is the number of digits of precision. The variable associated with an F format code must be of type REAL. The value stored in the variable location will be printed in a field of width w. A decimal point will be printed. The decimal point counts as part of w. P digits will be printed to the right of the decimal point; p also counts as part of w. The printed number will be right-justified in the output field. If the value is smaller than the field, the left-hand side of the field will be filled out with blanks. If the fractional part of the output number has fewer than p digits, the right-hand part of the field will be filled out with zeros. If the fractional part has too many digits, it will be rounded to fit.

EXAMPLE

```
REAL VAR, MOP
VAR=123.876
MOP=3.9
WRITE(*,8009) VAR, MOP
8009 FORMAT(1X,F8.2,5X,F5.3)
```

OUTPUT

```
  123.88     3.900
```

ERROR

If the *significant* digits of the value to be printed will not fit into the available room to the left of the decimal point in the output field, the entire field will be filled out with asterisks.

Spaces and Lines [X] [T] [/]

The X code outputs blanks. The general form is nX, where n is the number of blanks to be printed. Notice that in this case, the n specifier comes *in front of* the format code.

The T is used to *tab* to a specified position on the print line. The general form is Tc, where c specifies the column position where the *next* character to be printed is to go.

The / code causes the printer to move to the beginning of the next line. No numeric specifier is used with /. If, for example, you want to generate three / codes, you write ///. Since the / starts a new print line, a carriage control character must be supplied. As we noted above, we favor using 1X to supply a blank for "normal" single spacing.

```
EXAMPLE    1             INTEGER QBIT
           2             WRITE(*,9000)
           3             DO 100 QBIT=1, 5
           4                 WRITE(*,9001) QBIT, QBIT**2
           5        100  CONTINUE
           6       9000  FORMAT(1X,T5,'NUMBER',T15,'SQUARE'
           7       9001  FORMAT(1X,T7,I2,T17,I3)
           8             END
```

```
OUTPUT     NUMBER       SQUARE

             1             1
             2             4
             3             9
             4            16
             5            25
```

Here the WRITE statement at line 2 is used to provide the heading. By using the T code in the two FORMATs, we are able to line the headings up over their respective output columns. The / at the end of the heading FORMAT provides a blank line under the headings. This makes the output easier to read. Notice that both of the I format codes supply a wider field than is needed. This is done to provide a bit of insurance in case the program is later modified to print larger numbers.

Groups

If a format code is preceded by an integer number, FORTRAN will *repeat* the code the specified number of times. For example:

```
           INTEGER VAR
           VAR=5
           WRITE(*,8) VAR, VAR+1, VAR+2
        8  FORMAT(1X,3I5)

   Output  5   6   7
```

Any set of format codes may be enclosed in parentheses and preceded by a repeat specifier.

```
EXAMPLE        INTEGER VAR
               VAR=5
               WRITE(*,8) VAR, VAR+1, VAR+2
            8  FORMAT(1X,3(4X,I1))
```

OUTPUT   5   6   7

Notice that both of the forms shown above produce the same output. Repeating groups may be used to produce a bewilderingly large number of different possible format specifications. We recommend that you use the more simple single forms to get started, and then try out the more complicated forms later on. Skill in using FORTRAN format codes can be gained only with practice.

PRACTICE

1. Find the section of your *FORTRAN Language Reference Manual* that deals with format codes and look it over. Make sure that you read the sections of the manual that deal with the codes discussed in this chapter. If you are going to use formatted output, you should expect to have to refer to the manual *often*.

2. Modify three or four of your earlier programs so that they use formated output. Your objective should be to *decide ahead of time* what you want the output to look like, and *then* write FORMATs to produce that output.

SUMMARY FOR PART IV

Once an algorithm grows to be more than 30 or 40 steps long, it becomes more effective to design it as a *set* of smaller algorithms called *modules*. In commercial environments almost all large programs are written in modular form.

Good modular design produces modules that are small (each module does just one task) and independent (each module can be written and tested on its own). To do this, the designer must pay close attention to the module *interfaces*. One way is by means of a process called "top-down design." In top-down design, modules are first sketched out in a form that omits technical details. At this stage the modules are checked to make sure that, working together, they will be able to solve the problem, and while this is going on, the interfaces are also defined. In the succeeding stages more and more detail is added to the modules until each is a complete algorithm. A trace is then done, and if it succeeds, the program is coded and tested. Modular design involves a lot of work in the planning stages, but saves time in the debugging and testing stages. Modular programs are also the easiest to maintain once they're running. It is for these last two reasons that modular programming is so widely used.

FORTRAN was originally designed to be a numerical processing language. In FORTRAN IV it was very easy to process numbers but exceptionally difficult to process characters. FORTRAN 77 provides a CHARACTER data type and a number of character-handling functions, but it is still oriented toward numbers. If you *must* do character processing in FORTRAN, the best approach is to define the set of processing operations you wish to have the computer perform and then design a set of functions and subroutines to handle those operations. (This is often called the "programming tools" approach. An excellent discussion of character processing with programming tools is given in *Software Tools'* Kernighan and Plaugher, Addison-Wesley, 1973).

The FORTRAN FORMAT instruction gives the programmer total control over the form of a program's output. Unfortunately, however, there is a bewildering array of different codes, variations within codes, and input/output instructions. We make two suggestions:

1. Design your output pages first without worrying about *which* actual FORMAT codes you'll need to use. It's easier to fit the codes to the output form than to do it the other way around.

329

2. Do the FORMATTING last. Constructing FORMAT codes isn't difficult, but it is tedious. There's nothing more frustrating than putting in hours of work to get the FORMATs *just right,* only to find that a bug in the design requires a change in the output page. Start out by having the results dumped in an approximate form; then, after the program is thoroughly tested, go back and supply the exact FORMATs.

Formal output design is an important part of commercial programming. It is not as important as algorithm design, however, and we would suggest that beginners are better off concentrating on the latter.

PROGRAMMING PROBLEMS

1.0

PROBLEM
STATEMENT

Write a program that reads a text file and keeps counts of the occurrences of characters. Print the count for each letter, a count of the punctuation, and a count of "other" characters.

SAMPLE
OUTPUT

```
ENTER FILE NAME
TEST.DAT

A: 23    B: 8   C: 5  D: 3  E: 31

F: 6     G: 3   H: 2  .... etc.
          .
          .
          .
          .
      etc.

PUNCTUATION: 45

OTHER:
      #: 1

      $: 8

      +: 2
TOTAL OTHER: 11
```

1.1. Alter the program to include a statistical analysis of the results. Print a bar graph or other frequency diagram.

2.0

PROBLEM STATEMENT Write a program that will input two words and decide if they are anagrams of one another.

SAMPLE OUTPUT

```
ENTER WORD #1, WORD #2 -- USE *,* TO EXIT
BRAIN, FROG
            NO

MODE, DOME
            YES
*, *
            (END)
```

2.1. Compare the amounts of time it takes your program to process the following inputs:

INPUT	NUMBER OF CHAR- ACTERS	IS IT ANAGRAM?
ABCD,xxxx	4	NO
ABCDEFGH,xxxxxxxx	8	NO
ABCDEFGHIJKL,xxxxxxxxxxxx	12	NO
ABCD,DCBA	4	YES
ABCDEFGH,HGFEDCBA	8	YES
ABCDEFGHIJKL,LKJIHGFEDCBA	12	YES

If your program is optimal it shoud take twice as long to verify an eight-character anagram as it does to verify a four-character one. A 12-character anagram should take three times as long to verify. Each non-anagram should take the *same* amount of time to be rejected. Explain why this is the case. (If necessary, modify your program to improve its efficiency.)

3.0

PROGRAM STATEMENT Write a program that reads lines of text from a data file and checks to see if the first N characters in a line are the same as the first N characters of the previous line. N is an input to the program and is an integer between 1 and 80.

If two lines are found to match, they should be printed out along with their sequence numbers.

SAMPLE OUTPUT

```
ENTER DATA FILE NAME
TESTDAT
```

```
VERIFY HOW MANY CHARACTERS (1-80)
10

MATCHING LINES/TEXT

   4 AND 5

THE FROG SWAM IN THE DEEP POOL.
THE FROG SANG A SONG LATE AT NIGHT.

   12 AND 13

ALPHABETIC INFERENCES DEPENDENCIES AND ELEPHANTS
ALPHABETICALLY WE DANCED IN THE MOONLIGHT OF OUR DREAMS.

(END OF DATA)
```

3.1. Alter the program to allow the user to specify a match of strings N characters long, but beginning at column position C. (Note: C + N cannot exceed 80.)

4.0

PROBLEM
STATEMENT

The user should input the name of a text file at the terminal. The user should then input a string of characters. The program should scan the text file for occurrences of the input string.

    The output should include the row and column in the text at which the string occurs.

SAMPLE
OUTPUT

```
ENTER TEXT FILE
EXAMPL.TXT

ENTER SEARCH STRING -- USE *END* TO EXIT
DOG

LINE        COLUMN
1             5
3            17

ENTER SEARCH STRING -- USE *END* TO EXIT
*END*
```

Notes: For the example above, the text file would be something like this:

THE DOG WAS RUNNING DOWN THE STREET, JOHN
SAW IT AND WAS EXCITED. TURNING TO MARY HE
SHOUTED, "DO YOU SEE THE BLACK AND BROWN
DOG?" "YES," SHE REPLIED, "IT BELONGS TO OUR
NEW NEIGHBORS."

Test your program on a file of about 10 sentences. Along with your listing
and run, also hand in a listing of the text file.

4.1. Modify the program to replace occurrences of the search string
      with a new string. The search and replacement strings should be
      inputs.

4.2. Further modify the program so that when an occurrence of the
      search string is found, the string plus the 20 characters preceding it
      and the 20 characters following it are printed. At that point the user
      should have the option of replacing the string or not.

5.0

PROBLEM
STATEMENT

Write a program that will read data from a text file and count the number
of words. In this case define a "word" to be any string of characters with a
blank on either end. (Note that the first and last word of any line will be
the exception to this rule.)

  The program should also count the number of words of length 1, 2, 3,
and so on, and print out the totals in each category.

SAMPLE
OUTPUT

```
TOTAL NUMBER OF WORDS: 53

1: 8

2: 10

3: 12

4: 15

5: 10

6: 5

7: 2

8: 0

9: 1
```

5.1. Add a dictionary file to the system. Each time a word is found, it should be checked against the dictionary. If it is not there, it and its location in the text file should be printed out.

6.0

PROBLEM STATEMENT

The program should input one line at a time. Each line should be scanned, and strings of four or more blanks should be replaced with a tab code.

The tab code should consist of a special character (for example, ") that means "tab," a number indicating how many blanks were removed, then another character mark.

SAMPLE OUTPUT

```
ENTER DATA ONE LINE AT A TIME -- USE " KEY TO EXIT

THIS HAS 5        BLANKS.

THIS HAS 5"5"BLANKS.

        SIX IN FRONT,        SEVEN AFTER.

"6"SIX IN FRONT,"7"SEVEN AFTER.

TWENTY                    IN BETWEEN.

TWENTY"20"IN BETWEEN
```

This kind of program is called a filter. It inputs a stream of characters and "filters" out the excess blanks. Programs like this are used in word processing systems. (Why is four used as the minimum length?)

6.1. Alter the program to encode all strings of identical characters. (Four may no longer be the optimal maximum.)

6.2. Write a decoding program that will take the output from the above and print it in its original form.

7.0

PROBLEM STATEMENT

Write a program to input data from a data file. The data will represent the text of a letter.

The data will contain only English-language characters, except for the special characters:

"^", which means "start a new paragraph" (indent five spaces).
""3", """" means "skip lines"; the number tells how many lines to skip (up to a maximum of nine).
"*", which means "signature or heading line" (tab to column 50).

The program should reproduce the text exactly except that the special codes should be translated into their equivalent spacings. The letter should fit on a 78-character line. Words should be kept whole (i.e., words should not be broken across the end of a line).

SAMPLE
OUTPUT

```
ENTER DATA FILE NAME
TESTDAT

                                    567 MAIN ST,
                                    PHILADELPHIA, PENNA, 16334

                                    JULY 8, 1987

    MR, MALCOM WEST
    IMPORTS LIMITED
    3152 E, 15TH ST,
    NEW YORK, N,Y,  30408

    DEAR SIR:
         PLEASE SEND 500 GROSS OF PRODUCT #21567 BY THE FASTEST
    AVAILABLE MEANS,  CHARGE TO OPEN ACCOUNT #330; VERIFY AT
    608-445-3418 BETWEEN THE HOURS OF 8:00 A,M, AND 5:00 P,M,
         THANK YOU FOR YOUR PROMPT ATTENTION TO THIS MATTER,

                                    SINCERELY,

                                    JOHN SMITH
                                    CG12-B EXPEDITING
```

7.1. Alter the program so that * is always followed by a number indicating how deeply to indent. You will need to mark the end of the number (why?); *28*, for example.

7.2. Modify the program to do form letters. One data file should contain the text of the letter; use + to indicate places where the form data is to be inserted, as in:

```
DEAR +,
```

The form data should be kept in a second file. The program should:

- Read the text of the letter.
- Print the first letter reading and inserting form data as needed
- Print the second letter.
- Continue doing this until the form data is exhausted.

8.0

PROBLEM STATEMENT

Write a program to scan a text file and perform the following three grammar checks:

1. "i before e except after c."
2. Capitalization of the first letter in a sentence.
3. Two blanks after a period that ends a sentence.

The program should print the entire text. When the program finds a situation that appears incorrect, it should print the word or words on a separate line along with an appropriate message.

SAMPLE OUTPUT

Sample text: This is a test sentence. one mistake is that the "o" should have been capitalized. Such errors should recieve immediate attention.

```
ENTER TEXT FILE NAME
TESTDAT

This is a test sentence,

:: one ::    (word not capitalized)

mistake is that the "o" should have been capitalized,

:: Such ::   (only one space before word)

errors should

:: recieve ::  (i before e)

immediate attention,

::::(END OF DATA)::::
```

8.1. Alter the program to include ? and ! as sentence terminators.

8.2. Add additional rules of grammar to the set to be checked.

9.0

PROBLEM STATEMENT

Input a real number. Output the same number converted into scientific notation. The output should be of the form

```
a.bbbbEscc
```

where a is the first significant digit of the input, b b b b are the four digits following the first significant digit (they may be zero), and c c is the required power of 10 (where s is "−" if the number is negative, null otherwise).

SAMPLE
OUTPUT

```
ENTER VALUE TO BE CONVERTED -- USE 0 TO EXIT

1284.22739

RESULT: 1.2842E03


.04639527

RESULT: 4.6395E-02


.00004578993

RESULT: 4.5790E-05          (Note: Round up if necessary)


3057000060000450020.04

RESULT: 3.0570E18


0
```

9.1. Notice that the last example sacrifices considerable accuracy. What is the biggest integer number that you can force the computer to accept? Explain why the fact that there is a biggest possible integer can cause errors in computation within programs. Suggest at least two ways of dealing with such kinds of errors.

9.2. Write a program that will perform arithmetic operations on the numbers in their converted form.

10.0

PROBLEM
STATEMENT

Write a program that inputs a set of data in character form and attempts to convert each input into a number. If an input cannot be converted, an error message should be printed.

SAMPLE
OUTPUT

```
ENTER DATA -- USE *END* TO EXIT

12
-2.5
ABC
ERROR -- NOT A NUMBER

1.5
3.G8
ERROR -- NOT A NUMBER

-4.3
*END*
```

10.1. Modify the program so that it prints the average of the valid inputs.

11.0

PROBLEM
STATEMENT

Create a text file whose data is arranged as follows:

Line 1: FEDTAX, FICA, CITY, UNION, RETIRE

where FEDTAX = Federal Withholding Percentage
FICA = FICA tax percentage
CITY = City tax percentage
UNION = Union dues percentage
RETIRE = Retirement fund percentage

	Column	Item		
Line 2:	Data	Name	Data Item Description	Example
	1–10	LASTNAME	Employee last name	SMITH
	11–20	FIRSTNAME	Employee first name	CAROL
	21	WORKSIN	C=city S=suburbs	S
	22	UNIONCODE	M=union	\<blank\>
	23–27	EMPNO	Employee number	23216
	28–32	HOURS	Hours worked (to 0.5)	45.5
	33–37	REGRATE	Hourly pay rate	10.75
	38–42	OTRATE	Overtime pay rate	15.00
	43–44	DEPS	Number of dependents	2

Additional employees have the same form as line 2.

Your program should read the data file and compute:

1. Gross pay = (HOURS-up-to-40 * REGRATE) +
   (HOURS-beyond-40 * OTRATE)
2. Deductions:
   Federal Tax: (Gross pay – 10 * DEPS) * FEDTAX
   FICA: Gross Pay * FICA
   City Tax: Gross Pay *CITY, (only computed if WORKSIN=C,
   0 otherwise)
   Union Dues: Gross pay * UNION (only computed if
   UNIONCODE=M)
   Retirement Fund: Gross Pay * RETIRE
3. New Pay = Gross Pay – (Sum of Deduction)

Output

For each employee
Number, name, hours worked (reg and ot), pay rate, gross pay, list of deductions, net pay.

Summary
Number of employees processed, total gross pay, total of each deduction, total deductions, total net pay.

For testing purpose use: FEDTAX=.21, FICA=.07, CITY=.05,
UNION=.08, RETIRE=.1

11.1. Modify the program so that the data computed for each employee is written out to a data file. Write a separate program that reads this new file and prints a check for each employee.

11.2. Write a program that uses both files to compute the answers to the following questions:

- Do city workers make more or less than suburban workers (actual pay)?
- Do union members make more or less (actual pay)?
- Is there a relationship between number of dependents and number of overtime hours worked?

12.0

PROBLEM
STATEMENT

A computer dating service has decided to automate its "date selection" procedures.

Each applicant supplies the following information:

1. Name, address, phone number
2. Sex (M or F)
3. Interests:

S = sports	P = politics	D = dancing
M = music	X = science	R = religion
T = travel	K = skiing/mountains	B = sailing/beaches
J = jogging	F = films	A = art
N = nightclubs	V = video games	

Interests are supplied as a string of letters. The letters are given in order of importance to applicant.

The program should input data for up to 100 applicants and should print out a list of compatable couples. A couple is compatible if:

- The two people are of opposite sex,
- And one of the following is true:

(1) Their first two interests match exactly.
(2) Three of their first five interests are the same.

SAMPLE OUTPUT	NAME OF APPLICANT	MATCHES APPLICANTS	MATCHES ON CHARACTERISTIC
	SUSAN THOMAS 567 ROLAND AVE. BALITMORE, MD. 21213 301-446-7781	MICHAEL FRESTEL 1 CHARLES CENTER, #406 BALITMORE, MD. 21204 301-849-2126	M/A/S
		BRIAN SANDERS 153 AUGUST WAY COLUMBIA, MD. 21534 301-663-7935	S/F

12.1. Modify the program to print a match on a third condition—that the two people have any five interests in common.

12.2. Modify the program so that if a person has more than three matches, only the top three are printed.

13.0

PROBLEM STATEMENT

Write a program that will print out a happy-face design. The inputs should include a number to tell the program on which column to center the picture and the character which is to be used in the design.

SAMPLE
OUTPUT

```
CENTER ON WHICH COLUMN
15
USE WHICH CHARACTER
*
```

13.1. Alter the program to include an error test that makes sure the design will not "fall off the edge" of the paper.

13.2. Alter the program to allow the user to enter the approximate diameter of the design.

14.0

PROBLEM
STATEMENT

Write a program to print patterns of the following form:

```
        0
      1 – 1
    2 – – – 2
  3 – – – – – 3
4 – – – – – – – 4
  3 – – – – – 3
    2 – – – 2
      1 – 1
        0
```

where the largest number (4 in this case) in the input. The program should be able to handle inputs in the range of $(0 <= <9)$.

SAMPLE
OUTPUT

See above.

14.1. Modify the program so that it prints the design but omits the numbers

14.2. Modify the program to allow the user to specify the character to be used in the design and the column on which the design is to be centered. Provide an error check to reject designs that won't fit on the screen.

15.0

PROBLEM STATEMENT

Write a function that will print a character a given number of times. The character request should be in the form of an ASCII code value. The number of times should not exceed the width of the CRT screen. The function should return an integer value of 0 if it encounters an error condition; 1 otherwise.

Use the function to write another function that prints out triangles of characters as shown below. Use the same error convention.

Notice that the request to the user specifies that a character be input, not an ASCII number.

SAMPLE OUTPUT

```
ENTER CHARACTER, NUMBER OF ROWS
+ ,5


           +
          +++
         +++++
        +++++++
       +++++++++
```

15.1. Modify the program to start the printout at a column selected by the user:

```
ENTER CHARACTER, NUMBER OF ROWS, COLUMN POSITIO
,3,40

                              +
                             +++
                            +++++
```

The program should make sure that the printout will be able to fit on the screen before it begins to print.

15.2. Write a program whose inputs are a character and a string. The output should be the string reproduced as a large graphic composed of the character.

SAMPLE OUTPUT

```
ENTER CHARACTER, STRING
+ ,HI
```

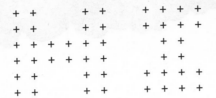

The length of the input string will be limited, depending on the size of the output graphics. (The output must fit on the screen.) If you wish, you can restrict the set of outputs the program can handle.

15.3. Expand the program to handle all of the capital letters, digits, and special characters on your keyboard.

15.4. Modify the program so that it adjusts the size of the graphic to match the length of the input string. As the string gets longer, the graphic will have to "shrink" in order to fit on the screen. The largest possible graphic should be printed.

15.5. Alter the program to provide hard-copy output.

16.0

PROBLEM
STATEMENT

Write a program that will input a word and print it out as a "magic triangle." The word may be up to 10 characters long.

SAMPLE
OUTPUT

```
ENTER WORD
COMPUTER
```

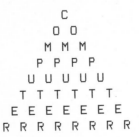

16.1. Include as an input a column number. Print the triangle with the apex in that column. (Be sure to check for "off-the-page" error conditions.)

16.2. Print the word in "hourglass" form.

```
R R R R R R R R
 E E E E E E
  T T T T T
   U U U U U
    P P P P
     M M M
      O O
       C
      O O
     M M M
    P P P P
   U U U U U
  T T T T T
 E E E E E E
R R R R R R R R
```

17.0

PROBLEM STATEMENT   Write a program to draw a graph of the function $f(x) = x$. Inputs should be starting and ending values for x.

SAMPLE OUTPUT
```
ENTER FIRST AND LAST VALUES FOR X

FIRST -3
LAST 5

GRAPH:
```

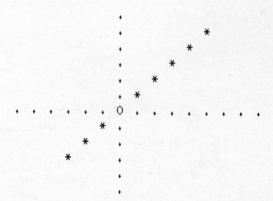

17.1.   Alter the program to graph the function $f(x) = x + b$, where b is an input.

17.2.   Graph $f(x) = mx + b$, where m and b are inputs.

17.3.   Alter the program so that the origin of the display is always the midpoint of the first and last x values. Label the axes accordingly.

18.0

PROBLEM
STATEMENT

Write a program that plays the game of Hangman. The program should read the words to be "played" from a data file. Allow the two players to make alternate guesses at the letters that make up the word. The game is over if a player guesses (or misses) the word, or if each player has guessed at a specified number of letters (the exact number should be an input).

SAMPLE
OUTPUT

```
ENTER NUMBER OF GUESSES PER PLAYER
7

ENTER LETTER -- USE * TO TRY TO GUESS THE WORD

PLAYER 1 GUESS A
THERE IS   1                  - - A - - - - -

PLAYER 2 GUESS E
THERE ARE 0                   - - A - - - - -

*** 6 GUESSES LEFT ***

PLAYER 1 GUESSES O
THERE ARE 2              - - A - - O O -

PLAYER 2 GUESSES P
THERE IS 1              - - A P - O O -

*** 5 GUESSES LEFT ***

PLAYER 1 GUESS T
THERE IS 1              T - A P - O O -

PLAYER 2 GUESS *
                       GUESS THE WORD TRAPDOOR

CORRECT: TRAPDOOR

PLAYER 2 WINS,
```

18.1. Alter the program to offer the user a choice of "difficulty" levels. The higher the level, the more difficult will be the words to be used.

18.2. Alter the program so that the more often the players solve the word, the more difficult the words become.

19.0

PROBLEM STATEMENT

Write a program to play Word Search. The game board is a square matrix of letters. The objective is to find all occurrences of a given word within the letters. Words can be formed by using any combination of vertically, horizontally, or diagonally connected letters as long as no letter is repeated.

Letter boards should be stored as data files. The object word should be an input. Output should include the numbers of the squares used to form each occurrence of the word.

SAMPLE DATA

A	T	H	E	D		1	2	3	4	5	
T	H	E	D	T		6	7	8	9	10	
H	D	T	A	E		11	12	13	14	15	(Number for
E	E	D	T	H		16	17	18	19	20	reference only)
D	H	T	A	E		21	22	23	24	25	

SAMPLE OUTPUT

```
ENTER WORD
?HEED

1:   3    4    8    9
2:   3    8    4    5
3:   7    8    4    5
4:   7    8    4    9
5:   11   16   17   12
6:   11   16   17   18
7:   11   16   17   21
8:   22   16   17   12
9:

        and so on ....
```

19.1. Modify the program to search for English words of a particular length. The input should be a number indicating how many letters—e.g., three-letter words, four-letter words, etc.—the output should be in the form above, but with the word printed after the set of reference numbers.

19.2. Modify the program to find all words of length three or more. Develop an estimate of the average running time for the program on a five-by-five-word square. See if you can rewrite the program so as to reduce the running time.

Index

Output
   defined in problem analysis, 8
   justification, defined, 317
   labeling, 103–05
   labels and headings, 315–18
   output design, 315–22
   sample (example), 10
   see PRINT * instruction; Format;
      Formatted output
   specifying output form, 319–21
   template (example), 320–21
   the need for sample output, 9

PARAMETER instruction
   defined, 108–10
   example, 112
PRINT * instruction
   examples, 41–42
   formatted form (no *), 46–50
   labeling input and output, 103–05
   with variables and strings, 46–49
Problem analysis, 6–14
   and program output, 8
   averaging numbers (example), 78–79
   definition of, 6
   even and odd numbers (example), 58
   grading exams (example), 244
   in commercial programming, 123–25
   powers and roots (example), 26–27
   program purpose, 7
   sorting (example), 184–89
   summing inputs (example), 96–100
   summing set of even numbers
      (example), 114–15
Problem solving
   differences among programming
      problems, 13
   in writing programs, 3
   modular, 272–77
Problem statement
   definition of, 6–14
   example, 26
   see Example programs
Processing, data into information, 10–13
Program
   as translation of algorithm, 15; 22–24;
      80–81; 99–100; 118–19
   coding and testing, 3

comment lines, 23
comments, 133; 135–42
commercial, 122–25
creating, 3
definition of, 2
design, 3
documentation, 23
layout, 121–34; 135–42
line numbers, 23
need for algorithm development, 15–25
organization and display, 121–34
output based on problem analysis, 8
problem analysis, 6–14
problem statement, 8
see Algorithm; Documentation;
      Example programs; FORTRAN;
      FORTRAN syntax
structure, 121–34
style, 31; 121–34; 135–42
syntax rules, 3
Program documentation, *see* Documenta-
      tion
Program logic, definition of, 2
Programmer
   major task of, 10
   minimum competencies required, 122
Programming languages, and structured
      programming, 126
Programming problems
   area of a triangle (16), 154
   balance a checkbook (4), 146
   bookkeeping (11), 338
   bookkeeping (5), 256
   bookkeeping (9), 259
   calendar construction (2), 254
   census analysis (8), 258
   change returned from a purchase (13),
      151
   complex numbers (21), 157
   compound interest (14), 152
   compressing text (6), 334
   compute a sum (1), 144
   compute mean, median, *s.d.* (3), 145
   compute value of *pi* (9), 150
   computing efficiency (18), 155
   converting to scientific notation (9), 336
   counting characters in text (1), 330
   counting sets of inputs (24), 159
   counting words in text (5), 333